Nations without States

To the memory of Ernest Gellner

Nations without States

Political Communities in a Global Age

MONTSERRAT GUIBERNAU

Polity Press

The right of Montserrat Guibernau to be identified as author of this work has been asserted in accordance with the Copyright, Designs and Patents Act 1988.

First published in 1999 by Polity Press in association with Blackwell Publishers Ltd.

Editorial office:
Polity Press
65 Bridge Street
Cambridge CB2 1UR, UK

Marketing and production:
Blackwell Publishers Ltd
108 Cowley Road
Oxford OX4 1JF, UK

Published in the USA by
Blackwell Publishers Inc.
Commerce Place
350 Main Street
Malden, MA 02148, USA

A catalogue record for this book is available from the British Library

Library of Congress Cataloging-in-Publication Data
Guibernau i Berdún, M. Montserrat (Maria Montserrat)
  Nations without states : political communities in a global age / Montserrat Guibernau.
    p. cm.
  Includes bibliographical references.
  ISBN 0-7456-1800-6. — ISBN 0-7456-1801-4 (pbk.)
  1. Nationalism Case studies. 2. National state Case studies.
  I. Title.
JC311.G783 1999
320.54′09′049—dc21   99–22431
                                                                  CIP

Typeset in 10/12 Palatino
by SetSystems Ltd, Saffron Walden, Essex
Printed in Great Britain by
MPG Books Ltd, Victoria Square, Bodmin, Cornwall

This book is printed on acid-free paper.

Contents

Acknowledgements

I owe a great debt to Tony Giddens for actively supporting this project; his advice and criticism have proved invaluable. Christopher Dandeker, Anthony D. Smith and Salvador Giner have each made lengthy, insightful and very helpful comments on a draft of the book.

I have also greatly appreciated and benefited from my conversations with Joan Manuel Guinda, Maria del Mar Serrrano, Simon Williams, Emmanuel Kattann, Wendy Alexander and Francesc X. Puig Rovira.

I wrote this book while holding an ESRC senior research fellowship at the Centre for Research in Ethnic Relations (University of Warwick). Among my colleagues there I would like to thank Zig Layton-Henry for his constant encouragement and support. I am also grateful to John Rex for the sheer fun of intellectual friendship and for so many stimulating conversations on nationalism and ethnicity.

This book began life in the shape of a shorter version which was awarded the 1998 Trias Fargas Prize (Barcelona).

Among those who have contributed in the preparation of this book I would like to thank Gill Motley, Pam Thomas and Julia Harsant. Particular thanks are due to Steve Curtis for a thorough copy-editing.

Introduction

Is it possible to refer to nations without states as new political actors
in the global age? Is the traditional nation-state system being replaced
by a system of nations integrated within larger political institutions?
Will nation-states become nations without states in a world organized
around supranational institutions to whom nation-states are progressively surrendering significant aspects of their sovereignty? What are
the reasons for the current strengthening of nationalism in nations
without states? How does globalization impinge upon the reshaping
of political institutions? Nationalism is thriving in nations without
states such as Catalonia, Scotland, Quebec and Flanders. A series of
factors contribute to this. They include: the fragmentation of the
former Soviet Union and the nationalist feelings it has sparked off in
places such as the Baltic Republics, Georgia and Chechenia; the
proliferation of transnational institutions such as the European Union;
the pressure exerted by an increasingly globalized culture capable of
reaching the remotest corners of the world; and the invigoration of
multinational corporations which break the boundaries of national
economies. Contemporary politics are grounded upon a constant
tension between pressure exerted by sub-state movements which put
forward nationalist claims, thus questioning the state's legitimacy,
and the growth of supranational organizations which require the state
to surrender relevant attributes of its traditional sovereignty.

In this context, I refer to nations without states as cultural communities sharing a common past, attached to a clearly demarcated
territory, and wishing to decide upon their political future which lack
a state of their own. These communities are included within one or

more states which they tend to regard as alien, and assert the right to self-determination, sometimes understood as further autonomy within the state, though, in other cases it involves the right to secession. I employ the expression 'nations without states' rather than 'stateless nations' to avoid the specific meaning that the latter term has within anthropology.

The origin of the consciousness of forming a distinct community among members of nations without states can, in most cases, be traced back to a more or less distant past in which the nation enjoyed its own political institutions, as was the case in Catalonia, the Basque Country, Wales and Scotland. Often this involves going back to an era previous to that of the emergence of the nation-state system. As Anthony D. Smith has stressed, the ethnic origin of most nations can be traced back to a time when the 'core' of ethnicity which resides in certain 'myths, memories, values and symbols' transmitted through different generations was established. Smith lists six main attributes of an ethnic community or *ethnie*: (1) a collective proper name; (2) a myth of common ancestry; (3) shared historical memories; (4) one or more differentiating elements of common culture; (5) an association with a specific 'homeland'; and (6) a sense of solidarity for significant sectors of the population.[1] In my view, to acknowledge that there is an ethnic origin to most contemporary nations is far from assuming that all pre-modern political communities turned into nations or nation-states, and does not imply that nations are perennial entities.[2] Extremely complex processes lead to the disappearance of some nations and to the emergence of new ones. What is relevant about the current strength of nationalist movements in nations without states is that, in many cases, they emerge within nations which once enjoyed a separate political and/or cultural identity which is now being invoked, revitalized and adapted to the new socio-political circumstances in which the nation lives and evolves.

In spite of the significance achieved by nations without states, no attempts have been made to offer a systematic analysis of them as emerging new political actors. One of the major obstacles for this is the lack of a clear-cut distinction between the concepts of nation and state in the literature about nationalism. In this sense, the general approach of this book is highly relevant to the contemporary political situation in as far as one of the central themes is the problem of separating the idea of a nation from that of the state – in other words, the problem of the preservation and perpetuation of communities with their own distinct culture in a world in which most political units are larger than national.

Three main approaches can be found in the restricted literature considering forms of sub-state nationalism. The first focuses on single case studies. It includes writings of a monographic or comparative nature in which one or more particular case studies are subject to an in-depth analysis. In such works very few, if any, theoretical considerations are made which go beyond the specific features of the cases involved.

The second approach comprises more general studies about the relevance of the regions and regionalism within Europe. These analyses tend to display a highly empirical outlook and focus on the implications of political decentralization for the areas concerned. The third is a more abstract, theoretical approach which examines the profound transformations affecting the nation-state. In so doing, most studies consider what is generally referred to as 'peripheral nationalism' and the role of a globalized economy as two major factors contributing to the emergence of sub-state units. The focus of attention is not the rise of nationalism in nations without states but the ways in which the traditional state is being recast.

(1) The first approach examines the re-emergence of nationalism drawing on specific case studies. It explores the reasons for the renewed strength of the nationalist movement and the social structure of the societies involved. The history of the relationship between the national minority and the state which contains it as well as the components of the specific national identity defended by the nationalist movement are carefully examined. I distinguish between two types of studies within this approach. The first contains works in which different case studies are compared. The second refers to monographic analysis concerned with a single case study.

Michael Keating offers one of the most sophisticated accounts within the first category. His book *Nations against the State* compares nationalism in Quebec, Catalonia and Scotland. In his view, the nationalist movements now emerging in these three nations should be interpreted as a response both to the changes in the capacity and legitimacy of the states containing them, and to the reconfiguration of territorial politics after the two World Wars. These nationalisms, which are historically rooted and have developed within states, offer a pragmatic solution to cultural or territorial questions. Keating argues that Catalan, Scottish and Quebec nationalism contains ethnic as well as civic elements in its doctrine, the political strategies it tries to advance and the support base it receives, although, in his view, its civic dimension has been strengthened over the years.[3]

For Keating, it is essential to distinguish between ethnic particularism and minorities' nationalism. In the three societies he studies, he considers national identity to be an organizing principle for the society as a whole, even if not all its members are committed nationalists. He argues that, in the past, Catalonia, Quebec and Scotland were politically and economically dependent on the states containing them, a situation which now has been reversed. He writes, 'This dependence has lessened as the states have lost their capacity for territorial management and the minority nations have become more self-assertive'.⁴ For Keating, these three nations emphasize social solidarity as a main value of the political culture while, at the same time, being strongly committed to their continental regimes, NAFTA in one case and the EU in the other two. These nationalisms, Keating argues, interpret their relationship with the state as a pact which is open to re-negotiation, a perspective which is commonly shared by the states containing them where it has proven a very conflictive point. Within this first approach, David McCrone's *Understanding Scotland: the Sociology of a Stateless Nation* is a good example of a monographic study about the specific features of nationalism in a single area. He describes the different elements which have contributed to the generation of a specific Scottish national identity throughout time and focuses upon the novel factors which are currently contributing to a renaissance of Scottish nationalism. In his view, Scottish nationalism should be understood not simply as the assertion of linguistic or cultural distinctiveness, but as a political challenge to the authority of the central British state.⁵

(2) The second approach examines regions and regionalism in Europe where since the early 1960s there has been a revival of sub-state nationalist movements. These studies focus on different decentralization experiments carried out within the European Union and considers whether regions have become or are in the process of becoming an essential level of government in Europe.

This approach is well represented by Christopher Harvie's *The Rise of Regional Europe*. In this book, Harvie considers different EU regions and focuses upon the ways in which history is being employed by their nationalist movements. He also looks at elites and regional cultures, and he concentrates on the economic dimension of the re-emergence of what he refers to as 'regionalism'. He does not employ the term nation, and includes under a single denomination 'region', areas with a cultural and historical basis and areas which are merely determined by economic or geographic factors. He is sceptical about the possibility of creating a Europe of the Regions due to the great inequalities existing among them.

Patrick Le Galès and Christian Lequesne in their recent book *Regions in Europe* also challenge the notion of a 'Europe of the Regions' and argue that 'the dynamics of particular regions and the discourse of Europe of the regions, have led one to overlook the fact that regions are structurally weak in terms of government and governance'.[6] They argue that only a small number of regions (and cities) are on their way to becoming collective political actors in European governance. In their view, most regions are weakly institutionalized, endowed with a weak political capacity, and are destined to manage scarcity or economic decline, as well as to protect culture, the environment and identities. They consider the Europe of the Regions as a myth whose importance should not be exaggerated, though the thesis they defend does not refer to the decline of regions in Europe, 'but to decline of causes that logically converge to reinforce regions'.[7]

(3) The third approach includes a substantial number of theoretical works which from different perspectives concentrate on the changes affecting the traditional nation-state. These studies do not address the rise of nationalism in nations without states in a direct way, however. Their analysis almost invariably contains some references to what is often referred to as 'peripheral nationalism' and considers the role of sub-state units within a progressively globalized economy.[8] This approach embraces some works which relate the nation-state's crisis to the intensification of globalization processes. David Held offers the best of these accounts.[9] In his view, the state is suffering a double crisis, one of rationality in so far as it is unable to fulfil its traditional functions, and a legitimacy crisis in that it is no longer able to achieve massive loyalty. Held argues that the number of groups which claim the principle of democratic legitimacy when demanding the right to control their political destiny is increasing. At the same time, the relevance and content of this principle is being altered by the intensification of globalization processes. In his view, it is essential to recognize three elements of regionalization and globalization. First, the changes in the nature, scope and capacity of the modern state produced by processes of economic, political, legal, military and cultural interconnectedness. Second, changes to the nature and dynamics of national political systems brought about by regional and global interconnectedness which links different states and their citizens in chains of interlocking political decisions and outcomes. Third, the transformations experienced by cultural and political identities as

a result of such processes, that have led many local and regional groups and nationalist movements to question the nation-state's legitimacy.[10] It is in this context that Held refers to new patterns of local and regional government and development and argues that while national sovereignty, even in regions with overlapping and divided authority structures, has not been wholly subverted, 'political domains clearly exist with criss-crossing loyalties, conflicting interpretations of rights and duties, and interconnected authority structures which displace notions of sovereignty as an illimitable, indivisible and exclusive form of public power'.[11]

From a different perspective, Horsman and Marshall provide one of the most illuminating accounts of the changes affecting the nation-state and the possible alternatives to its traditional structure. In their view, 'the decline in nation-state autonomy has compromised the pact between citizens and the nation-state ... Any solution will require ways of managing the multiple links between and among the citizen, the state, regional and international organizations, and the global economy. It will require a rethinking of communities and their rights and responsibilities.'[12] Notwithstanding such affirmations, Horsman and Marshall in some sections of their book refer to the Scots, the Catalans, the Basques and the Lombards' demands for autonomy as a sign of growing tribalism.[13] Michel Maffessoli and Eric Hobsbawm[14] also refer to the re-emergence of nationalism in what I call nations without states (they usually refer to them as regions) as an anachronism and a sign of backwardness. In my view, one should be wary of the theories which label the resurgence of sub-state nationalism as tribal, while often legitimizing state nationalism. From their perspective, 'the nationalists' are always the 'other people', those who 'generate trouble', 'show dissatisfaction', 'pose a threat to the state's integrity' and 'question the state's legitimacy'. I argue that to employ the term 'tribal' to describe the nationalism of nations without states disregards two crucial points.

First, it ignores the fact that contemporary forms of nationalism differ substantially from the classical nationalism which contributed to the constitution and consolidation of the nation-state in the nineteenth and early twentieth century. A sizeable number of the nationalisms which are now gaining salience in nations without states are grounded upon the defence of democracy and collective rights and, as I will show later on in the book, are intimately connected with the transformations brought about by globalization. A considerable number of these nationalisms claim the right to freely develop their nation's specificity within a framework of respect and tolerance and, in so doing, they challenge the nation-state by questioning its legitimacy.

It is true that not all nationalisms in nations without states are democratic and for this reason we should be attentive to the urgent need to distinguish between those which are based upon democratic principles and those which defend an ethnocentric world view grounded upon the implementation of exclusion mechanisms which often involve the use of force. My point is that, at present, there is a sufficient number of democratic sub-state nationalist movements for the social sciences to reflect on them as distinct phenomena which deserve particular attention.

Second, the very use of the term 'tribalization' to refer to the resurgence of all types of sub-state nationalism is an anachronism because it implies a return to the past which is no longer possible and neglects the connections between the rise of sub-state forms of nationalism and current alterations affecting the nation-state system.

Nationalism has traditionally been an uncomfortable topic for social scientists. In the nineteenth century and early this century we encounter numerous examples of great scholars who paid scant attention to what clearly was one of the major political forces of their time. As I have shown elsewhere, Max Weber, a German nationalist himself, never provided a systematic theory of nationalism. Émile Durkheim and Karl Marx predicted that nationalism would soon disappear.[15] History has proved them to be wrong. Instead, nationalism has played a key role in the modern age and it currently manifests itself as a potent force. Nationalism, however, has often been portrayed in intellectual circles as a sign of backwardness and as a doctrine opposed to the cosmopolitan ideal once formulated by Kant.[16] Such uneasiness towards nationalism stems from its potent emotional dimension which clearly differs from the ideal of rationality defended by the *philosophes* which has up to now remained unquestioned. On these grounds, indiscriminate rejection of sub-state nationalism should be carefully assessed, since it often hides strong and not always declared forms of 'state nationalism'.

The study of nationalism requires the analysis of the specific situations in which it arises. The political ideologies to which nationalism is attached are crucial to understanding the significance and character of nationalism in each particular case. Above all, we should realize that the complexity and flexibility of nationalism are connected to its multifaceted character. Therefore, nationalism is sometimes associated with those who advocate xenophobia and ethnic cleansing, while in other cases it is applied to describe those who defend their right to exist and peacefully cultivate a particular culture which makes them 'different' from other groups. The eighteenth-century concept of popular sovereignty was designed for the 'whole people'. When the revolutionaries stated that the principle of sovereignty resides essentially in the nation, they may be taken to have asserted that the nation was more than the king and the aristocracy. National self-determination turned out to be one of the most frequent interpretations of popular sovereignty.

The new ideas of the *philosophes* emphasizing liberty, equality and, in particular, the idea of state power rooted in popular consent were initially applied to the construction and consolidation of the nation-state. At present, democratic nationalist movements in nations without states invoke the principle of consent and the idea of popular sovereignty to legitimate their claims for self-determination, a concept which, as we shall see later on in the book, may be subject to significantly different interpretations. The idea of self-determination has the capacity to challenge the nation-state as a political institution which, in most cases, has been created upon the attempt to seek the cultural and political homogenization of its citizens, paying scant attention to its own internal diversity.

It is my contention that, although the accounts included in the three approaches I have just briefly summarized have made significant contributions to understanding current changes affecting the nation-state while examining with varying depth the unexpected force of sub-state nationalism, they lack a systematic account of the re-emergence of nationalism in nations without states and fail to consider the crucial role that it is likely to play in the near future. I consider the re-emergence of nationalism in Western nations without states as the result of a multidimensional process which requires a specific examination of the conditions of modernity which have brought it about. The main weaknesses of the literature I have mentioned stem from its inability to focus upon nations without states as a primary subject of analysis.

At present a significant number of nations without states are struggling to become global political actors in a changing world within which they enjoy the capacity to provide individuals with a strong sense of identity. Nations without states open up the possibility for individuals to play a more active part in the political life of their communities through participation in autonomous institutions. In so doing they contribute to the dynamization of civil society and encourage civic coherence. Emphasis upon identity is of paramount importance, but it is also crucial to take on board the sound economic arguments for decentralization which are in favour of the creation of sub-state units. In my view, there are strong cultural, political and economic arguments for nations without states to become global political players.

Objectives and structure

This book focuses upon the re-emergence of nationalism in nations without states in Europe and North America. The empirical focus includes Catalonia, Scotland, Wales, the Basque Country, Quebec and Northern Ireland as well as First Nations in the United States and Canada, although there are spot references to some other cases. All these nations have ethnic origins that can be traced back to an era previous to the rise of the nation-state. They are all evolving within industrialized societies endowed with democratic institutions, Western democratic nation-states that grant them varying degrees of autonomy and recognition. Thriving nationalist movements exist in all of them. Most of these nations without states are, in fact, included in the European Union, a pioneering political institution which might play a part strengthening them and their various nationalisms if it decides to implement a much debated decentralization policy in favour of a Europe of the Regions.

I am aware that there are sub-state nationalist movements emerging in many parts of the world, the former Soviet Union, Asia and Africa, as well as native movements among native peoples in Australia and New Zealand which deserve much attention and offer interesting examples of new forms of nationalism. For the reasons I have just mentioned, their analysis is beyond the scope of this book.

This book has four main aims. First, to offer a definition and a typology of the different political scenarios in which nations without states find themselves in the West. Second, to advance a systematic analysis of the processes leading to the generation of nationalist movements in nations without states paying particular attention to the role of intellectuals and the impact of the media in the construction and reproduction of nationalist messages. Third, to establish a clear-cut distinction between cultural resistance and armed struggle as major strategies employed by different nationalist groups in the advancement of their goals. Fourth, to assess the factors which might contribute to generating a completely new political environment in which nations without states are likely to become global political actors.

The book is divided into seven chapters. Chapter One focuses upon the concepts of nation, state and nationalism as three terms closely related to each other. It explains the link between these concepts which are presented as forming a triad characterized by constant tension and interdependence. Here, I relate the unfolding of nationalism in nations without states to the profound metamorphosis currently being experienced by the nation-state and the intensification of globalization processes. The pre-eminence which the nation has achieved in late modernity is connected to the role it played in the Romantic era. Following this line of argument, questions about the value of diversity, the need for civic coherence and the restoration of a sense of community are examined. The nationalisms of nations without states are studied as social movements seeking the recognition of the communities they represent as distinctive cultural units with a territorial dimension and the desire to decide about their political future.

Chapter Two offers a typology of the different political scenarios in which nations without states find themselves, paying particular attention to the nature of the state containing them and the aspirations expressed by the nationalist movements studied. References to Catalonia, Quebec, Northern Ireland, Scotland, Wales, and Kurdistan, among others, are made here to illustrate the various political environments in which nations without states live and develop. It should be emphasized that this is not an exhaustive typology. It does, however, offer sufficient elements of analysis to permit a general classification of the radically distinct options faced by nations without states.

Chapter Three examines recent expressions of nationalism emerging among Native peoples in the United States and Canada. From an historical perspective, these peoples are very different from the well-documented ethno-historical European nations without states, but they share enough features with them to be included here. This chapter expands the traditional definition of nations without states to include American Indians as nations which have appropriated the language of nationalism and adapted it to their own non-Western realities. Conflicting definitions of self-determination employed by Canadian indigenous communities are considered here to illustrate the complexity of current debates on sovereignty and self-determination.

Chapter Four's focal point concerns the role of intellectuals in the construction of nationalist discourses seeking to re-create a sentiment of community among the nation's members. Intellectuals are under pressure to generate, wherever it is absent, or increase, wherever it already exists, the intensity of national consciousness. Their task is to construct a political discourse critical and subversive of the current state of affairs and put forward a set of principles which should favour the strengthening of the community as distinct and separate from the state containing it. Intellectuals are crucial in the configuration of the nationalist movement, but they are insufficient to guarantee the survival and development of a particular culture and language as something more than a piece of ethnographic curiosity and philological interest. To be successful, a nationalist movement, which generally starts as an elite movement, has to obtain a mass following. Elite nationalisms are bound to disappear if they fail to transform themselves into mass social movements.

Chapter Five investigates different strategies employed by nationalist movements in nations without states to counteract the homogenizing policies of the state and advance their goals ranging from cultural resistance to armed struggle. Here, I examine different types of action which are generally included within cultural resistance. This chapter goes on to study the so-called 'dark face' of nationalism, its relation with violence. Political terrorism and 'total war' as well as 'state terrorism' are carefully analysed in this section.

Chapter Six explores some of the main features of the traditional nation-state which are being altered by increasing globalization. It introduces the concept of the 'post-traditional nation-state' to refer to a nation-state which is being forced to make fundamental changes to its traditional concepts of sovereignty, territoriality, control of the means of violence and the administration. A careful analysis of the relationship between the European Union and its member states illustrates the changes and dilemmas faced by nation-states in these four crucial areas. The chapter then moves on to consider the reasons which permit us to envisage a medium term future in which nations without states might become global political actors. Questions about national identity and geopolitics, as well as the economic viability of nations without states are discussed here.

Chapter Seven sums up the main arguments expounded throughout the book and concentrates on what I consider the main questions and dilemmas currently faced by nations without states which are likely to be intensified in the near future. These are: internal diversity; the possible use of violence as a mechanism to advance their goals; and excessive bureaucratization. Multiculturalism, procedures to avoid the use of force and the implementation of subsidiarity as a political principle are examined as useful tools in confronting these three major challenges.

Questions about legitimacy, the desire to reconstruct a sense of community among otherwise isolated individuals, and the disintegration of traditional sources of identity are crucial factors to consider when studying the renewed vigour which nationalist movements in nations without states are experiencing. The transformation of the economy, communications technology and a rising awareness of global interdependence design a novel political scenario in which new actors are coming on stage. To begin with I turn to the relation between nation, state and nationalism as three interdependent concepts in constant tension with each other and offer a definition of what I mean by nations without states. In recent times the pre-eminence of the nation seems to be on the increase. Individuals have embarked upon a quest for identity which often seems to take them away from a progressively weaker state and back to smaller cultural communities which in many cases seek to play a political role. At present, identity is closely connected to politics.

1

State and Nation

The nation has become one of the most contested concepts of our times. Different cultural, political, psychological, territorial, ethnic and sociological principles underlie the multifarious definitions of the nation provided by the various scholars, politicians and political activists willing to shed some light on this much disputed term. Their lack of agreement suggests a major difficulty in dealing with such a complex phenomenon. The crux of the matter probably resides close to the link which has been established between nation and state, and to the common practice of using the nation as a source of political legitimacy. To be or not to be recognized as a nation entails different rights for the community which claims to be one, since being a nation usually implies the attachment to a particular territory, a shared culture and history and the assertion of the right to self-determination. To define a specific community as a nation involves the more or less explicit acceptance of the legitimacy of the state which claims to represent it, or if the nation does not possess a state of its own, it then implicitly acknowledges the nation's right to self-government involving some degree of political autonomy which may or may not lead to a claim for independence.

The nation, however, cannot be viewed in isolation. I argue that a clear-cut distinction needs to be drawn between three main concepts: nation, state and nationalism. By 'state', taking Weber's definition, I refer to 'a human community that (successfully) claims the *monopoly of the legitimate use of physical force* within a given territory',[1] although not all states have successfully accomplished this, and some of them have not even aspired to accomplish it. By 'nation', I refer to a human group conscious of forming a community, sharing a common culture, attached to a clearly demarcated territory, having a common past and a common project for the future and claiming the right to rule itself. This definition attributes five dimensions to the nation: psychological (consciousness of forming a group), cultural, territorial, political and historical. By 'nationalism' I mean the sentiment of belonging to a community whose members identify with a set of symbols, beliefs and ways of life, and have the will to decide upon their common political destiny.[2] But yet another term needs to be defined and distinguished from the ones I have just mentioned, the nation-state. The nation-state is a modern institution, characterized by the formation of a kind of state which has the monopoly of what it claims to be the legitimate use of force within a demarcated territory and seeks to unite the people subject to its rule by means of cultural homogenization.

Nation, state and nationalism form a triad characterized by a constant tension between its three components. Hence, changes in the definition of one of the constituents have the capacity to influence and, to some extent, even alter the definitions of the other two. For instance, if belonging to a nation is defined in terms of common blood, the definition of the state and with it that of citizenship, as an attribute conferred upon its members, will have to include blood as a *sine qua non* condition for membership. Consequently, any nationalist movement emerging in these specific circumstances will focus upon common blood as a requisite for exclusion and inclusion in the nation that they want to defend and promote. In other cases where common ancestry is replaced as the primary condition for membership of a particular nation by birth or residence within its territory or by the simple wish to belong to it, the definition of the nation and the character of nationalism are altered accordingly.

This example refers to conditions for membership, that is, to elements which are considered to be indispensable to establishing a distinction between those who belong and those who do not belong to the nation. But alterations in the definitions of nation, state and nationalism are not restricted to conditions for belonging or criteria for membership.

The state's self-definition as a unitary, a federal or even a multinational political institution holds significant consequences for the peoples living within its boundaries. Once one of these self-definitions is adopted by a specific state, it has the capacity to influence the definition of the nation. This is particularly evident when a people is confronted with a state that declares itself to be multinational, thus assuming the coexistence of more than one nation within its territory. Such a position entails an automatic distinction between nation and state which challenges the commonly accepted coincidence between the two. A multinational state explicitly acknowledges its internal diversity and, in so doing, it influences the diverse definitions of nationalism that may emerge within its territory. First, in these cases, the nationalism instilled by the state will necessarily involve the acceptance of the diverse nations included within its borders. This type of nationalism tends to focus on shared constitutional rights and principles as elements able to hold together an otherwise diverse citizenry. Second, the nationalism emerging from some of the national minorities included within the state is strongly influenced by the state's recognition of their status as nations. The minorities' nationalism is bound to focus upon demands for greater power and resources which will allow them to further the degree of self-government they enjoy – assuming that they are already entitled to some political autonomy.

In a similar way, alterations in the definition of nationalism also have the power to impact upon the definitions of both the state and the nation. Therefore, a nationalist discourse based upon the rejection, dehumanization, and portrayal of those who do not belong to the nation as 'enemies' and as a 'threat' will feed xenophobia and ethnic hatred. This type of nationalism is likely to foster a narrow definition of the nation based upon the exclusion of the different and the belief in the superiority of one's own nation above all others. A state endorsing this sort of nationalism is likely to base its policy on the marginalization or sometimes even the elimination of 'others' within its territory, and/or the pursuit of a consistent assimilation policy. This type of state often engages in conflicts with other states as a result of an aggressive economic and/or territorial expansionist policy.

So far I have offered some examples showing how differences in the nature and definition of one of the constituents of the triad motivate substantial variations in the definitions of the other two. A further consideration suggests that different definitions of nation, state and nationalism coexist simultaneously in different parts of the globe. Hence, the relation between the three components of the triad can be analysed by focusing upon two different levels. The first, as I have shown above, involves the study of how changes in the definition of one of the constituents affects the other two. The second moves on to consider the eventual emergence of external factors capable of altering the very nature of the triad by shifting the balance of power between its members and even threatening to undermine one of them at the expense of another. Here we are confronted with radical transformations able to alter the more or less stable equilibrium existing between the triad by affecting their relationship at a structural level well above the particular situations considered when analysing individual cases.

At present, the main challenge to the relationship between the triad concerns the radical and rapid transformations altering the traditional nature of the state. The proliferation of supranational institutions, the increasing number of multinational corporations, and the emergence of sub-state nationalist movements contrive a novel political scenario in which the traditional role of the state is being undermined in a fundamental way. The signs of this have already become apparent; the radicalization of state nationalism, the proliferation of ethnic and national conflicts and the state's resistance to giving up substantial aspects of its sovereignty represent but a few examples which hint at the state's urgent need to recast its nature. At this moment in time, we are witnessing the rise of what I call 'nations without states' as potential new political actors able to capture and promote sentiments of loyalty, solidarity and community among individuals who seem to have developed a growing need for identity. Sound political and economic arguments may also be invoked in trying to account for the relevance that nations without states may acquire in the foreseeable future.

Nations without states

By 'nations without states' I refer to nations which, in spite of having their territories included within the boundaries of one or more states, by and large do not identify with them. The members of a nation lacking a state of their own regard the state containing them as alien, and maintain a separate sense of national identity generally based upon a common culture, history, attachment to a particular territory and the explicit wish to rule themselves. Self-determination is sometimes understood as political autonomy, in other cases it stops short of independence and often involves the right to secede. Catalonia, Quebec, Scotland, the Basque Country and Flanders represent only a few of the nations without states currently demanding further autonomy. It could be argued that some of these nations do have some kind of state of their own since a substantial number of powers have been devolved or one in the process of being devolved to their regional parliaments. But, in my view, political autonomy or even federation fall short of independence since they tend to exclude foreign and economic policy, defence and constitutional matters, and this is why it continues to make sense to refer to them as nations without states. The main qualities of the nation-state which, in one way or the other, favoured the assimilation of otherwise culturally diverse citizens were: its power to confer rights and duties upon its citizens; to provide for their basic needs – a function which since the Second World War materialized in the establishment of more or less generous welfare systems; and to maintain order in society while controlling the economy, defence, immigration and foreign policy, education and communication systems.

A nation without state, as the term indicates, is based upon the existence of a nation, that is, a community endowed with a stable but dynamic core containing a set of factors which have generated the emergence of a specific national identity. The state, that is, the political institution with which the nation should ideally identify, is missing. This creates a picture in which we have the cultural unit but lack the corresponding political institution regarded as legitimate by the members of the nation. The relationship between nation and state seems to have shifted from a time in which the state and its role in nation-building was given pre-eminence. In contrast, contemporary nationalist movements in nations without states are actively involved in 'state-building'. We should note, however, that the state they seek to create differs from the classical model of state. We shall come back to this particular question in the concluding chapter.

The rise of nations without states is closely connected to two interrelated factors, the intensification of globalization processes and the transformations affecting the nation-state. The nation-state has traditionally based its legitimacy upon the idea that it represents the nation, in spite of the fact that often the state once created had to engage in nation-building processes aiming at the forced assimilation of its citizens. It now becomes apparent that, in many cases, these processes have largely failed; the re-emergence of nationalist movements in nations without states proves it. At present, the state seems to become increasingly unable to fulfil its citizens' needs, and as a result of this they turn away from it and search for alternative institutions.

Most so-called nation-states are not constituted by a single nation which is coextensive with the state;[3] internal diversity is the rule. The nation-state, after a long process of consolidation which has involved the construction of a symbolic image of the community endowed with a particular language and culture, and the creation of symbols and rituals destined to emphasize its unique character and the fixing of territorial borders, is being forced to respond to challenges from within.

The nations or parts of nations included within a single state do not share similar levels of national awareness. What is more, while some will define themselves as nations, others will be happy to be referred to as provinces or regions. Nations are not unique and fixed, and throughout history it is possible to record the disintegration of some nations which have played a prominent role during a particular period and the creation of new ones.

The state has a strong tendency to absorb functions and a great reluctance to delegate control over any of the tasks it considers as an integral part of its sovereignty. The argument for state centralization is closely connected to the idea of state sovereignty understood as full control over all matters concerning the social, political and economic life of the citizens living within its boundaries. The increasing number of international organizations, multinational companies, supranational social movements and the technical sophistication of modern warfare are currently challenging this classic concept of state sovereignty. The state is exposed to pressure from above while at the same time it lays itself open to increasing internal strain to modify its traditional centralist nature and acknowledge the existence of territorially circum-scribed cultural communities within itself which show a varying degree of national self-consciousness and put forward different socio-political demands. The origin of most of these communities can be traced back to an era previous to the founding moment of the nation-state when diversity was generally diluted under the centralist and homogenizing practices of a then incipient nation-state.

The nationalism of nations without states emerges as a socio-political movement that defends the right of peoples to decide upon their own political destiny. Pressure for change and the nature of political demands are not homogeneous and depend upon each case, but what all these movements seem to share is the will to develop their specific culture and language, whenever it exists, and the desire to feel represented by the institutions deciding upon their future. The number of people involved in the movement can measure the strength of this type of nationalism; thus a massive following is more difficult to ignore if the state wants to maintain its credibility as a democratic institution.

Globalization and the nation

In *The Consequences of Modernity*,[4] Giddens argues that the undue reliance which sociologists have placed upon the idea of 'society', understood as a bounded system, should be replaced by a starting point that concentrates upon analysing how social life is ordered across time and space. He writes, 'in the modern era, the level of time-space distanciation is much higher than in any previous period, and the relations between local and distant social forms and events become correspondingly "stretched"'.[5] He defines globalization as 'the intensification of world-wide social relations which link distant localities in such a way that local happenings are shaped by events occurring many miles away and vice versa'.[6]

Globalization is a dialectic process which results in local happenings being influenced by, and at the same time holding the capacity to influence, distant events. The rise of sub-state forms of nationalism in Europe and elsewhere can be interpreted as a product of the dialectic nature of globalization which consists in mutually opposed tendencies. Thus the globalization of the economy and social relations which contributed to the weakening of the nation-state, also seems to have contributed to the intensification of regional forms of nationalism.

According to Albrow, we have entered the 'global age', this is a period which will redefine the human condition and where 'the technical reason of modernity will no longer occupy the prime place in the moral ordering of social relations'.[7] For him, the global age means the emergence of a new political order characterized by the pulling apart of society and the nation-state. Albrow argues that 'the modern nation-state is neither the only possible form of state nor the crowning political achievement in human history'.[8] In his view, the nation-state has failed to confine sociality within its boundaries, both territorial and categorical, and regards it as a 'timebound form' which 'no longer contains the aspirations nor monopolizes the attention of those who live on its territory'.[9] Albrow introduces the concept 'global state' and argues that it exists at every moment when the individual takes account of and seeks to act in the interests of a common interest spanning the globe.[10] The global state is constructed from below, and relies on the global consciousness of countless individuals. In my view, the nationalist claims of democratic movements emerging in nations without states can be interpreted as an expression of Albrow's transnational movement challenging the traditional nation-state.

In contrast with the theories which confer on globalization a major function in transforming politics, Hirst and Thompson are among those to espouse a sceptical attitude towards globalization itself. They consider it as a myth which suits both the right and the radical left for different reasons. Thus, for the right, it justifies government inaction, a position also defended by Will Hutton.[11] For the radical left, globalization provides release from a different kind of political impasse. It can interpret it as a continued reality of the world capitalist system and a confirmation of the futility of national social democratic reformist strategies. In Hirst and Thompson's view, 'nation-states are still of central significance since they are the key practitioners of the art of government as the process of distributing power, ordering other governments by giving them shape and legitimacy'.[12] They argue that the state's exclusive control of territory has been reduced by the international economy and new communication media. They stress, however, that the state still has the power to regulate populations since 'people are less mobile than money, goods and ideas: in a sense they remain "nationalized", dependent on passports, visas, and residence and labour qualifications'.[13]

The recent intensification of globalization processes has accelerated the demise of the nation-state, as new organizations such as NATO, NAFTA, the European Union or the United Nations are based upon the principle of states giving away some aspects of their sovereignty. As a result, the nation-state, which throughout many years tended to accumulate more and more functions to the point of almost collapsing, is being forced to surrender some of its traditional powers. In so doing, the nation-state has to acknowledge that the reasons for it to participate in and favour the organization of supranational and international organizations stem from its own increasing weakness. The re-emergence of nationalism in nations without states is directly related to the intensification of globalization processes which have proven capable of altering the political, economic and cultural structures of current societies.

Globalization involves greater awareness of diversity, and stresses interdependence between peoples, markets, and cultures. But globalization is not an even phenomenon since access to the technology which allows globalization to take place is restricted to those – nations, individuals, groups – who have sufficient means and resources to use it. Globalization contains the potential for creating a world in which a greater number of cultures become known and interact with each other, but it also contains the potential for cultural homogenization based upon the expansion of a single global culture to the detriment of others which are to be reduced to a folkloric tourist attraction.

The perceived threat of cultural homogenization is one of the factors contributing to the revitalization of minority cultures struggling to find a niche in the global net. Control over education and the media are crucial for nations who wish to promote their own languages and specific cultures; however, these nations should acknowledge that their languages and cultures will have to survive alongside more powerful ones which are progressively invading all aspects of life. Minority cultures struggling to survive know that they can only do so by entering an unequal contest with a major global culture which will undoubtedly influence their own.

From a financial perspective, globalization has broken up the classic nation-state's monopoly of the economy. Interdependence and the proliferation of multinational firms cutting across state boundaries permit nations without states to be considered as economic players. To succeed, they have to compete for foreign investment and encourage production of high-quality and specialized products. Economic viability and the capacity to provide a sense of identity to its members are the two key issues which are likely to determine the relevance of nations without states in the near future.

At present, different criteria and definitions apply to the nation when compared with earlier periods. As Hobsbawm argues, the liberal criteria of nation-making employed in the nineteenth century and in the early twentieth century assumed that only what were considered as culturally and economically 'viable' nations could enjoy the right to self-determination. 'To this extent', he notes, 'Mazzini's and Mill's idea of national self-determination was fundamentally different from President Wilson's'.[14] Real great nations should survive, small and backward ones were doomed to disappear and with them their specific cultures and languages.

Van Dyke argues that the liberal tradition ignores the existence of other groups between the individual and the state. In his view, the individualism that permeates liberalism is its main flaw and has so far prevented liberal thinkers from supplementing liberalism with a theory of collective rights.[15] But, this is not a position restricted to liberal thought since a somewhat similar stand can be found in Marx and Engels. In 1848–9 they supported the national causes of the 'historic' or 'great' nations such as Hungary, Poland and Germany, all of which sought to establish large, stable national states. At the same time, Marx and Engels voiced their hostility towards the aspirations of 'non-historic nationalities' such as the smaller Slavic nations, particularly the Czechs.[16] The nation-state's consolidation process entailed the assumption that heterogeneous nation-states would impose a unifying language and culture upon its citizens while presuming that 'especially small and backward, nationalities had everything to gain by merging into greater nations, and making their contributions to humanity through these'.[17]

Hobsbawm argues that this position did not arise from chauvinistic motives but described the general attitude. In his own words,

> it did not imply any hostility to the languages and culture of such collective victims to the laws of progress (as they would certainly have been called then). On the contrary, where the supremacy of the state-nationality and the state-language were not an issue, the major nation could cherish and foster the dialects and lesser languages within it; the historic and folkloric traditions of the lesser communities it contained, if only as proof of the range of colours on its macro-national palette.[18]

The criteria for deciding what is to be considered a 'viable' nation have substantially changed since a time when most nationalist movements aimed at the creation of large states. In the nineteenth and early twentieth centuries, nationalist movements sought unification and expansion while aiming to create large powerful states often encompassing different nations within their territory. At the end of the twentieth century, we are confronted with the unpredicted revitalization of nationalism in nations without states. This type of nationalism questions the legitimacy of the state and tends to reject unification and expansion. Instead, it often favours the fragmentation of the state's power and resources monopoly while invoking the right of small nations to self-determination. Nowadays, relatively small size does not seem to be an obstacle for a nation's viability as an autonomous or even independent political institution. Furthermore, small units make sense in a world in which economy and culture are no longer the monopoly of the state.

Romanticism and the nation

There is a connection between the contemporary upsurge of nationalism in nations without states and the nationalism brought about by Romanticism in the first part of the nineteenth century. The Romantics endorsed an idea of the nation 'as natural division of the human race, endowed by God with its own character, which its citizens must, as a duty, preserve pure and inviolable'.[19] Herder himself argued that states 'sin against the principle of diversity, for in them the different nations always run the risk of losing their identity, and are not able fully to cultivate their originality'.[20]

The primary conviction of Romantic nationalism is that culture, a particular way of life and the more important social institutions are essentially formed and shaped by the nation. They are expressions of a unitary force which is usually referred to as the soul, mind or spirit of a people; in Hegel's language, the *Volkgeist* or the character of a nation. Reflecting the uniqueness of a nation, a language is viewed as the form of expression of a particular perception of the world. And alongside an interest in language, there emerges a specific interest in history – the glorious past, myths of origin, customs, ways of life and ideas of a particular people.

Contemporary forms of nationalism in nations without states also invoke the pre-eminence of the nation, and consider minority cultures and languages as valuable, but there is a fundamental difference between the nationalisms of both periods. While Romantic nationalism was primarily concerned to advance the cultural claims of small nations, the nationalism of nations without states at the turn of the twenty-first century is by no means confined to the defence of minority languages and cultures, rather it claims the right of nations without states to some kind of political autonomy which may or may not involve independence.

According to Nipperdey, Romantic nationalism could be understood as a reaction to the European intellectual hegemony based on the cultural predominance of the French-styled Enlightenment, as well as to the imperial tendencies of the Jacobins and Napoleon illustrated by the occupation and exploitation of nations and the threat of European uniformity.[21] In an analogous way, the nationalism of nations without states is linked, among other factors, to a perception of a potential threat of cultural homogenization prompted by the intensification of globalization processes. The selective exclusion of most cultures from access to the means of globalization due to their lack of power and resources adds to the fears of global assimilation. The threat of an Americanization of culture and the use of English as a main language has provoked diverse reactions in different nation-states as well as in nations without states. They are all concerned about their cultures being progressively replaced by an increasingly pervasive global culture which tends to permeate public life and which, to a certain extent, even intrudes in the private sphere.

Romantic nationalism contributed to the creation of new nation-states, such as Germany and Italy. It also achieved prominence among the peoples of Western Europe who lived in national states as was the case with the French; and had a profound effect in nations without states such as Catalonia where it favoured the revitalization of their vernacular cultures and languages. The nationalism of nations without states could contribute to the generation of new political institutions and structures formed by representatives of smaller nations which prove to be economically viable and possess a strong sense of national identity. For Catalan, Scots, Welsh and Basque people, among many other European national minorities, the prospect of a Europe of the Regions stands as a pioneering political structure within which they could enjoy a substantial degree of autonomy. A Europe of the Regions would encourage regional development and allow for sub-state cultures to be preserved.

A further element should be examined when comparing the relevance of the nation and that of nationalism in the Romantic era and today. Romanticism sought to protect relatively untouched traditions at a time when cultural isolation was still possible. In the global age, interdependence and awareness of difference have resulted in the creation of complex societies whose cultures engage in a constant dialogue with other cultures. They welcome some new influences, they reject others, they clash and constantly adapt to a changing socio-political environment. Only cultures with enough power and resources are equipped to survive in the global age where cultural homogeneity has become a feature of the past.

The quest for recognition

The nationalism of nations without states currently employs two major sets of arguments to legitimize its discourse. First, a political argument stemming from the French and American Revolutions. It concerns the endorsement of democracy and popular sovereignty as leading principles to legitimize the construction of the modern state. In late eighteenth-century France, sovereignty was taken away from the king and the aristocracy and placed in the hands of the nation which was understood to include the 'whole people', even though in the first instance it was assumed that the most educated and enlightened citizens would have to guide the people and bring them gradually into political life. Second, a cultural argument closely related to the principles subscribed by Romantic nationalism. It refers to the value of cultural and linguistic diversity together with the relevance of the different identities which now attain a new and unprecedented salience.

The combination of political and cultural arguments in the articulation of nationalist discourses in nations without states possesses a proven capacity to challenge the nation-state's legitimacy at a time when it is most vulnerable. Hence, the progressive weakening of the state sharply contrasts with the renewed relevance acquired by the nation. The current proliferation of definitions and accounts of what is to be considered a nation often fails to establish a clear-cut distinction between nation, state and nation-state, as three different but closely interrelated political concepts to which that of nationalism should be added.

The principle of autonomy stated by Kant means giving laws to oneself, being free from coercion and having the right to choose. He formulated his doctrine to defend the idea that individuals are an end in themselves. As Berlin argues, Fichte quickly applied Kant's plea for self-determination to the group, the nation, which he soon began to identify with the state.[22]

Social movements struggle for recognition, be it the recognition of equality between men and women, the rights of gays and lesbians, animal rights, or environmental rights. The main objective of social movements is to bring attention to a particular issue, to make it relevant, to denounce the unfairness and ill-treatment suffered by somebody or something, whether a group of people, animals or the environment and to put forward a set of measures to reverse their situation. The nationalism of nations without states, when based upon democratic principles, can be considered as a progressive social movement seeking the recognition of a particular community as culturally distinct and having the right to rule itself.

Recognition is the paramount objective of nationalist movements in nations without states. But, we should ask, recognition by whom? I argue that recognition by the state in the first instance, and then by the international community, are the foremost goals of nations without states, since most of them are included within the boundaries of states which are reluctant to acknowledge their status as nations. Not in vain the main objective of nearly all state-elites in the last two hundred years has been to generate a single nation living within the state's territory to legitimize their power over an originally heterogeneous population.

The nationalism of nations without states often clashes with ignorance, neglect or lack of will on the part of the state which tends to resist pressure to grant the right to self-determination to national minorities living within its borders. In most cases, nations without states possess memories of a past in which they enjoyed their own autonomous institutions. The processes which brought that time to an end are not free from conflict and experiences of oppression. Berlin defines nationalism as 'the result of wounds inflicted by someone or something, on the natural feelings of a society, or of artificial barriers to its normal development'.[23] In the nationalist discourses of nations without states which are currently seeking recognition, it is common to find a detailed description and a list of grievances against the state. In Berlin's words: 'Nationalism springs, as often as not, from a wounded or outraged sense of human dignity, the desire for recognition'.[24] The struggle for recognition entails the desire to be regarded and treated as an equal, as someone who has a voice and is able to participate in the political processes affecting his or her future. Recognition involves many dimensions which sometimes overlap. There are moral, social, political and even financial consequences for a state which decides to acknowledge the existence of different nations within its territory. In the process of recognition, pride and moral sentiment take precedence over economic compensation. Berlin writes,

> Recognition is demanded by individuals, by groups, by classes, by nations, by States, by vast conglomerations of mankind united by a common feeling of grievance against those who (they rightly or wrongly suppose) have wounded or humiliated them, have denied them the minimum demanded by human dignity, have caused, or tried to cause, them to fall in their own estimation in a manner that they cannot tolerate. The nationalism of the last two hundred years is shot through with this feeling.[25]

The nationalism of nations without states seeks to halt a relationship with the state which is often marked by: (1) political dependence (sometimes involving also financial dependence); (2) limited or frequently non-existent access to powers and resources; (3) restricted or no financial powers or no financial powers at all, and (4), in many cases, a restraint is placed upon the nation's capacity to develop and promote its own culture and language. Nations without states claim the right to be recognized as political actors and have a say in different forums entrance to which has been up to now restricted to nation-states. Some may argue that the recognition of nations without states adds a further complexity to current international structures, they may add that this might lead to increasing fragmentation and is opposed to the advancement of internationalism.

I argue that such positions ignore the right of peoples to preserve and develop their cultures and decide on their political future. Contemporary democratic nationalist movements in nations without states invoke the right to self-determination, a principle advanced by Woodrow Wilson after 1918. It involved, at first, 'equating the popular principle of sovereignty with the attack on the remaining dynastic empires in Europe, and later with anti-colonialism generally. Secondly, it involved abandoning the constitutional mode of settling disputed claims in favour of political settlements'.[26] In Mayall's view, the historical fate of the principle of national self-determination is doubly ironic: it has tended to legitimize the state and only the state; and it has elevated and institutionalized the progressive view of human affairs by attempting to freeze the political map in a way in which has never been previously attempted.[27] He points at two major challenges to the internal order; irredentism as the main essentialist challenge, and secession as the main rationalist challenge. Irredentism, in modern political usage, has come to mean any territorial claim generally based on historical and/or ethnic arguments made by a sovereign state to lands within another. Secession refers to the creation of an independent state out of a territory previously included within another state from which it has now separated. The term is also often employed to describe unsuccessful separatist rebellions against the state, which may or may not involve the use of violence.

A crucial distinction between irredentism and secession concerns the level at which they both take place and originate. Irredentism is usually instilled by state elites and emerges within the existing system of inter-state power rivalries. 'Secession', as stressed by Mayall, 'depends on group sentiment and loyalty not just on a disputed title to land or a doctrine of prescriptive right'.[28] Secession constitutes a standing challenge to an international order based on the sovereign state.

> It does so because, on the one hand, it belongs to the modern "rationalist" world in which the right to self-determination is held to be a fundamental human right, while, on the other, aggressive war, and therefore the possibility of acquiring title by conquest, is proscribed under the United Nations Charter. The only way out of this impasse is to resort to the conventional interpretation of national self-determination as reflected in the existing state order. This is so obviously a fiction that it must in turn constitute a provocative invitation to secessionist nationalists.[29]

In my view, the recognition of nations without states as global political actors does not necessarily involve them becoming independent. My argument is that while some nations without states may secede most of them are likely to achieve greater political autonomy within the political institutions which are currently being developed. For instance, there are strong chances that further European integration will favour a greater presence of nations without states such as Catalonia, Scotland, the Basque Country or Flanders in the international political arena.

The international community of states is reluctant to undertake territorial revision. There have been four great waves of modern state creation. In Latin America in the nineteenth century; in Europe after the First World War (1914–18); in Asia, Africa, the Caribbean and the Pacific after the Second World War (1939–45); and in Eastern and Central Europe after the break up of the Soviet Union (1989). In each case, state creation has been connected to the collapse of empires although in the case of the Soviet Union, it is not accurate to speak of it as a formal imperial structure, but as an hegemonic system of economic and political influence.

The rise of Quebec nationalism and the pledge of the Parti Québécois, elected in the November 1998 provincial election, to hold a second referendum on Quebec sovereignty might provide a test case for Western nations without states which, in spite of enjoying a substantial degree of political autonomy, decide to demand independence.

After failure to obtain a majority in the 1995 referendum on Quebec sovereignty by about 50,000 votes, the Canadian federal government asked the Supreme Court of Canada whether, under the Constitution, Quebec can secede from Canada unilaterally, whether it has that right under international law, and, in the event of a conflict between Canadian and international law, which takes precedence. On 20 August 1998 the Supreme Court of judges stated that 'A clear majority in Quebec on a clear question in favour of secession would confer democratic legitimacy on the secession initiative which all participants in Confederation would have to recognize. The other provinces and the federal government would have no basis to deny the right of the government of Quebec to pursue secession.'[30] The Federal judges affirm that after a Yes vote, Canada would have to negotiate with Quebec. In the case of an impasse, Quebec would unilaterally declare sovereignty and appeal for international recognition. The path to an independent Quebec, if a clear majority of Quebeckers were to vote for sovereignty, seems to be open. In this case, self-determination is understood by Quebec nationalists as the right to decide upon Quebec's political future within or outside Canada.

Civic coherence and the nation

But, why do nations acquire a special relevance at this particular time? So far I have mentioned globalization, the weakening of the classical state and the proliferation of all sorts of supranational institutions and bodies as some of the major features which continue to generate radical transformations affecting collective life. Now I would like to highlight what seems to me one of the major challenges faced by contemporary societies, this is the survival of what I call 'civic coherence'. By 'civic coherence' I mean a situation in which a minimum set of values and principles able to maintain a sense of unity and common purpose are shared among the members of a particular society. Social movements and political ideologies have, to a certain extent, sought to instil a common body of values and beliefs aiming to unite their members and followers in order to favour the emergence of a sense of solidarity among them. In the early twentieth century Durkheim was already emphasizing the need for secondary organizations to exist between the individual and the state. Their role involved, among other things, professional functions, mutual assistance and educational activities, supposing that ultimately 'the corporation will be called upon to become the foundation, or one of the essential foundations, of our political organization'.[31]

The current longing for the nation and the renewed strength of nationalism in nations without states focuses upon the wish to restore a sense of community among individuals who share a common culture. The nation is portrayed as an ideal community which, in fact, could be seen as sharing many of the attributes which Ferdinand Tönnies placed upon *Gemeinschaft* as opposed to *Gesellschaft* which could somehow be identified with the state. Tönnies offers one of the most exhaustive accounts of the degradation of kinship ties in industrial societies. His distinction between community (*Gemeinschaft*) and society (*Gesellschaft*) is based on the different degree of coherence and solidarity which regulates life in both situations. He writes:

> The theory of the *Gesellschaft* deals with the artificial construction of an aggregate of human beings which superficially resembles the *Gemeinschaft* in so far as the individuals peacefully live and dwell together. However, in the *Gemeinschaft* they remain essentially united in spite of all separating factors, whereas in the *Gesellschaft*, they are essentially separated in spite of all uniting factors.[32]

In *Gesellschaft*, individuals are isolated and 'there exists a condition of tension against all others'. People only have and enjoy what belongs to them to the exclusion of all others, 'something that has a common value does not exist'.[33] In Tönnies view,

> *Gesellschaft*, an aggregate by convention and law of nature, is to be understood as a multitude of natural and artificial individuals, the wills and spheres of whom are in many relations with and to one another, and remain nevertheless independent of one another and devoid of mutual familiar relationships adding that, this gives us a general description of 'bourgeois society'.[34]

A contractual relation lies at the basis of *Gesellschaft*. In a similar way, individuals acquire certain rights and duties by becoming citizens of a particular state without necessarily entering in a personal relationship with other citizens. Despite the fact that the state seeks to foster a sense of community between its citizens by creating a culturally homogeneous nation within its boundaries, the renewed strength of the nationalism in nations without states proves that, often, the state has been unsuccessful.

Tönnies would go even further and argue that 'before and outside convention and also before and outside of each special contract, the relation of all to all may therefore be conceived as potential hostility or latent war'.[35] Although I will not go as far as to describe the relations between citizens of the same state as hostile and close to war, we should be aware of the deep antagonisms which sometimes emerge between citizens of the same state who consider themselves as belonging to a nation other than that promoted by the state. To illustrate this we can consider some Irish nationalists in Northern Ireland and their relation with Britain, and certain Basque nationalists and their relation with Spain. In both cases the state is considered as an alien, foreign power which has colonized Northern Ireland in the first case, and the Basque Country in the second. This leads not only to the rejection of the state's laws and principles, but to the determination to fight what they consider as a foreign army of occupation. The peace process in Northern Ireland and the recent unilateral ceasefire declared by the Basque separatist group ETA (September 1998) seem to have opened the way for the substitution of violence by dialogue in the search for a peaceful solution in both cases.

A further dimension when considering intra-state conflict corresponds to antagonisms arising between different ethnic groups who coexist within the same state. Migrant communities who have settled within the state's boundaries and who may or may not have acquired citizenship may form some of these groups.

Gesellschaft describes a society in which individuals compete most of the time, except when they form a coalition to confront a common enemy. All relations are permeated by material interests and 'based upon comparison of possible and offered services'.[36] For Tönnies, the economic system was a perfect example of *Gesellschaft*, while 'the corporations of the arts, churches and holy orders represented a prototype of *Gemeinschaft*'.[37]

'Blood, place (land), and mind, or kinship, neighbourhood, and friendship' are, according to Tönnies, the three pillars of *Gemeinschaft* which are encompassed in the family. He stresses the primordial role of the land, as the place where the community's life evolves. The land is the area occupied by the community throughout different generations and links individuals to their ancestors prompting the hallowing of certain shrines. What Tönnies writes about the land when applied to *Gemeinschaft* can perfectly be applied to the territory of the nation as portrayed in nationalist discourses.

Habits, mores and folkways are also attributed particular significance in a *Gemeinschaft*. Similarly, customs and beliefs are an important component of the nation. The image of the family employed by Tönnies to exemplify *Gemeinschaft* has often been employed to portray the nation as an extended family.

A final and crucial consideration concerns Tönnies's warning against a decaying culture of *Gesellschaft*, and an increasing claim for *Gemeinschaft*. In an analogous way, the state seems to be currently challenged by the national claims of some of the nations integrated in its territory. The strength of nationalism in nation without states stems from its capacity to portray the nation as a community with which individuals can identify. Only when the nation is perceived as a community, are individuals able to develop a bond of sentiment and a feeling of solidarity among them. But this does not imply that nations without states are ideal communities free from internal conflict and diversity, rather their members may hold differing images of how the nation should be defined and what the national project should be. Democratic nationalist movements in nations without states accept and encourage dialogue between people who may differ in their conception of the nation but who share a sense of belonging to a common nation, membership of which remains open, and are ready to engage in a dialogic process of national development. It would be naive to ignore that in the same way as some nation-states seek to enhance their unity by implementing undemocratic homogenization policies, some nationalist movements in nations without states may be tempted to do the same and adopt non-democratic practices.

The nationalism of nations without states attempts to restore and enhance a sense of community which most states have proven unable to foster. It is in this sense that Tönnies's distinction between *Gesellschaft* and *Gemeinschaft* becomes relevant when trying to account for the relation between the state and the nation. The former is a political institution based on rational laws and principles which define its relation with its members in terms of citizenship. The latter is a cultural community capable of creating a bond of sentiment and a sense of belonging among individuals who share a common national identity and demand the right to be considered as political actors.

I shall now move on to examine the different political scenarios in which nations without states find themselves. This will emphasize the huge differences existing between the recognition they seek and obtain from diverse nation-states. It will also shed some light upon the various relationships states develop with the national minorities they contain.

2

Nations without States:
different political scenarios

At present we are witnessing a dynamic re-emergence of some old nations which currently lack a state of their own but possessed an independent status in a more or less remote past, Catalonia and Scotland among them. They are both integrated within larger states and have developed significant nationalist movements, which initially focused upon cultural demands that progressively turned into political claims. How does the state respond to such claims? What are the main arguments employed by national minorities to promote their right to self-determination? How can the claims advanced by one or various national minorities within a single state be harmonized? Is it possible to restrict political autonomy to some areas within a single state, or is it necessary to develop symmetric models which grant autonomy to all of the state's regions?

A key feature when considering nations without states is the degree of dissatisfaction felt by their members concerning their present situation. They tend to regard the state within which they are included as 'alien', as an 'obstruction' to the development of their nation, or as a 'burden' which takes a great deal of their resources and does not provide them with sufficient benefits. The articulation of such feelings provokes the emergence of nationalist movements with differing political aims ranging from devolution and autonomy to secession and independence. Such movements are based upon the denunciation of an unsatisfactory situation with regard to economic, social, political or security matters stemming from the relationship between the state and its national minority or minorities. The particular nature of the state, which differs in each case, determines the status of the national minority, while the strength of the minority's nationalist movement heavily influences a possible reshaping of its relationship with the state.

This chapter considers cultural recognition, political autonomy and federation as three possible political responses to the nationalism of nations without states. Independence may indeed be the outcome of nationalist pressure, but in what follows I shall focus upon these three alternatives which are capable of accommodating the national minorities' demands without in principle leading to secession. Cultural recognition, political autonomy and federation presuppose the acceptance of democracy understood in a broad sense and the readiness of the state to recognize varying degrees of difference within itself. There are many intermediate solutions to the three main political scenarios I wish to study. In this sense, I will consider regionalization, devolution, and decentralization as variations either within cultural recognition or political autonomy depending upon each case. A further political response refers to a state of affairs in which the national minority's existence is not recognized as such by the state or states containing it. This is what I call 'denial and repression'. In these circumstances, lack of recognition is often accompanied by the active implementation of policies destined to homogenize the population and to eradicate the cultural and political specific traits of the minority. There are many ways in which repression can be exerted ranging from social and political to overt military measures.

In this chapter, I examine different political scenarios and feasible solutions to the nationalism of nations without states in Western countries. Although I will make occasional references to some post-colonial societies, I am aware that for these references to be fully accurate, a careful analysis of what colonialism means, and how the concepts of nation, state and nationalism were exported to these areas and appropriated by the new local elites to fit into a radically distinct environment from that of the West where they had originated, should be included. But this is an area of study that is far beyond the scope of the present book.

Cultural recognition

The acknowledgement of certain cultural traits as specific characteristics of a territorially-based national minority, which the state may refer to as 'region', 'province', or 'département', stands as a 'soft' option in the state's process of recognizing its internal diversity. Two

main issues need to be considered before exploring this option. First,
cultural recognition presupposes the existence of a unitary state which
excludes the possibility of considering its internal diversity as the
outcome of more than one nation living under the umbrella of a single
political institution. Almost invariably, the state promotes a common
language and culture through a more or less efficient national education system. In this context, internal differences do not pose a threat
to the state's integrity, rather, they are incorporated into the state's
culture and are considered as part of it. Second, cultural recognition
seems to work wherever national minorities have a weak sense of
identity, or are unwilling to articulate or prevented from articulating
social and political movements in defence of their specificity. But how
are we to explain a weak national self-consciousness? Three main
causes can be identified: (1) a successful assimilation programme
implemented by the state which has resulted in a considerable degree
of integration of the national minority involved; (2) a situation in
which the national minority has been repressed over a substantial
period of time, taking into account that repression can be exerted in a
myriad of ways which do not necessarily involve the use of physical
force and; (3) historical accident. This last refers to unspecified circumstances which can be considered entirely as a matter of chance. For
example, the death or lack of a successor to the crown and the need
to find a new monarch outside the nation; a high influx of migrants
taking over the economy and, later, the political system; or the
massive migration of young members of the nation forced to find
work elsewhere.

Cultural recognition involves a minimal degree of decentralization,
if any. The state may decide to appoint a special representative for the
area in charge of the distribution of state subsidies and the administration of the region according to the state's legislation. This person is
usually accountable to the parliament for issues concerning the region.
The state's nominee is not elected by the region's inhabitants as
members of the regional government and the president himself are in
the case of political autonomy.

This has been the case in Scotland up to May 1999, when the first
members to the newly created Scottish Parliament will be elected.
In Scotland, a Secretary of State was appointed in the first post-
union Government (1707). After 1745, however, no such appointment was made; and while responsibility for Scotland during the
majority of the ensuing period lay with the Home Secretary, most
of the effective political power was exercised by the Lord Advocate.
This System lasted until 1885 when the office of Secretary for Scotland

was created, its status being enhanced in 1926 to that of Secretary of State.

Cultural recognition, as mentioned above, involves a unitary state which does not delegate its sovereign powers, except on very specific issues – this was the case in Scotland which maintained its separate education system, religion and civil law.

The citizens of the state exert their sovereignty in general elections which affect the life of the entire population, the region is never considered as a separate entity enjoying the right to directly decide upon matters affecting it. There are no regional elections, sovereignty is exercised at a single level and it is not devolved. The integrity of the state is well preserved since the possibility of internal challenges is ruled out by a firm unitary state structure.

Cultural recognition usually involves the protection and promotion of the regional language, if there is one, and culture. It is relatively easy and uncompromising for the state to sponsor some folklore events which reflect the specific traditions of the area and present them as a constitutive part of the nation-state's broad culture. Such manifestations are aimed at pleasing those members of the region who consider themselves satisfied with this level of recognition.

The protection and encouragement of a regional language which is only spoken by a small minority, or relegated to a private sphere, is more controversial. The degree of controversy is directly connected to the strength and resources allocated to this end, and to the social impact of an increasing use of the language in the public sphere. Wherever the regional language has been lost, difference is maintained by other distinctive features of the community such as law, religion, etc., but undoubtedly, wherever a language still exists, it becomes one of the most prominent features of identity.

The recognition of internal difference, be it in the form of cultural recognition, political autonomy or federation, is bound to provoke opposition from those who sustain a closed image of the state as a political institution which aims at the annihilation of difference within itself. In many multinational states we encounter what I call a 'colonization of the regions'. By this I mean a process of active assimilation of regions to the mainstream culture and language. The presence of the state's representatives in the administration and the army contributes to the consolidation of such policies.

Further to this, a subtle and to a certain degree unintended form of colonization of poor areas occurs when a substantial number of second residences are acquired by people from outside the region who enjoy a higher standard of living and benefit from the region's lower prices in the house market and services. The impact of their presence depends very much on the number of new 'part-time' residents. A few people are easier to assimilate into the uses, traditions and even the language of a particular region. The various attitudes of those entering certain communities through their second homes makes a great difference. Thus, some people are respectful of regional cultures, while others are indifferent to them. There are also those who clearly despise regional cultures as inferior, primitive or retro-grade and a sign of the region's backwardness. In these circumstances, the autochthonous people's reactions towards the 'newcomers' range from open hostility, which sometimes can lead to violence, to admir-ation and a sense of inferiority.

Political autonomy

Political autonomy refers to a situation in which a unitary state decides to put into practice a certain degree of decentralization by devolving some of its powers concerning a specific number of issues to all or some of its constituent regions, provinces or nations – the terminology varies a great deal depending upon the individual's perspective. Some key concepts connected with the idea of political autonomy are: subsidiarity, decentralization, and devolution. They all refer to the transformation of a unitary state into a political institution able to delegate some functions while still retaining a strong core of attributes. These concepts can be understood as a means to deepen democratic practices by bringing decision-making processes closer to those who will be directly affected by them. The main argument for decentralization is the implicit belief that transferring certain functions to sub-state institutions with a territorial basis could increase effi-ciency and legitimacy. However, and although there are practical reasons for defending the partial autonomy of certain areas within a single state, it should never be taken for granted that the state will automatically accept such a principle.

The combination of democracy with Woodrow Wilson's 1918 prin-ciple of a people's right to self-determination has so far resulted in different political arrangements attempting to acknowledge both cri-teria while preserving the nation-state's integrity. Political autonomy should be regarded as a state's response to its national minorities' nationalism which goes beyond cultural recognition. It usually emerges as the result of pressure exerted by the national minorities involved and it is never a smooth process. Political autonomy requires the amendment of the state's constitution to specify the degree of decentralization and the specific powers which will be transferred to the regions. It also requires the establishment of clear guiding principles for the allocation of the resources which will make the new political dispensation possible. Sovereignty is not shared by the constituent parts of the state as expected in a federation. Instead of this, the state transfers some of its functions to newly created regional institutions with or without a previous historical existence, which must always be accountable to it. Matters relating to culture and welfare seem to be easier to transfer than those concerning taxation, security and international relations. Powers over the latter, if ever ceded, are always partial and are kept under close supervision by state agents and institutions. There is not a fixed rule as to how much power should be devolved when autonomy is conferred upon regions; this explains why the concept and content of this political arrangement vary substantially when applied to different political environments. In what follows I shall address some of these issues by examining two particular cases in which political autonomy has been put into practice, Catalonia and Scotland.

Catalonia, in northern Spain, shares Scotland's history of having been independent until the early eighteenth century and then subsequently integrated within a larger state. A separate sense of identity based on a particular culture, which in the case of Catalonia includes a distinct language, and the desire for some type of political recognition have been at the heart of Catalan as well as Scottish nationalist demands. A brief historical reminder should prove useful when tracing back the origins of both nations, and will shed some light on the major issues which have contributed to the emergence of distinct national identities in both Catalonia and Scotland.

The making of the Catalans Fundamental to the history of Catalan nationalism is the fact that Catalonia became a nation without a state only after a long period from the ninth century up to 1714 during which it enjoyed its own political institutions and laws. Rather than offering a complete history of Catalonia, I shall focus upon certain events crucial in the process of formation of the Catalan nation which become invested with particular meaning when Catalans *'tell their history'* and think of themselves as *'different'* from others.

After the Roman Empire and three centuries of Gothic rule, the Moors invaded the Iberian Peninsula in 711. As a direct result of the confrontation with the Moors, the inhabitants of the North-Eastern corner of *Hispania* allied themselves with the Franks across the

Pyrenees, taking a first step in a course of events which would lead to the emergence of an independent Catalonia. The Franks called this territory the *Marca Hispánica*, respected the rights of its inhabitants and left the government in the hands of local elites. While the power of the Carolingian empire decreased, that of the Catalan counts steadily grew and the Count of Barcelona took precedence over his fellows. Wilfred the Hairy (*Guifré el Pilós*) was the last count of the *Marca Hispánica* to receive his commission from the Frankish king (878). The independence of Catalonia, or more accurately, of the House of Barcelona, was first recognized by a French monarch in 1258 when James I The Conqueror (*Jaume I el Conqueridor*) and Louis IX signed the Treaty of Corbeil. By this treaty, Louis IX of France renounced claims to the counties of Roussillon and Barcelona, while James I gave up his aspirations to the fiefs of the viscounties of Carcassonne and Narbonne, thus reducing Catalan dominion north of the Roussillon. The union of Catalonia and Aragon in 1137 was the result of a pact, and for this reason both parts maintained their separate political identities; that is, their territorial integrity, laws, habits, institutions and rulers. The Counts of Barcelona became kings of Aragon and from this moment onwards, the historiography refers to their possessions as the Crown of Aragon. It is significant that, together with England, Catalonia was one of the first societies to grant itself what amounted to a written feudal constitution. Yet, the English *Magna Carta* was preceded by almost one century by the Catalan *Usatges* of 1150 whose very title (the *uses*, that is, established customs and practices) betrays the fact that the laws the document proclaimed had already been in existence for a very long time. The *Usatges* was an essentially pactist law code.[1]

During the thirteenth and fourteenth centuries Catalonia built up a powerful Mediterranean empire of a primarily commercial character. It included Valencia, Majorca, Sardinia, Corsica, Sicily, Naples, Athens and Neopatria, as well as French territories beyond the Pyrenees particularly Roussillon and Cerdagne. When Martin the Humane (*Martí l'Humà*) died without a successor in 1410, Fernando de Antequera (*Fernando I*) from the Castilian family of the Trastámara was elected to the throne (Compromise of Casp, 1412). Fernando I confirmed the pactist character of the Catalan Principality that dated from 1150 when the *Usatges* were drawn up, defining the mutual rights and responsibilities of the ruler on the one side and of his subjects on the other. The *Usatges* were reinforced by the formation in the thirteenth century of the *Corts* (Parliament).

The joint rule of Isabel, queen of Castile and Fernando, king of the

Crown of Aragon (*Reyes Católicos*) over their territories from 1479, put two very different nations under the same monarchs. As Elliott argues, the gulf between the two was made still wider by their differing political traditions and institutions. Although each possessed parliamentary institutions (Corts), the Castilian Corts had never attained legislative power and emerged from the Middle Ages as isolated and weak, while those of Catalonia, Valencia and Aragon (component parts of the Crown of Aragon) shared the legislative power with the Crown and were well buttressed by laws and institutions which derived from a long tradition of political liberty.[2] Thus, apart from sharing common sovereigns, neither Castile nor the Crown of Aragon underwent any radical institutional alteration.

However, in practice the equality between Castile and the Crown of Aragon did not long survive the death of Fernando el Católico and a widening gap between Castile and all the other territories, including the states of the Crown of Aragon, began. A radical change in the Castilian policy towards Catalonia took place when Philip IV (*Felipe IV*) appointed the Count Duke of Olivares as chief minister in March 1621. His objective was to create a powerful absolutist state. Clashes between Catalan and Castilian culture and institutions intensified when Philip IV, in need of fiscal revenues, tightened up centralism. The increasing tension between Castile and Catalonia reached its climax in the Revolt of the Reapers (*Revolta dels Segadors*) in 1640 which would acquire a particular significance in the Catalan nationalist literature. Scholars of Catalan history argue that, as early as 1640, the Catalans led what can be considered one of the first nationalist revolutions. They united against the harsh treatment received from Castile, emphasized their difference from Castilians, and if they did not object to the figure of Philip IV as their king, they claimed that he had to acknowledge Catalan institutions, law and customs, since monarchy had a pactist character according to the Catalan Constitutions.[3]

In the War of the Spanish Succession, Catalonia supported the cause of the Austrians against Philip V (*Felipe V*) of the Bourbon dynasty. The Treaty of Utrecht (1713) confirmed Philip V as king of Spain and Catalonia was left alone to face the might of the Franco-Spanish armies. Catalonia maintained its rights and liberties until 1714, when on 11 September after a massive Franco-Spanish attack that followed a siege of fourteen months, Barcelona surrendered. Philip V ordered the dissolution of the Catalan institutions – the *Consell de Cent* (Council of One Hundred), *Diputació* and *Generalitat* – and Catalonia was subject to a regime of occupation. Catalan was forbidden and Castilian

(Spanish) was proclaimed as the official language. On 19 January 1716, Philip V promulgated the *Decreto de Nueva Planta*, a new ground plan for the centralized government of Catalonia and its integration with the rest of Spain. The abolition of Catalan institutions, rights and liberties involved the practical disappearance of the Catalan aristocracy – only very few were absorbed into the Spanish nobility. This fact, together with other factors such as the demographic recovery of Catalonia, the existence of a free *pagesia* (land-owning farmers and peasants) entrenched in their properties, and the Catalan *menestrals* (artisans, shopkeepers, workshop owners) who combined individualism, familism, commitment to hard work and respect for the methodical accumulation of wealth through savings, was the basis for the transformation of Catalonia into an industrial society. The industrialization of Catalonia in the nineteenth century was accompanied by major social changes along patterns similar to those that were taking place in other industrializing Western European countries and resulted in the creation of a sharp contrast between Catalonia and the rest of the Peninsula, with the exception of the Basque Country. This originated a very peculiar scenario in which the most economically developed part of a country, Catalonia, found itself politically subject to an anachronistic and backward state, Castile, that held political power. Although differences have diminished, Catalan nationalists claim that this is still the case.[4]

By the end of the nineteenth century, the influence of Romanticism favoured the *Renaixença*, a movement for national and cultural renaissance, and soon prompted demands for Catalan autonomy, first in the form of regionalism and later in demands for a federal state. Catalan nationalism did not emerge as a unified phenomenon. Rather, diverse political ideologies and cultural influences gave rise to different types of nationalism, from the conservative nationalism of Balmes, to the federalism of Pi i Margall, the Catholic nationalism of Torres i Bages, or the Catalan Marxism of Andreu Nin, among many others.[5]

Catalonia enjoyed a certain degree of autonomy under the administrative government of the *Mancomunitat* (1913–23), suppressed in 1923 after the *coup d'état* of Miguel Primo de Rivera, and the *Generalitat* (1931–38), abolished by General Francisco Franco's decree of 5 April 1938. After Franco's dictatorship, Catalonia would recover its autonomous government, the *Generalitat*, only in 1977 and sanction a new Statute of Autonomy in 1979. The president of the Catalan government in exile, Josep Tarradellas returned from France (1977). Jordi Pujol, leader of the Convergence and Union coalition (*Convergència i Unió* or CiU) became the first president of the

Catalan parliament in the first democratic election after Francoism (1980).

Catalonia and the Spanish Autonomous Communities System The Spanish Autonomous System stands as a good example of how devolution works once it is applied to the whole territory of a state. During the Francoist regime (1939–75), nationalism and democracy stood together as part and parcel of the Catalan and Basque demands for the transformation of Spain into a democratic state able to recognize diversity within itself and ready to alter its recalcitrant centralist nature. After Franco's death in 1975, the national question became a pressing matter and a compromise among all political forces engaged in the process of drawing up a new democratic constitution for Spain had to be achieved. The makers of the Constitution opted for a model based upon symmetry, what has been called 'coffee for everyone' (*café para todos*), and instead of directly responding to the nationalist claims of Catalonia and the Basque Country as nations, they decided to implement a system which would allow for the creation of seventeen autonomous communities, some historically and culturally distinct – Catalonia, the Basque Country and Galicia – others artificially created where no sense of a separate identity had ever existed – La Rioja and Madrid among many others. While Catalonia, the Basque Country and Galicia were immediately allowed to initiate the process towards full autonomy, other regions had to fulfil a five-year 'restricted autonomy' period before initiating it. Once full autonomy is achieved, however, the Constitution makes no distinction between the communities. This involves assuming the indissoluble unity of Spain while recognizing and guaranteeing the right to autonomy of its nationalities and regions.

Each Community has a regional legislative assembly consisting of a single chamber. Deputies are elected on the basis of proportional representation and usually the leader of the majority party or coalition assumes the presidency of the Community. The President heads a regional executive of ministers in charge of departments which mostly, but not always, follow the Spanish state's pattern. In many ways the Autonomous Governments act as states. In Catalonia and the Basque Country, for example, they provide services in education, health, culture, housing, local transport, agriculture and they have even gained control of their Autonomous police force. The Spanish Government holds exclusive jurisdiction over defence, the administration of justice, international relations and general economic planning. A Compensation Fund administered by the government

allocates special resources to poorer regions and is intended to promote equilibrium and solidarity among them. After almost twenty
years of autonomy, some Catalans and Basques are not fully satisfied.
They still want to stress their specificity and be recognized as nations
within Spain. They demand special treatment and show increasing
reluctance to blindly accept the 'coffee for everyone' option. Pressure
to change the Constitution is already accumulating; the Catalan
nationalist coalition, the Convergence and Union (CiU, or *Convergència
i Unió*), that has ruled Catalonia since 1980, is pushing for the
recognition of Catalonia as a nation within Spain and demanding the
granting of a special status for it. Asymmetry is regarded as an
arrangement which would reflect the Spanish reality in a more accurate manner. In spite of current criticism and increasing pressure to
modify the Autonomous System by conferring a special status on
Catalonia and the Basque Country, in my view the Spanish Auto-
nomic System deserves a positive evaluation as an instrument which
permitted a peaceful accommodation of regional nationalism during
the Spanish transition to democracy. Political autonomy seemed a
dream to those who fought against a dictatorship which never seemed
to come to an end (it lasted from 1939 to 1975). Furthermore, political
autonomy applied to the whole territory of the Spanish state has
avoided, although not completely, some of the issues which are
currently being discussed when considering the presence of Scottish
MPs in Westminster once Scotland's Parliament is established.

Catalonia and the Basque Country base their claims for further
autonomy on historical and cultural grounds, and the same applies to
Scotland and Wales. In Spain, it has proven very hard to avoid conflict
whenever special treatment for the Basque Country and/or Catalonia
has been discussed or arranged. Other regions tend to interpret it as a
sign of favouritism which promotes some parts of the state to the
detriment of others.

The tension between the acceptance of Catalonia as part of Spain
and the desire to extend its degree of autonomy lies at the core of
the CiU's nationalist discourse. It has been in power since 1980. Its
leader, Jordi Pujol, has since then been re-elected six times as president of Catalonia. It defines Catalonia as a nation but does not
question Spanish unity. The CiU supported the Socialist government
(1993–95) when it lost its majority in the Spanish Parliament, and is
currently backing the Conservative Popular Party which did not
obtain a majority in the 1996 general election. This illustrates Jordi
Pujol's idea that it is feasible to be a Catalan nationalist and at the
same time to contribute to the governance of Spain. Pujol granted

support to the PSOE (Spanish Socialist Workers Party) in a climate fraught with constant political corruption scandals affecting socialist leaders. During this period he managed to attain a substantial development of the Catalan Statute of Autonomy. The right to retain 15 per cent of the taxes collected in Catalonia was probably his greatest achievement. Since 1997, and after negotiations with the Popular Party, the Catalan Government (*Generalitat*) has been directly collecting 30 per cent of the taxes. In Catalonia decentralization has not bred extreme nationalism, on the contrary setting channels for participation has greatly enhanced the Catalan economy and quality of life.

The making of the Scots   Scotland enjoyed political independence until 1707, and the survival of many of its institutions, notably law, religion and education, after the Union contributed to the preservation of its singular identity.

Opposing myths of origin were invoked by English and Scots in accounting for the origin of Scotland. The former claimed superiority on various grounds, and attributed great significance to the myth which considered the Scots as descendants of the younger son of Trojan Brutus, while Britain had been founded by his eldest son; the consequence of this being that Scots owed loyalty to the English. The Scots' alternative myth of descent related them to the Greek prince Gedyl-Glays who married Scota, the daughter of a Pharaoh of Egypt who came via Hispania to Ireland, and then to Scotland.[6]

Roman influence in Scotland was persistent up to the fourth century, but it was limited to the Lowlands, where they built Hadrian's Wall as a northern frontier of Roman Britain. Four peoples inhabited the land now called Scotland: the Picts, the Scots from Ireland, the Britons and the Angles.[7] Their union took centuries to accomplish and this accounts for the difference in the sense of Scottish identity, felt by the inhabitants of the Highlands and the Lowlands, which still persists. Christianity was introduced in Scotland in late Roman times and was firmly established by the Celtic clergy. The Church in Scotland remained Celtic until the eleventh century.

Viking raids were frequent from the eighth century, and Norse earls ruled Orkney, Shetland and the Hebrides. In 834 Kenneth MacAlpin became the first joint king of the Scots and the Picts. King Duncan I was the first to rule over most of Scotland when he came to the throne in 1034. Malcolm Canmore became king in 1058, and founded a dynasty which was to rule in Scotland for over two centuries. During this period, the Celtic monarchy evolved into an organized feudal state which received strong English influences. It is during this period that, according to Llobera, 'the generation of a feudal state, the unifying role of the Scottish Church and the constant threat of an Anglo-Norman invasion contributed to generate a Scottish "national spirit" '.[8]

After the Maid of Norway's death (1286), thirteen claimants for the Scottish crown emerged. Edward I of England undertook to judge the various claims and presented himself as a feudal superior of the Scottish monarch. He named John Balliol as king of Scotland. In 1296, Edward I forced the submission of Balliol and of Scotland with ease. National resistance against the English was led by William Wallace who defeated the English at Stirling Bridge (1297), lost at Falkirk (1298) and was executed in London (1305). In 1306 Robert the Bruce (Robert I) rose in revolt and was crowned king of Scots. He defeated the English army of Edward II at Bannockburn (1314).[9]

In 1320 the Scots nobles sent a letter to Pope John XXII trying to persuade him of the legitimacy of King Robert the Bruce. This was a patriotic address known as the Declaration of Arbroath, invariably quoted as the first nationalist statement in Western Europe: 'For as long as one hundred of us shall remain alive we shall never in any wise consent to submit to the rule of the English, for it is not for glory we fight, for riches, or for honours, but for freedom alone, which no good man loses but with his life.'[10] The Declaration referred to Robert the Bruce as 'king of Scots', not king of Scotland, thus portraying him as a limited monarch of a people and not as lord and owner of the land. It was not until 1328 that Robert the Bruce was fully absolved by the Pope who had excommunicated him when he was crowned king of the Scots. By that time Scotland had finally gained independence.

James VI King of Scotland became king of England in 1603 and adopted by proclamation in October 1604 the title of 'King of Great Britain, France and Ireland'. James VI united the crowns of England and Scotland, and it was legally recognized that subjects born after his accession to the English crown had a common nationality.

After King Charles I was sentenced by a court he did not recognize and beheaded on 30 January 1649, England was proclaimed a free Commonwealth ruled by the army under Oliver Cromwell's leadership. Scotland reacted by immediately proclaiming King Charles II. War between Scotland and England broke out and Cromwell invaded Scotland, which was finally defeated in 1652. In the first instance, conquered Scotland was to be treated as a mere province, but a Declaration of the English Parliament stated that Scotland and

England were to be made into one Commonwealth. The expenses
incurred by England were to be met by confiscation of the estates of
those who had fought against Cromwell and the whole nation was
to enjoy all the privileges of English subjects. But soon the Scots
found that they were to be seriously underrepresented in the joint
Parliament in London and other Commonwealth institutions. Thus,
in 1652, Cromwell imposed on Scotland a full and incorporating
union with England, but the Act of Union of Parliaments did not
take place until 1707.

In 1706 violent protest against the draft Union Treaty broke out in
Edinburgh, Glasgow and Dumfries. Concern about the future of the
Kirk (Scottish Church) was raised and numerous petitions were
presented to the Scottish Parliament. In response to this, the Parliament passed an Act for Securing the Protestant Religion and Presby-
terian Church Government, which was to be regarded as part of the
Treaty; at the same time the English Parliament passed an Act for
securing the Church of England. The Scots lost political independence
after the Treaty of Union in 1707. It is open to controversy how the
Scots reacted to the Union, and whether they consented to it, or
whether it was imposed upon them.[11]

The Act of Union preserved the Kirk, Scottish law, the education
system and the judicial system, which have since then contributed to
the maintenance of a distinct Scottish identity. According to Mackie,
'in theory after 1 May 1707 there was no English Parliament, but a
wholly new "British" legislature, in practice, the English Parliament
simply absorbed the Scottish one'.[12] In his view, hostility to England
among the Scottish governing class rose after the English showed a
patronizing attitude towards Scotland often misinterpreting and
sometimes even ignoring the Treaty of Union. The idea that Scotland
was 'sold' spread among opponents of the Union who argued that the
sums Scotland had received when signing the Union Treaty were an
act of bribery of the Scottish Parliament. Political, economic, constitutional and ecclesiastical grievances against the English began to
increase. Lynch points to two unflattering images of the post-Union
Scot in the minds of London governments – 'the Scot on the make,
usually in London, and the whinging ingrate, already caricatured by
cartoonists as "sister Peg" or "Sorley"'.[13]

The Jacobites attempted in 1715 and again in 1745 to break the
Union, but without success. In the eighteenth century Scottish culture
flourished and Scotland stood in the forefront of the European
Enlightenment.[14] The economy took off and by the end of the eighteenth century cotton spinning and weaving on the new power

machinery of the Industrial Revolution became Scotland's leading industries.

The nineteenth century witnessed several development:

1 The three main institutions which protected Scotland's identity – the Kirk, education and the law – were all forced onto the retreat. In 1853 the Association for the Vindication of Scottish Rights was created. It was the first concerted 'nationalist' protest whose main aim was to defend the place of Scotland in British politics.

2 By the end of the nineteenth century the metallurgical industry had become dominant. A new middle class and urban working class emerged, and severe social and economic distress led to outbreaks of unrest in city and countryside alike. From Scotland emerged some of the first leaders of the British labour movement.

3 In 1885 a Secretary for Scotland was appointed, however he did not command a place in the Cabinet until 1892 and the office did not become a full Secretaryship of State until 1926.

In 1928 the Scottish Nationalist Party was established. The movement for home rule for Scotland received an impetus after the Second World War when the Scottish Liberal Party published a scheme for the establishment of a Parliament for Scotland. In 1954 the Royal Commission on Scottish Affairs recommended increased powers for the Secretary of State for Scotland, but rejected devolution. The nationalist movement gained prominence in 1966 with the discovery of North Sea oil.

Scotland within a decentralized Britain   Scotland has endured a long and complicated process towards self-determination. In the 1979 Referendum, the Scots voted in favour of the Labour Government's proposals to establish a Scottish Assembly. The Act was repealed because a special majority provision required that at least 40 per cent of the registered electorate should vote in favour. Only 32.9 per cent of the electorate voted positively in the referendum.

Since 1988 the Scottish Constitutional Convention comprising Labour, Liberal Democrats, Nationalists, churches, unions and other civic groups has been campaigning for change. In 1995 they published a plan for a Scottish Parliament. In the light of the unhappy memories of earlier attempts at major constitutional reform, the Convention opposed an establishing referendum considering it as a high-risk strategy. Once in power, however, the Labour Government decided to hold a referendum (11 September 1997) which had a positive outcome: 74 per cent of the Scots voted for a Scottish Parliament and

63 per cent voted to give it tax-varying powers. This has transformed
Scotland's status within Britain, and will see an end to the Secretary
of State for Scotland. The Scots will elect their own representatives to
the Scottish Parliament (May 1999). The First Minister will head the
Scottish Executive and will be appointed by the Queen on the advice
of the Presiding Officer after the Scottish Parliament has nominated a
candidate, who will normally be the leader of the party able to
command the majority support of the Scottish Parliament. The affirmative referendum result cannot deliver constitutional entrenchment,
but it might reinforce its moral and political legitimacy. Ultimately
Scotland's Parliament will have to secure its future in the UK constitution by convincing the population of its relevance to their lives.

One of the main concerns of British politics when discussing devolution is the continuing role of MPs sitting for devolved areas at
Westminster. This issue became prominent when Tam Dalyell posed
the so-called 'West Lothian Question' in the House of Commons. It
refers to 'the anomaly whereby Scottish MPs would retain the right to
vote on matters affecting only England and Wales but no Westminster
MP would have such a voting entitlement on the same issues for
Scotland (these having been transferred to the Edinburgh Parliament)'.[15] The current over-representation of Scotland at Westminster
by around fourteen seats, justified by the need to compensate sparsely
populated regions, should also be corrected. The absence of a written
British constitution where answers to these questions could be found
leaves open a wide range of options to be discussed in dealing with
these crucial issues. The creation of a devolved parliament in Edinburgh does not alter, in principle, the unitary character of the British
state since sovereignty continues to reside in Westminster. An SNP
majority in the Scottish Parliament could, of course, put pressure for
further autonomy and even call for a referendum on Scottish
independence.

The creation of a Scottish Parliament undoubtedly establishes an
asymmetric structure in the UK through recognizing Scotland as
distinct from other areas of Britain on the basis of its specific culture,
tradition and ways of life stemming from its separate past as an
independent territory.

The British Prime Minister, Tony Blair, in his preface to the *Scotland's Parliament White Paper* refers to Scotland as 'a proud historic
nation in the United Kingdom', thus acknowledging the multinational
character of the British state. Throughout the *Paper*, Scottish devolution is presented as part of the Government's comprehensive programme of constitutional reform which will strengthen the United

Kingdom. Scotland will remain an integral part of the UK, and the Queen will continue to be Head of State of the United Kingdom. Westminster is and will remain sovereign. The Scottish Parliament will have law-making powers over a wide range of matters which affect Scotland. Westminster will retain powers and responsibilities for the constitution of the UK, UK foreign policy including relations with Europe, UK defence and national security, the stability of the UK's fiscal, economic and monetary system, employment legislation, social security, and most aspects of transport safety and regulation.

For most English people it is hard to establish a clear-cut distinction between an English and a British identity; this explains their difficulty in understanding the Scottish perspective. In Britain devolution has become a highly contentious issue which automatically provokes passionate reactions. Lack of solidarity, unfair treatment, favouritism, and threat to the integrity of the state, are some of the expressions which have been used about a decentralized Britain. These assertions ignore the argument that granting political autonomy to national minorities represents a deepening of democracy. If the Scots want to decide upon their own future and are ready to defend this option by peaceful means, as they proved in the 1997 devolution referendum, it will be extremely difficult for any future British government to abolish the Scottish Parliament.

A key economic issue distinguishes the position of Catalonia and the Basque Country from that of Scotland and Wales. The former are net contributors to the state's coffers, the latter depend on state subsidies. This makes a substantial difference when considering the Spanish and the British prospects for further decentralization.

An asymmetric political structure such as the one being set up in Britain is likely to provoke conflict, and states are usually reluctant to accept it because it implies, in one way or another, the acceptance of a special status for some areas. Few states define themselves as multinational, although there may be strong arguments for them to do so. In this sense, political autonomy is regarded as an intermediate option which goes further than simply acknowledging the cultural specificity of some regions, but stops far short of the sharing of sovereignty involved in federation. For the state and the areas which do not benefit from it, asymmetry is hard to accept. However it might come to be regarded as the only acceptable alternative for some nations without a state if they are to be discouraged from seeking independence. Their plea for a more generous interpretation of the right of peoples to self-determination, excluding a watering down of their national aspirations by the creation of a system based on the homogeneous decentralization of the state, becomes a pressing matter when the region has a nationalist movement which enjoys a mass following. In these circumstances the state, to sustain its democratic reputation, has to respond to such claims and avoid favouring the emergence of regional nationalisms demanding secession. In Europe, the strength of nationalism in nations without states and the different state reactions to it need to be contrasted with the impact of further European political integration. I shall discuss this particular topic later on in the book.

Federation

The main difference between federation, as a form of government of a country in which power is divided between one central and several regional governments, and political autonomy lies in the much higher degree of decentralization which is constitutionally established and guaranteed whenever a federal structure is set up. In objective terms and from the point of view of the degree of self-determination a nation without a state can enjoy without becoming independent, this is the most advantageous arrangement. However, there is not one sole interpretation of federalism, or, at least, there are remarkable differences between different federal structures. In Graham Smith's view, federalism is both a political ideology and an institutional arrangement.[16] As a political ideology, it assumes that the ideal organization of human affairs is best reflected in the celebration of diversity through unity. As an institutional arrangement, federations vary widely in their content depending upon historical, economic, social and political circumstances.

Federalism represents an ideological commitment, this is why the mere creation of federal structures does not necessarily lead to a federalism which assumes both respect for diversity and a strong commitment to accept the union of the federation. In some cases, the commitment of political leaders to federalism produces a 'federalizing influence' in the articulation of the state without arriving at federation. Spain is a case in point.

Federation embodies a particular articulation of political power within a clearly demarcated territory, which is informed by the desire to acknowledge, protect and encourage diversity within it, while at the same time maintaining the territorial integrity of the state. The constituent units of a federation, as Burgess writes, are not mere local authorities subordinate to a dominant central power, 'On the contrary, they themselves are states with states rights'[17]. As Elazar puts it, 'the very essence of federation as a particular form of union is self-rule plus shared rule.'[18]

At the centre of the federalist idea lies the assumption of the worth and validity of diversity. For this reason federations have often proved highly useful political tools in protecting national minorities concentrated in particular territorial areas within the federal state. For instance, Quebec, the only French enclave in North America, is one of the most active nations without a state in struggling to secure its linguistic and cultural development, in principle, within the Canadian federation.

In the case of Switzerland, most cantons are, for the most part, homogeneous from a linguistic standpoint.[19] There are four major linguistic areas in Switzerland, and each of them comprises several of the twenty-six cantons into which the territory of Switzerland is divided. Ethnonationalism within language communities is discouraged by primary powers being vested in the cantons. Political parties do not correspond to language regions and the voting behaviour of cantons on constitutional issues is primarily associated with sociopolitical patterns rather than language. Recently there have been some exceptions to this; voting on participation in the developing European Economic Area corresponded to language divisions. A further crosscutting cleavage in Switzerland derives from the division between Protestants and Catholics.

Quite often there is a tension between the desire of some members of the federation to expand the scope of self-determination and the state's wish to increase federal control. This tension varies in each case and its intensity depends a great deal on the reasons which prompted the creation of the federation. Ideally, federations should be the outcome of an agreement between independent states which freely decide to start a federal project which allows them to shoulder common interests jointly while dealing separately with their domestic affairs. Quite often, however, federations are born out of the pressure exerted by territorially circumscribed ethnic groups which are dissatisfied with the treatment they receive by the unitary state containing them, and have enough power to force its transformation. This is the case in Belgium, where a strong Flemish nationalist movement has progressively pushed for the recognition of its specificity within a once unitary Belgian state, which has recently turned into a federation to accommodate Flanders' nationalist demands. In other cases federations are not the result of pressure from below, but are created from above. The Soviet Union and India illustrate this point.

An exception to this is the regionalization of the German political system and the role of the *Länder*. Gunlicks argues that German federalism today does not reflect a society divided by significant ethnic, social, cultural, or religious tension, rather it is designed to reduce the power of the central government and guarantee a stable democracy.[20] This explains the greater emphasis which the German Basic Law places on the sharing of powers, responsibilities and resources, when compared, for example, with the Constitution of the United States, which stipulates a separation of powers between the federation and the states. In Germany, federal and *Länder* governments are forced to collaborate by a system of joint policy-making or 'interlocking politics'. Benz argues that the cultural or historical basis of the *Länder* is rather weak due to the vicissitudes of German history throughout which the territorial patchwork was in constant flux.[21] He emphasizes the role of the two World Wars in overturning the territorial boundaries of the state and its parts. He writes: 'After the Second World War, the regional structures of the German state were re-established in a territorial setting primarily defined by the artificially created occupation zones. The *Länder* which formed the Federal Republic after 1949, as well as those which existed in the GDR until 1952 and which were re-established in 1990, were for the most part pragmatic creations of the Allies and lacked traditions'.[22] Benz argues that cultural regions exist but they are more fiction than reality from a political point of view since the *Länder* do not coincide with them, except in a very few cases.

The territorial grouping of its citizens is a major feature of a federation; in King's words: 'what is distinctive about federations is not the fact that the people are viewed as sovereign, but that the expression of this sovereignty is tied to the existence and entrenchment of regional, territorial units'.[23] Thus, federation is a useful device in the articulation of large political institutions formed by the will of several independent founding units, as was the case in Canada, which is regarded, at least by Quebec nationalists, as the merging of two founding nations, one of French and the other of English culture and language. But, as I have already mentioned, federation is also instrumental in responding to the claims for self-determination of nations without states.

The role of federation in a multiethnic or in a multinational society where cultural groupings are non-territorial requires a different approach. The Austro-Marxists, Otto Bauer and Karl Renner, addressed this subject by trying to establish valid channels of representation for the numerous ethnic groups scattered around the Austro-Hungarian empire. They suggested the creation of non-territorially based institutions through which ethnic groups could be represented and find institutional support. Once more, this emphasizes the main aim of federation, that is, the preservation of diversity within unity, a feature present in Lenin's Soviet Union, Nehru's India, Trudeau's Canada or even, as Smith points out, in Delors' European Union.[24] Diversity and unity, not uniformity, are two constituents of federalism which are constantly being negotiated in a federation. Centralization and decentralization are also core features in defining federations considered as an expression of democratic practice.

Federation does not eliminate conflict. To a certain extent it could be argued that the acknowledgement of diversity is in itself a source of conflict, but, as Burgess stresses, this 'does not have to be conceived as a weakness'.[25] The success of federal systems is not to be measured in terms of the elimination of social conflicts but instead, in their capacity to regulate and manage such conflicts.[26] Federations seek to resolve conflict through democratic means, by encouraging tolerance and respect for ethnic diversity. This is why federations cannot be the result of force or an imposition from above. Awareness of the extremely complicated process of creating a federal state which will defend diversity and promote a sentiment of union between its constituents becomes crucial to secure and maintain its legitimacy.

In Kriek's view, the main dangers threatening federations are: (1) the possibility that a cultural or religious minority will exceed its opposition role and end up calling for secession; (2) the dominant position of certain groups within the federation holding enough power to push for centralization, a threat which could be avoided by the creation of strong regional or group parties, and (3) the dependence of one constituent on others for its resources, a factor capable of provoking either unitary trends or separatist movements. Consequently financial autonomy is usually regarded as a highly desirable characteristic of the units forming a federation.[27]

To prevent disintegration, federations need to combine a strong but minimal federal government with a genuine policy of decentralization and respect for their members. A rational division of functions and powers is decisive in establishing an effective coordination system able to avoid a redundant bureaucracy. Decisions need to be taken collectively and the relations between the federal state and its constituents clearly established in a constitution sanctioned by all. A state may adopt some federal elements, but it cannot be referred to as a federation unless the federal principle is stated in its constitution. Once federation is established, in principle, all its components hold symmetric rights and duties. But symmetry is a feature which is currently being questioned in several federations. The Quebec nationalist movement has since the 1960s sought a special status for Quebec within the Canadian federation and is currently defending the right of Quebec to decide about its political future, which includes the right to break away from Canada. Before addressing current issues, it might be worth considering the origin of Quebec and relations between its French and English inhabitants as they affect contemporary Quebec nationalism.

The making of the Quebec people   The original inhabitants of Quebec came from Asia about 22,000 years ago, during the last Ice Age. They divided into tribes and clans who spoke different languages. These were self-governing and politically independent groups, who created a mixed subsistence economy of hunting and agriculture supplemented by trade. Although there are no written records detailing the history of American Indian society prior to the first contact with Europeans, archaeological evidence and oral tradition give a reasonably complete picture of the precontact period. Both the Huron and the Iroquois formed political and religious confederacies, and alliances with other groups.

The Europeans first came to North America in the sixteenth century, at that time Iroquois, Cree, Algonquin, Huron and Montagnais were the main Indian nations living at the site of present-day Quebec. Jacques Cartier, sponsored by Francis I, king of France (1515–47), explored the Gulf of St Lawrence and stopped at the Indian settlements of Stadacona (Quebec City) and Hochelaga (Montreal). It was not until 1608 that a permanent French settlement was duly established in Quebec City by Samuel de Champlain. Economic, political and religious motives led the French to colonize this area. Champlain developed trading links with the Algonquin and Huron Indians and came into violent conflict with the Iroquois. The French colony made very slow progress until 1665 when it was returned to direct royal power, after a period during which it was administered by the French Colonies of Commerce. In 1663 New France was proclaimed a royal province by Louis XIV, and in 1665 Jean Talon became its intendant.

During the first half of the eighteenth century, the colony made slow but steady progress, the population reached 55,000 in 1754. In that period many French settlements were established along a line of military posts including almost half of North America.

In the late eighteenth century, France and England were engaged in a protracted struggle in Europe (the Seven Years War 1756–63; in

America the war was known as the French and Indian War 1754–63), and the confrontation extended to French and English dominions in North America. One of the main objectives of the English was to destroy the French chain of military and trading posts. The English colonies contained more than 1,000,000 people, compared to the 70,000 of New France which was economically weak, dependent on France for trade and defence and strategically vulnerable. Some indigenous nations fought with the French against English attacks from the south, but the English gained ground. On 13 September 1759 English forces under General James Wolfe defeated French troops commanded by Louis, Marquis de Montcalm at the Plains of Abraham just outside Quebec city. Montreal was to be conquered within a year. From then on until 1982 the English monarch was Canada's head of state.

By the Treaty of Paris (1763) Quebec became a British colony and was ruled under the terms of a Royal Proclamation (7 October 1763). The conquest's immediate effect was to bar Catholics (the French were Roman Catholics) from public office because of the oath requiring allegiance to the British monarch as head of the church. Although the Conquest and its aftermath were benign by the standards of the day, it had long-term consequences for Quebec society. The British victory led to the dismantling of the French Canadian merchant elite and the emigration of many of the old land owners.[28] During this time, society was deprived of secular leadership and the Catholic Church emerged as a protector and defender of French culture and language. Quebec society became increasingly homogeneous and rural.

The Quebec Act of 1774 was a complete reversal of the policies in the Royal Proclamation of 1763. It granted permission for Catholics to hold public office in Quebec. The Act restored the boundaries of the colony to their pre-Conquest dimensions. It extended to the Labrador coast and included in the west and south the areas of the present-day US states of Michigan, Wisconsin, Illinois, Ohio and Indiana. The 1774 Quebec Act allowed French Canadians to cultivate their language, maintain their old civil law – although English criminal law was imposed – and gave them freedom to practise their religion; it explicitly forbade the creation of an elected assembly. Instead an appointed council to advise the governor was established. The demand for an elected assembly therefore united the English and French Canadians against London and the local administration elite.

In 1775 the Americans invaded Canada, the failure of that invasion ensured that, on the recognition of American independence, the territories North of the Rio Grande would be divided between the British and the Americans.

The Constitutional Act of 1791 imperfectly divided the English-speaking and the French-speaking population into Upper and Lower Canada, respectively. The Act allowed for elected assemblies but appointed governors and councils. It soon became clear that the governor's executive authority extended as far as overriding decisions of the colonial parliament. In Lower Canada the English minority had considerable influence on political decisions, while the French-speaking residents, the *Canadiens* as they were often referred to, formed a rural-based majority.

In 1837–8 Louis Joseph Papineau led a violent rebellion against the establishment. Papineau was forced into exile, martial law was declared and a period of repression under Sir John Colborne concluded with London sending Lord Durham as a plenipotentiary envoy. Lord Durham published a report in 1839 calling for the assimilation of the *Canadiens* into the British community. He also recommended the union of Lower and Upper Canada.

The Act of Union of 1841 united Upper and Lower Canada into a single colony; Kingston became its capital. French was denied official status as a language either of public record or of debate in the assembly, though this policy was to be reversed in 1848. A very high property qualification was established for eligibility to run for election resulting in the exclusion of most French Canadians. Governor and council were appointed. French civil law and the religious rights of the Catholic Church were respected. Education was under local control.

The Intercontinental Reciprocity Agreement between Canada, New Brunswick, Nova Scotia and Prince Edward Island providing preference for each colony's products in the others was signed in 1850. A further reciprocity agreement with the USA was signed in 1854.

Constitutional reformers emerged in both language groups. In 1847 the two principal leaders, Louis Hippolyte La Fontaine and Robert Baldwin established a unified administration with both men sharing the title of prime minister. In 1867 the British government approved the British North American Act establishing the Dominion of Canada formed by the three colonies of Nova Scotia, New Brunswick and the Canadas (now the provinces of Quebec and Ontario).

The uprising of the Métis (people of half French and half Indian descent) in 1885 was viewed by nationalist French Canadians as an uprising for French Canadian rights beyond Quebec's territory. The rebellion concluded with the hanging of its leader Louis Riel, a Métis. This caused a bitter division between French and English Canadians which sparked off nationalist feeling strong enough to defeat the

Conservative provincial government in Quebec and ruin the federal Conservative party in Quebec for almost one hundred years.[29]

In the First World War, Canada, which was a dominion of Britain, automatically entered the war. French Canadians opposed conscription; they did not want to fight for the British Crown and did not want to be forced to do so. There were riots in Quebec city (29 March–2 April 1918), martial law was declared and a battalion of English-Canadian soldiers from Toronto were sent there; five civilians were killed in the confrontations.

In the Second World War, initially there was no conscription, but pressure increased and the then Prime Minister Mackenzie King held a plesbicite in which English Canada gave a resounding 80 per cent in favour of conscription and Quebec a 73 per cent against it. Only volunteers were sent overseas until 1944 when King agreed to send conscripts to the front to reinforce the army's infantry units. Despite these negative reactions toward conscription, it must be emphasized that many French Canadians fought and gave their lives during the two world wars, and especially the second, since they fought in Dieppe and on Juno Beach for the liberation of France.

The rise of Quebecois nationalism   Quebec, one of the ten provinces of Canada, considers itself distinct from the other provinces. It enjoys a specific French culture and language together with a separate historical tradition and has developed a strong sense of identity closely linked to a flourishing nationalist movement.[30] Quebec's demand to be recognized as a 'distinct society' within Canada exemplifies a claim for asymmetry founded upon a bicultural and bilingual conception of Canada. The recognition of the right to self-determination of indigenous peoples within the Canadian territory adds further pressure to explore asymmetric forms of federation and alter the traditional conception of Canada.

Federation should be regarded as a dynamic process which evolves as a result of internal as well as external transformations affecting its constituents. Substantial changes can be identified in the case of Canada, specially since the 1960s 'Quiet Revolution'[31] took place in Quebec awakening a nationalist movement which denounced the second-class treatment received by French Canadians within the federation.[32] Education, employment and language appeared as three major areas in which French Canadians were discriminated against. The 1969 Official Languages Act granted equal status to French and English in federal institutions, guaranteed federal services in both languages across the country, and established the Office of the Commissioner of Official

Languages to police implementation.[33] The same year, the Royal Commission on Bilingualism and Biculturalism revealed that the cultural and linguistic privileges of the English minority in Quebec were combined with a considerably better economic situation. The average English-speaking male in the labour force earned just under 50 per cent more than the average French-speaking male.[34] Unilingual anglophone males in Quebec were portrayed as the most privileged group in all Canada. The public exposure of the inferior status of francophones sparked nationalist feelings and contributed to the reinvigoration of the nationalist movement.

The constant activity of a rising Quebec nationalism precipitated some transformations in the treatment of French Canadians – progressively referred to as Quebecois – thus territorially circumscribing them. In 1971 Pierre Trudeau, then Prime Minister, declared Canada to be a multicultural state, a measure highly disputed by Quebecois circles who argued that multiculturalism was an instrument to water down their nationalist claims and the primarily bilingual and bicultural nature of the Canadian federation.

The inclusion of a constitutional amendment which affects Quebec, the Canadian Charter of Rights and Freedoms, was enacted in 1982 when Canada patriated its Constitution without the consent of the people of Quebec through their representatives in the provincial assembly. This constituted an injustice from the Quebec perspective because it violated one of the fundamental rules of federation: what affects all must be agreed to by all or by their representatives. As Tully emphasizes, 'although the Supreme Court ruled that the convention would be breached, nine provinces and the federal government, all of whose consent was given, proceeded without the consent of the Quebec Assembly, and with its express dissent, even though Quebec was affected the most. This was unprecedented'.[35] Since then, several attempts have been made to solve this anomalous situation. In 1987, under the auspices of Prime Minister Brian Mulroney, the premiers of the ten provinces drafted the Meech Lake Accord which increased provincial power and contained a clause in which Quebec was defined as a 'distinct society' within the Canadian federation. Much concern and unease emerged about the meaning and significance of the term 'distinct society' exclusively applied to Quebec. The accord attracted growing opposition and it finally collapsed in June 1990.

In 1991 constitutional negotiations reopened, and in 1992 the premiers of the nine English-speaking provinces drafted the Charlottetown Agreement. It substantially increased provincial powers and weakened the federal government while granting Quebec a 'distinct society' status. Decentralization went further than it did in the Meech Lake Accord. In the Charlottetown Agreement, the so-called 'Canada clause' proclaimed the 'equality of the provinces', Canada's 'linguistic duality', and proposed to entrench the inherent right of aboriginal self-government in the constitution. The most irreparable damage to the Charlottetown Agreement resulted from the stand adopted by the Native Women's Association of Canada (NWAC). Their major concerns were the exclusion of women from the negotiating table, and the primacy given by the Agreement to native culture and traditions over gender equality rights. Charlottetown attracted further opposition from the Indian chiefs' caution about the possible erosion of treaty rights. In Quebec, the 'Canadian clause' insistence on the 'equality of provinces' re-awakened an ever present resentment which would re-emerge whenever Quebec was treated as a province just like the others. In the 26 October 1992 Referendum on the Charlottetown Agreement, Quebec and the rest of Canada (commonly referred to as ROC) voted 'no' for opposite reasons.

The 30 October 1995 Referendum on Quebec's sovereignty was lost by only 54,288 votes, giving a 1.16 per cent majority for the 'no'.[36] The substantial increase in the number of people backing sovereignty, however, confirmed the strength of the Quebecois nationalist movement and is currently forcing the Canadian federal government to find a solution to Quebec's claims.[37] In Gagnon's words: 'attempts at reducing Quebecois to the status of one minority among others in Canada simply denies the fact that Quebec forms one of the main pillars upon which Canada was established in the Confederation agreement of 1867'.[38] A recent investigation shows a distinct profile of citizenship attitudes found among residents from Quebec who expressed the lowest preference for a Canadian identity while they strongly identified themselves as Quebecois.[39]

The relationship between Quebec and the Canadian federal state illustrates the dynamic character of federation. Change is intrinsic to federation as a political arrangement which is not only based upon respecting diversity but which also acknowledges its non-permanent nature.[40]

Denial and repression

There is a fundamental qualitative shift between the meaning and implications of the three political scenarios we have just analysed and the study of what I shall refer to as 'denial and repression'. Through cultural recognition, political autonomy and federalism, the state acknowledges varying degrees of internal difference. These options may not fully satisfy the aspirations of the nations without states concerned in each case; however, there is a tremendous difference between the struggle for further recognition and the fight to defend the right to exist.

Denial concerns the state's refusal to acknowledge the existence of any sort of cultural, historical or political *national* minorities within itself. In this situation, internal diversity is ignored, and assimilation is actively encouraged. The state imposes a unique language, culture and institutions which are presented as the only ones which both exist and can exist within the state's territory. Any remaining cultural or linguistic difference is portrayed as a regional characteristic, as a sign of the past, and given a folklore status. In this section, I mention some examples of denial and repression in Europe, and focus on the analysis of two particular cases: the homogenizing policies implemented by the French state in the period leading to its consolidation as a modern nation-state, and the active repression endured by Kurdish people.

We encounter numerous examples of denial and repression when we examine the fate of Western national minorities. Catalans and Basques during the Francoist regime and Lithuanians, Estonians and Latvians under Soviet domination constitute but two examples.

Catalonia and the Basque Country Catalans and Basques had to endure the harsh repressive measures imposed by Franco's regime (1939–75).[41] The immediate effects of the Francoist victory in the Spanish Civil War (1936–39)[42] on Catalonia and the Basque Country entailed not only the suppression of all their political institutions and laws, but also the prohibition of the Catalan and Basque languages and all sorts of symbolic elements (flags, anthems, etc.) of their specific identity.[43]

The Francoist, 'nationals', fought to impose a closed 'image' of Spain, an image that emphasized unity and condemned all forms of diversity. Their nationalism emerged as a reaction against modern ideologies such as socialism and anarchism which were threatening the traditional socio-political structure of Spain. The Spanish Second Republic (1932–39) had already implemented some progressive policies and was seeking to construct a state within which national minorities were taken into account and which conferred a substantial degree of cultural and political autonomy upon them.

The reaction of the Catalans faced with a repression that pervaded their day-to-day activities was one of passive resistance. They had been defeated. Their country was destroyed and they were living in precarious conditions after the Civil War. They had to endure the presence of a Spanish army and an imported Castilian-speaking bureaucracy. The official public sphere was occupied by the new regime.

The Baltic Republics The Baltic Republics, Lithuania, Estonia and Latvia, saw independent statehood abolished by the signing of the Molotov-Ribbentrop Pact on 23 August 1939. The agreement provided for the Soviet takeover of Estonia, Latvia and part of Finland and, later, Lithuania, in return for Nazi Germany's assuming control over most of Poland. Soviet rule involved the expropriation of property, the 'Russification' of cultural life and the integration and adaptation of local agriculture and industry, where it existed, or its development where it was lacking, into the all-Union economy. Forced collectivization included mass deportations. In Estonia, on 25–26 March 1949 some 8 to 12 per cent of the rural population, with estimates ranging from 20,000 to 80,000 people, was deported to labour camps in various parts of the Soviet Union.[44]

Russified Latvians and Estonians who had spent most of their lives in Russia, returned to their home republics and filled the ranks of the local Communist Parties, a feature which contributed further to the Russification of the Baltic Republics. Lithuania was quite exceptional in that it was allowed to develop its own national intelligentsia.[45]

Immigration, primarily from the Russian republic into Latvia accounted for over two-thirds of Latvia's demographic increase throughout the 1970s.[46] This prompted fears that the Latvian language and culture would progressively be relegated to a secondary position. Russification was singled out as the greatest threat to the Latvian nation.

The Lithuanians were also subjected to mass deportations (June 1941) which lasted into the early 1950s. The Soviet regime left little space in which people could try to resist. The threat of deportation to Siberia or the loss of one's job was aimed at eliminating dissent. The Catholic Church, closely supervised by Soviet authorities played a key role in maintaining Lithuania's national identity. The Lithuanians were the major Catholic people in the Soviet Union.

After these two very brief examples of denial and repression within twentieth-century Europe I would like to consider the linguistic homogenization of France and the repression suffered by Kurdish people in more detail.

France: linguistic homogenization and the consolidation of the nation-state The defence of a unitary state with a strong tendency to homogenize its population was a common feature of most nation-states in their foundational moment. At that particular time, states struggled to eliminate internal difference and to turn themselves into political institutions which sought to create cultural and emotional links among their citizens. France is a case in point. Immediately after the French Revolution, decrees were translated into the major dialects and languages spoken in the territory of the French state. The First French Republic (1793–1804), initiated a change in attitude directed at establishing 'one people, one nation, one language'. In 1793 the abbé Grégoire presented his *rapport* on the need and means to universalize the use of French to the Convention's Committee of Public Instruction. According to him, only 3 million people, out of a total population of 26 million, could speak the 'national' language, that is French, correctly, while the percentage of those able to write in French was still lower.[47] In Citron's view, 'the Third French Republic (1870–1940) played a crucial role in the process of *francisation* of the French people. Jules Ferry created a free, compulsory and secular school system which promoted French language, history and values. At school, the use of patois was strictly forbidden and "severely punished"'.[48] Citron writes: 'the leaders of the Third Republic, heirs of the revolutionaries, were like them, impervious to the idea of a possible existence of cultures other than their own in France'.[49] At the same time Gallicization involved the imposition of a certain image of France as a 'single and indivisible nation' through the teaching of a unified history which left aside the particular histories of the peoples included within the French Republic.[50]

As Graff mentions, with the spirit of national linguistic development and increased intolerance of dialect, class differences in language and literacy were reinforced. Resistance did not prevent linguistic change. The power of the state to impose a language and expand it through a school system was the key to initiating the slow decay of minority languages and dialects. French represented the advance of civilization and progress, and its use in 'urban and white-collar work, armed-forces training, and the growing volume of print materials stimulated the increase in French speaking, reading and writing in the countryside'.[51] Similar policies were implemented in nineteenth-century Prussia, where Bismarck expanded the Prussian school system into the Polish regions of Poznan and Silesia and allowed only the German language as a medium of instruction.[52]

In my view, the states' rejection of linguistic diversity and the imposition of a single 'national' language by making it a necessary and compulsory means to get by in ordinary life has several major consequences: (1) the folklorization of minority languages by restricting their use to festive or literary contexts in which they are portrayed as signs of cultural difference, but not as everyday markers of national identity;[53] (2) the perception of minority languages as having a lower status, which is directly connected to restrictions in their use; (3) the progressive lack of interest in the cultivation of minority languages not only as part of a high culture but also in everyday use: public and private utilization of the language tends to decrease; (4) the labelling of the minority language as a remnant of the past, as a sign of backwardness and even resistance to modernization; (5) the portrayal of the desire to maintain a language other than the official one as an indication of betrayal of the state and one's own fellow countrymen and women.

Denial involves the exclusion of the minority language and culture from the state's school system, sentencing them to a slow and so to speak 'natural' death. But for any language to become the vehicle of expression of the most intimate emotions and feelings of a people, it takes more than its expansion through the school system and its compulsory character. It requires a long and complex process at the end of which people should come to regard a particular language as their own and not as something which has been imposed upon them.

The association of a particular language with a certain superior status is closely connected to the self-image of the nation-state it represents. The attachment of prestige and power to a specific language is crucial if it is to attain popular acceptance. To illustrate this point one could refer to the Catalans of the Cerdanya (a Catalan valley divided between France and Spain by the Treaty of the Pyrenees and its addenda in 1659–60). As Peter Sahlins mentions, 'French Catalans were bound to the French state by its ability to satisfy their needs. The French state had created the ties of loyalty and identity instrumentally, by fulfilling the material needs of its citizens', in particular after the French Revolution.[54] In sharp contrast with this, the inefficiency and backwardness of the Spanish state was unattractive. Sahlins writes, 'it is practically unthinkable for natives of the Spanish Cerdaña to identify themselves as "Spanish Catalans"'. In his view, these people identify themselves exclusively as Catalans. For them Catalonia is the 'nation', the Catalan language its defining characteristic. Spain is the 'state' or, worse still, 'the empire'.[55] Thus, while Catalans on the French side of the border came to define themselves as French-Catalans, those living on the other side never identified with Spain and kept their own distinctive Catalan identity unchanged.

Denial is not only practised by nation-states in the process of being formed, as in post-Revolutionary France. There are contemporary states which actively implement homogenization policies of various kinds. Contemporary France continues to promote French strongly to the detriment of other existing minority languages. Occitan, Basque, Catalan and Breton can be considered as active but extremely locally circumscribed languages.

Spain reversed its centralist homogenizing policy towards Catalan, Basque and Galician in 1978 when a new Constitution acknowledged the need to recognize and guarantee the right to self-determination of the nationalities and regions included within the Spanish state.

The Kurds: the repression of difference   Often the denial of difference is accompanied by measures directed at the elimination of internal diversity. Repression has many faces, and it ranges from mere socio-economic to political measures which may include the use of force. To forbid a language and a culture, and to dissolve, wherever they already exist, the political institutions of a national minority are common strategies employed by some states seeking to annihilate internal diversity. The punishment of those who trespass the state's laws regarding these matters is intended as a deterrent. Random intimidation and attacks on members of the national minority seek to destroy any kind of nationalist revival which could eventually turn into a real threat to the state's integrity. The use of force stresses the power of the state and the vulnerability of those subject to it. It also reveals the state's inability to put forward its cause for homogenization by means other than the use of force. Violence, which sometimes is publicly displayed while on other occasions it is used in a more surreptitious fashion, reflects the absence of rational arguments and dialogue.

The intensity, frequency and the means applied to implement repression are likely to provoke divergent outcomes which are closely related to the characteristics of the national minority in question. The degree of national consciousness and the solidarity among the minority's members is likely to increase during periods of repression when experiences of collective intimidation need to be constantly integrated into the political discourse of resistance. A pervasive and prolonged repression usually undermines the national minority's capacity to resist and favours its assimilation. Individuals' political resistance might be debilitated to the point of extinction. On some occasions, individuals may even try to hide their origin by fitting into the state's imposed pattern of what it means to be a proper citizen: by speaking the state's language and being attached to the state's culture and values. In contrasting cases, the state's actions stimulate the emergence of active resistance movements, which often respond to the state's violence against their community with armed struggle.

The repression suffered by the Kurds illustrates this point. The land the Kurds claim as their own stretches across five nation-states: Iraq, Turkey, Syria, Iran and Armenia. There are an estimated 23 million Kurds.[56] After the First World War and the consequent dismantling of the Ottoman empire, the Kurds were promised a state (Treaty of Sèvres, 1920), however, the influence of Woodrow Wilson's principle of the self-determination of peoples was to be forgotten when the Treaty of Lausanne (1923) determining the new borders of Turkey was ratified. The Kurds have always been regarded as a threat to the modern Turkish state founded by Kemal Atatürk. Guided by Atatürk's nationalism, Turkey attempted the forcible assimilation of Kurds. As Ignatieff writes, 'they were denied the right to speak their own language, educate their children in it or even call themselves Kurds'.[57] In Zubaida's words, 'Turkey has maintained a stubborn denial of Kurdish identity and has severely suppressed cultural and linguistic expressions of Kurdishness'.[58] In 1984 the Kurdish Workers' Party's (PKK) leader, Abdullah Ocalan, declared war on the Turkish government and demanded independence. Guerrilla activity was resumed in south-eastern Turkey. 'A very dirty war began', O'Ballance writes, 'and atrocities were committed by both sides'.[59]

The Kurds were also regarded as a tribal and backward people by the modernizing nationalism of the Shah of Iran. Their condition as Sunni Muslims, while most Iranians were Shias, contributed to a marginalization which acquired an even darker side after the fundamentalist revolution of the Ayatollahs in 1979. Violence has often been employed against Kurdish villages inside the enclave.[60]

The history of Kurdish repression in Iraq since the 1970s, when Saddam Hussein came to power, is a long, violent and complicated one in which internal Kurdish differences have been exploited by both the Iraqi and the Turkish governments. Anticipating Saddam Hussein's defeat in the Gulf War, a Kurdish popular uprising occurred in Iraq in 1991. Saddam Hussein retaliated causing a mass exodus of Kurds who sought refuge in remote mountains, and in Turkey and Iran. The creation of the enclave of Kurdistan in 1991 constituted the first United Nations attempt to 'protect a minority against the genocidal intentions of its nominal ruler'.[61] The enclave of Kurdistan is not a state, it has no flag of its own and it is not even allowed to call itself Kurdistan. Technically, the enclave remains a part of Iraq and is protected by forces which set up an air exclusion zone north of the 36th parallel.

The following stand as examples of violent repression against the Kurds:

(1) After the fall of Mulla Mustafa Barzani, the most famous contemporary Kurdish tribal and national leader, the Iraqi regime intensified its repressive actions against the Kurds. In 1975, the Iraqi government embarked on a sweeping campaign to Arabize the areas that had been excluded from Kurdistan under the offer of autonomy – an effort that had first begun in 1963. Hundreds of Kurdish villages were destroyed during the mid-1970s in the northern governorates of Nineveh and Dohuk, and about 150 more in the governorate of Diyana, the southernmost spur of Iraqi Kurdistan, where there are significant oil deposits.[62]

(2) In July 1983 the Iraqi troops abducted between 5,000 and 8,000 males aged twelve or over. According to Human Rights Watch (HRW)/Middle East, 'none of them has ever been seen again, and it is believed that after being held prisoner for several months, they were all killed'[63] leaving women and young children on their own in the camps of Kushtepe and Diyana.

(3) HRW/Middle East has recorded forty separate attacks using chemical weapons on Kurdish targets between April 1987 and August 1988. 'Each of these attacks was a war crime inasmuch as it involved the use of a banned weapon; the fact that the victims were often non-combatants adds to the offence'.[64] The largest chemical attack took place on 16 March 1988 when Iraqi planes dropped mustard gas, nerve gas and cyanide killing 5,000 people in the city of Halabja.[65]

So far, I have analysed the different political scenarios in which sub-state nationalism emerges and develops ranging from cultural recognition to federation. I have also given some examples of nations without states which are subjected to the denial of their own specificity and suffer different forms of repression as a consequence of it. I shall now examine if the terms nation without a state and nationalism can be applied to Native peoples in North America and discuss autonomy and independence as two possible responses to the nationalist claims of Native peoples in Canada.

3

Nations and Nationalism in Native America

The aim of this chapter is to analyse the nature of the nationalist claims of Native peoples in North America and consider if the term 'nation without a state' could be applied to them. Although there are substantial differences between the Western nations we have studied so far and Native nations, I shall argue that in both cases we encounter cultural communities with a consciousness of forming a group, memories of a common past and the desire to decide upon their own political future. They are communities which define themselves as nations and do not identify with the states within which they are included. Native as well as Western nationalist movements put forward different demands ranging from further autonomy to independence.

In what follows I offer a definition of indigenous peoples and examine the new impact of their demands upon the nation-states which contain them. The text then moves on to present a brief historical account of the relationship between Native peoples and European settlers in North America. The latter part of this chapter discusses Native nationalism in Canada. There the Mohawk of Kahnawake's nationalist movement for independence is contrasted with the endorsement by the Royal Commission Report on Aboriginal peoples of Canada's of a new relationship between Native peoples and Canada.

Indigenous peoples and the nation-state

The prominence of indigenous peoples as international actors made possible by the expansion of ideas of democracy and self-determination and the awareness of difference prompted by globalization is a recent phenomenon. The first working definition of the term goes back to 1974 when the first conference of the World Council of Indigenous Peoples took place. Since then, several indigenous groups in different parts of the world have gained prominence and organized themselves into active social movements. However, what characterizes indigenous peoples across the world is their lack of power when trying to defend their existence and particular way of life which hardly ever coincides with the state within which they are included.

The broadest definition of indigenous peoples might be: peoples with tradition-based cultures, who were politically autonomous before colonization, and who, in the aftermath of colonization and/or decolonization, continue to struggle for the preservation of their cultural integrity, economic self-reliance, and political independence by resisting the assimilationist policies of nation-states.[1] In 1982 the United Nations Working Group on Indigenous Populations issued the following definition:

> Indigenous populations are composed of the existing descendants of the peoples who inhabited the present territory of a country wholly or practically at the time when persons of a different culture or ethnic origin arrived there from other parts of the world, overcame them and, by conquest, settlement or other means, reduced them to a non-dominant or colonial situation; who today live more in conformity with their particular social, economic and cultural customs and traditions than with the institutions of the country of which they now form a part, under a State structure which incorporates mainly the national, social and cultural characteristics of other segments of the populations which are predominant.[2]

Indigenous groups may or may not be recognized as separate entities within the boundaries of contemporary nation-states and, in most cases, they are considered a problem. Usually portrayed as inferior and barbaric, they belong to what Wilmer terms the Fourth World. In her view, 'self-determination has at least nominally placed the states of the Third World on equal-footing as participants in the international system and protected their enjoyment of relative freedom from external control'.[3] In contrast, indigenous peoples have had little influence over the political forces controlling their fate.

Indigenous groups have been portrayed for a long time, and still are in many places, as incompetent, backward, inferior and an obstacle to progress. This poses fundamental questions to the ways in which cultures are classified from a Western perspective based upon values such as technological progress, capitalism and the consolidation of the nation-state. These are features which have been exported all over the world and to which even most Third World countries subscribe. The idea of progress is intimately linked with the concept of development. But, how should development be defined? What are the objectives of development? Is there a single route towards a common objective? And even more important, where does the moral legitimation to impose a certain model of progress on other peoples come from? Does progress justify the annihilation of communities through starvation or by force? Does it justify the imposed assimilation of indigenous peoples into mainstream cultures, their relocation and the expropriation of the elements lying at the basis of their economic structure? The way in which these questions are answered determines the future and the possibilities for survival of particular indigenous groups.

The prominence and novelty of the topic arises from the impact of globalization and the current questioning of the traditional values of modernity. The intensification of globalization processes has brought about increasing interdependence and has broken the isolation in which most cultures found themselves in former periods. Indigenous peoples have suddenly become visible. The conditions of their existence are known, and the treatment they receive from the states they are part of belongs to the public domain. As a consequence of this, some states feel the need to justify their actions or neglect, while others sense the urgency of covering up and trying to limit the information available about their 'internal' problems. However, a degree of visibility which did not exist in previous times has brought to the fore a long forgotten or ignored reality.

Globalization opens up the possibility of establishing contact with, or at least being aware of, the existence of other communities suffering similar problems in other parts of the world. In the global age indigenous peoples use communication technology to advance their goals and increase the degree of awareness about their problematic existence.

Indigenous peoples are regarded as communities whose way of life is based upon a less aggressive relation with the environment. The lack of a sophisticated technology to transform their *milieu* favours a higher equilibrium between individuals and nature than that achieved within areas which have suffered the impact of Western civilization. Zones which have remained practically untouched for centuries can be critically damaged in a few years by the tools of progress. The continuous destruction of the rain-forest in the Amazon offers a dramatic example of the environmental changes caused by the intro-duction of advanced technologies to exploit natural resources. In this case, indigenous peoples and wildlife are suffering the consequences of an irrational exploitation of nature. According to scientists, the whole planet is being affected by human action in the rain-forest. Some indigenous peoples present their culture and values as having a more friendly relation with nature, and use this as a compelling argument to defend their existence. However, and for this reason, they are vulnerable to the type of romanticization linked with Rous-seau's idea of the 'noble savage' which actually ignores the hardship of life in the wild.

Without doubt, the progressive visibility of indigenous peoples and their 'idealized' image as 'unpolluted', oppressed and victims of oblivion makes a strong case for the defence of their right to exist and evolve. The international community can no longer ignore their demands since they are based upon the values the international community claims to endorse. Freedom, the right to exist and develop a particular culture, and access to the means to do so are preconditions for indigenous survival which can be linked with the idea of self-determination employed in the decolonization struggles of this century. Self-determination when applied to indigenous peoples challenges the sovereignty of the nation-state and gives status and prominence to cultures based upon non-modern principles. Besides, the sort of critical attitudes towards modernity we are witnessing increase the interest in alternative ways of life.

Amongst the arguments employed to legitimate the domination of indigenous peoples we might mention the whites' image of them-selves as a superior race, and the mission to fulfil a special duty, be it to civilize, or to indoctrinate, a 'barbarian population'. The United Nations Working Group on Indigenous Populations has rejected con-quest, discovery and *terra nullius* as 'no longer valid in international law'.[4] But indigenous people do not only inhabit lands conquered or occupied by white people. Colonial countries which have turned into independent nation-states and replaced European by autochthonous elites do, in many cases, continue white policies in their treatment of indigenous groups living within their territory. The marginalization and poverty of indigenous peoples is sometimes due to the scarce resources managed by postcolonial governments, on other occasions it results from obliviousness or the need to focus on other matters perceived as more pressing. However, oblivion grows into sudden concern if the areas occupied by indigenous peoples happen to contain valuable resources or are regarded as strategic military sites. Modernization, national economic development and national security are then presented as unquestionable arguments to impose the relocation, resettlement, or removal of indigenous communities.

In the United States, the period of relocation of Native Americans began in the 1830s and confinement to reserves in the 1850s. The settlers' demands for more land progressively pushed the Indians towards the West. The discovery of gold or any other valuable resource within Indian territory meant conflict and often Indians were forced to move from the lands that had been previously allocated to them once they had already been forced to abandon their native homelands. According to Wilmer,

> in Indonesia, the government program for forced transmigration in West Papua in order to facilitate economic development relocated approximately twenty-five thousand families between 1969 and 1974, and another sixty thousand between 1974 and 1979. In Southern Kenya, large areas of Masai homelands have been designated as national parks.[5]

These are only a few examples which illustrate the vulnerability of forms of life which are not compatible with or suitable to industrialization and capitalism, predominantly the latter. Again, questions about the concept of development arise. Can people be forced to adapt to ways of life alien to them? Is there a single path towards modernization and industrialization? Are there any strong enough arguments to sustain the indisputable superiority of a Western life-style when this involves the annihilation of minority cultures or the relocation of people who are not usually given the means to adjust successfully to their new forced environment?

Indigenous peoples are minorities within nation-states. Here the word 'minority' does not refer to the size of the group but primarily focuses on its lack of power and resources. Thus, a minority is a group which is subject to disadvantage and often racism. Spoonley makes this point when discussing the relationship between the Maori and the Pakeha – New Zealand-born people of 'European' descent – in New Zealand.[6]

The articulation of social movements defending indigenous rights poses a major challenge to the nation-state. Indigenous groups are based on common ethnicity, in the sense that they share a common ancestry (real or imagined), have a common culture and history and are attached to a particular territory. Contemporary indigenous movements demand the right to exist and to develop their cultures, to freely dispose of the natural resources of their lands, and to have a say in determining their own political status. This threatens the sovereignty of the nation-state, because, as Burger argues, while most governments might readily accede to the right to culture, language or education of indigenous peoples, so far most governments 'have resisted any unconditional agreement which would commit them to self-determination and full land rights for indigenous peoples'.[7]

The following section offers a brief account of the circumstances which brought Native peoples in North America to their current situation. It stands as a very good example of indigenous groups which progressively became marginalized within the territory they had inhabited for centuries when white settlers from Europe began to expand and dominate their lands. It is a story about two civilizations which confronted one another and, as had happened before in many periods and in many places, the newcomers alienated the Native peoples and founded their own states, kingdoms or dominions upon lands once alien to them. The original inhabitants lost their sovereignty and became minorities within their own land.

The Indian–European settlers relationship: an overview

Stephen Cornell in his book *The Return of the Native: American Indian Political Resurgence* writes:

> For four centuries non-Indians in North America have had an 'Indian problem'. In its most basic form this problem has had three aspects. First, it has been an economic problem: how best to secure access to Indian resources, land in particular. Second, it has been a problem in cultural transformation: how best to accomplish the cultural transformation of Indians into non-Indians. Third, and consequently, it has been a political problem: how to maintain an effective system of controls over Indian groups so that problems one and two could be satisfactorily resolved.[8]

The initial relation between Indians and Europeans was based on the fur trade. This lasted for about two centuries, from the latter part of the sixteenth century to the eighteenth century. Cornell argues that Indians pursued their incorporation as producers into the transatlantic political economy unaware of its possible consequences and high cost. By the nineteenth century, the United States had been founded and white expansion was being carried out at the expense of a progressive Indian marginalization. White settlers appropriated the most fertile lands, restricted Indian hunting territories, increased the pressure on game, diverted waters to irrigation and were firmly pressing Indians to the West.

In *Democracy in America*, Alexis de Tocqueville speaks of the Negroes and Indians as 'two unlucky races' which have nothing in common except their misfortunes. 'Both occupy an equally inferior position in the land where they dwell; both suffer the effects of tyranny, and, though their afflictions are different, they have the same people to blame for them'.[9] Tocqueville points to the effect of slavery on the Negro, and the independence enjoyed by the Indian as fatal influences in both cases. According to him 'the Indian lives on the extreme edge of freedom'[10] and 'regards all our crafts merely as the labor of slaves'.[11] He refers to the Indians as nations and describes their increasing difficulty in surviving within a land which is gradually taken away from them: 'Isolated within their own country, the Indians have come to form a little colony of unwelcome foreigners in the midst of a numerous and dominating people'.[12] In his view, the final objective of the colonists was the expulsion of the Indians: 'If one studies the tyrannous measures adopted by the legislators of the southern states . . . one is readily convinced that the complete expulsion of the Indians is the final objective to which all their simultaneous endeavours are directed'.[13] Tocqueville also mentions the tension between Congress and individual states concerning Indian rights. Often the central government surrendered to individual states' pressure demanding lands which had been previously guaranteed to the Indians. He writes: 'no doubt within a few years that same white population which is now pressing around them will again be on their tracks in the solitudes of Arkansas; then they will suffer again from the same ills without the same remedies; and because sooner or later there will be no land left for them, their only refuge will be the grave'.[14] Tocqueville points to famine and war as two major causes of misery for Indians brought about by their forced removal:

It is impossible to imagine the terrible afflictions involved in these forced migrations. The Indians leaving their ancestral fields are already worn down and exhausted. The country in which they intend to live is already occupied by tribes ... there is famine everywhere ... their homeland has already been lost, and soon they will have no people; families hardly remain together; the common name is lost, the language forgotten, and traces of their origin vanish. The nation has ceased to exist. It barely survives in the memories of American antiquaries and is known to only a few learned men in Europe.[15]

The struggle between white settlers and Indians ended up with the consolidation of a nation-state founded upon lands which originally belonged to communities operating at a lower technological level than newcomers. The relation between Indians and whites was more equal at the time when trade between both groups was first established. However, by the early years of the nineteenth century, as Tocqueville describes, the imbalance between whites and Indians was patently clear and in favour of the former. President Monroe (1817–25) recommended to Congress the enactment of a law providing for the general removal of tribes east of the Mississippi. He feared their 'degradation and extermination' if they remained in the East and proposed that removal might be made honourable to the United States and attractive to the Indians.[16] Granting the emigrant Indians a permanent title to their Western lands together with certain economic benefits should encourage them to abandon their lands and hand them over to the United States. In the 1830s the Jackson and Van Buren administrations unsuccessfully attempted to create an all-Indian territory beyond the Mississippi.[17] At that time most Indian tribes were suffering the constant pressure of new white settlers who aimed to establish themselves in territories once given to the Indians as permanent. White expansion reached the West Coast and exerted continuous pressure on Indian land.

In 1849, to concentrate the Indian population and to bring intertribal peace to the Plains, the Commissioner of Indian Affairs proposed the creation of reservations as territories with clear-cut boundaries within which the Indians would be forced to live. Indians were forbidden to abandon their reservations and they were supposed to 'undergo civilizational transformation' within their new homes.[18] The army would patrol the borders of the reservations and make sure Indians did not leave them. However, the construction of roads and railways often disrupted reservation boundaries and on many occasions Indians were removed from their territories more than once. Berkhofer argues that by the end of the 1870s the United States government had completed the conquest of the Indians, although the last battle occurred in the massacre at Wounded Knee in 1890.[19]

The General Allotment Act of 1887 (Dawes Act) 'permitted individual assignment of lands on all reservations except for the Five Civi-
lized Tribes (Cherokees, Creeks, Choctaws, Chickasaws, and
Seminoles) and a few groups in Indian territory, Nebraska and New
York'.[20] Allotment meant Indian individual ownership of land, a
concept new to the Indians since their territories had always been
communal. Although allotment was originally conceived as a policy
which would favour the transformation of Indians into farmers, its
most immediate consequence was the loss of Indian land through
widespread leasing of allotments. In 1898 the Curtis Act terminated
tribal land tenure without Indian consent and laid out severe general
provisions concerning Indian land ownership. According to Parman,
'the most striking feature of severalty was its contribution to the
transfer of Indian land to whites in the final two decades of the
nineteenth century. In 1881 the Indian estate amounted to 155,632,312
acres. By 1890 it had fallen to 104,314,349 acres and by 1900 to
77,865,373 acres'.[21] The Indian population had declined by 82 per cent
from the time of contact in the sixteenth century to the 1930s.[22]

The appointment of John Collier as Commissioner of Indian Affairs
from 1933 to 1945 marked a turning point in Indian policy. He
defended cultural pluralism, stood against assimilation and recognized the disastrous consequences of allotment for Indians. Collier's
programme was embodied in the Indian Reorganization Act or IRA
of 1934. It took shape in the early 1930s and in the short term it was
quite successful in creating new jobs and in bringing funds to reservations. His aim was to preserve the Indian's tribal life. The period
from 1933 to 1945 is often called the era of reform in federal Indian
policy, or the Indian New Deal. The IRA ended the policy of allotment
and authorized the return to tribal ownership of lands. It entitled the
Secretary of the Interior to acquire additional lands for the tribes with
funds provided for that purpose, it encouraged the conservation of
Indian resources and established a credit fund from which tribes
could borrow for economic development purposes. The IRA's most
significant contribution from a political perspective was the idea that
'any Indian tribe or tribes, residing on the same reservation, shall
have the right to organize for its common welfare and to adopt a
constitution for that purpose'.[23] Vine Deloria refers to Collier's policy
as a 'total revolution in thinking which conceived of tribal governments as modern organizations with rights of substantial political
sovereignty'.[24] Wilmer points out that the Act 'was, and still is, very
controversial because it was supposed to give tribes self-government;
many of them never believed that they had lost it'.[25]

Mounting congressional opposition to the explicit goals of the Collier programme and its possible consequences led to a policy reversal after the Second World War. Some Indians took part in the two World Wars and fought for the United States. The impact of the wars varied in different reservations. A common factor which influenced Indian life was the wartime economic development and inflation. The Second World War proved crucial in prompting the massive migration of Indians from reservations to industrial areas due to an increasing demand for labour after 1939. The war reshaped the activities of the Bureau for Indian Affairs; Collier resigned in 1945 and a conservative reaction against New Deal policies evolved in the postwar era (1945–61).

Nations and nationalism in Native America

Native nationalism in the USA

The term nation was initially used by European settlers to refer to the different communities inhabiting North America. But, as we shall see, there have been subtle and significant differences in the ways in which the concept has been applied throughout the years. In 1789, Henry Knox, Secretary of War to George Washington wrote: 'The independent nations and tribes of Indians ought to be considered as foreign nations, not as the subject of any particular state'.[26] Tocqueville refers to the Indians as nations, except on some occasions when he uses the work 'tribe'. He quotes the Cherokee petition to Congress of 19 November 1829 in which the Indian speaker refers to them as a nation.

> Permit us to ask you humbly what better right a nation can have to a country than the right of inheritance and immemorial possession? We know that the state of Georgia and the President of the United States claim today that we have lost this right. But this seems to us to have a gratuitous allegation. At what time have we lost it? What crime have we committed which could deprive us of our homeland?[27]

Both quotes are representative of a time in which the term nation was still used on both sides as implying a certain Indian sovereignty. But the situation would change rapidly and Knox's definition of the Indians as 'foreign nations' would soon be challenged. In fact, the 1829 Cherokee speech contains a plea to defend their nation, to demand and maintain the recognition of its independence and of its right to a territory. In 1831 Chief Justice John Marshall wrote:

> Though the Indians are acknowledged to have an unquestionable, and, heretofore, unquestioned right to the lands they occupy, until that right shall be extinguished by a voluntary cession to our government; yet it may well be doubted whether those tribes which reside within the acknowledged boundaries of the United States can, with strict accuracy, be denominated foreign nations. They occupy a territory to which we assert a title independent of their will, which must take effect in point of possession when their right of possession ceases. Meanwhile they are in a state of pupilage. Their relation to the United States resembles that of a guard to his guardian.[28]

This text would be quoted time and again, although with different purposes, by US officials and also by Indian activists who in the 1960s initiated a vibrant movement for self-determination. To consider Indian tribes as 'domestic dependent nations' automatically changed the relation between the United States and the Indians. A situation of at least juridical equality in which they could sign treaties as equal partners was replaced by a relation in which the imbalance of power which existed *de facto* achieved an explicit recognition. To recognize Indian nations as distinct, independent political communities implied that their right to self-government was inherent to them and not the outcome of a delegation of powers from the US government. To legitimize control over Indians, their status had to be changed and their sovereignty extinguished or, at least, limited. In 1924 Congress granted citizenship to all Indians, this was a crucial move with decisive implications. Pressure to assimilate Indians into mainstream US culture increased and manifested itself in the termination policy implemented by Congress in the 1950s. Termination involved the extinction of treaty rights and tribal political existence. The supporters of termination argued that there was an implicit contradiction in the idea that a government could make treaties with some of its own citizens as some Indians opposing termination demanded. This particular point would be addressed in the 9 January 1973 response from the White House to the Indian's Twenty Points March (3–9 November 1972):

> Over one hundred years ago the Congress decided that it was no longer appropriate for the United States to make treaties with Indian tribes. By 1924, all Indians were citizens of the United States and of the states in which they resided. The citizenship relationship with one's government

and the treaty relationship are mutually exclusive; a government makes treaties with foreign nations, not with its own citizens. If renunciation of citizenship is implied here, or secession, these are wholly backward steps, inappropriate for a nation which is a Union.[29]

In the 1960s the controversy continued and many civil rights supporters regarded the Indian position as anti-American. Indians showed great scepticism and often hostility towards a policy which would give them civil rights while abolishing their treaty rights.[30] Increasing concern about the preservation of Indian identity and land became a key issue which attracted widespread support among Indians belonging to different tribes. A new Indian social movement immediately began to take shape. The Indian discourse defended their right to choose and live according to a set of values and traditions endangered by the progressive incorporation of Indians into American life and by a set of laws which were threatening their own separate status within the US. In 1960 30 per cent of Indians lived in urban areas; ten years later the percentage had risen to 45 per cent. The insistence on the need to preserve Indian identity, the opposition to assimilation and to the termination policy led Indians to demand greater political power. In their own words: 'We must recognize and point out to others that we do want to live under better conditions, but we want to remember that we are Indians. We want to remain Indian people. We want this country to know that our Indian lands and homes are precious to us. We never want to see them taken away from us'.[31]

The Indian movement was initially led by some young urban Indian activists. Most tribal councils were unsympathetic to their demands to revise old treaties. But support came from some fullblood Indians living in reservations. Fullblood Indians had opposed tribal councils set up under the Indian Reorganization Act of 1934 on the basis of treaty rights and usually acted as leaders in tribal religious ceremonies. With their support, the movement gained strength and attracted new followers. The 1969 Indian occupation of Alcatraz, the 1972 Twenty Points March, the 1973 confrontation at Wounded Knee and the 1978 Longest Walk to Washington are landmarks in the Indian movement.

The Indians insisted on the restoration of treaties, demanded the recognition of tribal sovereignty, and wanted to take an active part in the economic development of their areas. They were strongly against termination, since they considered that this would break the treaties signed between their ancestors and the US who had agreed to look after them. In return, Indians had ceded their lands to the US. The

Indians' argument was that, if their ancestors had known that the US would unilaterally abolish the treaties, they would have never signed them. In 1970 Richard Nixon shortly after being appointed president of the US abandoned the termination policy and referred to it as 'wrong'.[32] He also valued cultural pluralism as one of the strengths of the US and mentioned the need to develop Indian self-determination by encouraging Indians to take an active part in the decisions and projects which concern them.[33]

Probably the most pressing demand of the Indian movement is that tribes should be recognized as nations by the US government. Vine Deloria, a prominent Indian activist, writes: 'Affirmative action by the Congress of the United States to define Indian tribes as smaller nations under the protection of the United States would be the first step in defining the nature of the new relationship ... In effect, this action would mean a surrender by the United States of its right to extinguish Indian aboriginal title to land, and would freeze the present Indian lands within the context of national boundaries rather than reservation boundaries'.[34]

Deloria argues that there is no reason to reject the Indian demand for a sovereign status on the grounds of inadequate Indian land. There exist other nations which have smaller territories and whose lands are also landlocked by other countries. He also rejects population size, economic backwardness and poor education as reasons for preventing Indian communities being granted recognition as nations. Deloria provides a comparison of Indian nations with nations all over the world to strengthen his argument. In so doing, he puts forward the claim of indigenous people to be admitted as political actors by the international community.

Gerald Alfred points to the distinction between an Indian move-ment for enhanced self-government and the vindication of 'aboriginal rights', and Native nationalism. For him, the former reflects a narrow view which assumes that Native politics functions in an environment created exclusively by non-Natives. He argues that 'Lost on many observers is the fact that most Native peoples view non-Native institutions as transitory and superfluous features of their political existence'.[35] In contrast, Native nationalism seeks to re-establish polit-ical independence and preserve the separate national identities eroded through the impact of Western colonialism.

Rebecca L. Robbins defends the right of Native Americans to self-determination and acknowledges the diverse meanings which self-determination may adopt when applied to different communities.[36] She adds: 'In the event, should the United States finally and simply admit what has been true all along, that native nations are absolutely entitled to complete national sovereignty, it is likely that few (if any) American Indian peoples would elect to exercise it fully'.[37]

Donald Parman stresses the contradiction caused by the Indian's insistence that the federal government provide the full protections and services created by treaties and statutes, while demanding the right to be considered as 'autonomous bodies with independent powers'.[38] Indians have limited resources to exploit and are dependent on US funding. Water, oil and uranium are the most important natural resources present in some Indian land which permit some Indians to have a substantial source of income through direct exploitation or by leasing contracts with the US. Probably the most visible manifestation of Indian sovereignty, at least to the general public, has been Indian gaming. However, it seems that the cultural and political survival of Indians to a considerable extent depends on US support. Thus pressure for self-determination is mixed up with increasing demands for more elaborate links between tribal communities and the surrounding society.

A key problem faced by Indians is how to make their communities viable without destroying their indigenous identity, since the prospect of economic development often causes internal divisions. The communal sense is threatened when communities are to be reorganized on the basis of market needs. There are at least two sets of crucial issues concerning Native Americans. First, the tension between the demand for self-determination and the demand for support from the US. Second, the possibilities for survival of Indian identity and culture and their role within American society. Although Indian symbols have become more visible as a consequence of the success of the Indian movement, there are serious questions about whether this cultural re-emergence will be realized in actual patterns of life and action or whether it will remain at a superficial level. Indians are progressively being acculturated to the US life-style and values.

At the time when Indians are more integrated within the Western tradition, they have access to an alternative account of their past and are able to re-write their history. The strength of the Indian movement has managed to promote the rejection of the 'old ideology of the innate inferiority of the tribal culture'.[39] However, assimilation stands as a fascinating alternative for many Indians.

Parallel to a growing demand for enhanced self-government, we encounter a rising Native nationalism based upon the rejection of Western institutions and values with which Native communities have been forced to compromise. Native nationalism is based upon re-examining the roots of the political and cultural institutions and traditions which lie at the heart of Indian communities. It condemns the colonizing strategies imposed upon them by the newcomers and blames Western institutions and principles for the sometimes irreparable erosion of Native culture.

The abuse, exploitation and constant effort to assimilate Native people into the newly created order has finally backfired and a radical Native nationalism is currently questioning the legitimacy of the United States and Canada as nation-states constructed through suppression rather than integration of Native nations.

Alfred writes: 'Understood properly, native politics is the self-assertion of nationhood on different axes and to differing degrees by various distinct political communities'.[40] This acknowledges the diversity of Indian communities in North America concerning size, Native social and political structures, identity and resources. In Alfred's view, very few communities in North America are threatened with imminent extinction. He refers to the Mohawks of Kahnawake as a community which has advanced well beyond the survival model to an explicit assertion of nationalist goals, and sees a basic level of material well-being as a prerequisite for a movement seeking a more consciously political set of objectives.

Native nationalism claims the right to independence of the Indian nations, and puts forward an alternative social and political community structure based upon some elements of the Native tradition. However, there is a sharp contrast between those who defend a traditionalist image of the nation, and those who stand for a non-static interpretation of Native culture. Alfred analyses these differences within the Mohawks and sharply criticizes the traditionalists, who, in his view, defend a fundamentalist position anchored in the idea of applying 'historic concepts to the modern situation without modification in any way. This includes governing forms, process and social organization as well as the framework of relationships deriving from historic treaties between the Confederacy and non-native polities in North America'.[41]

In contrast to this traditionalist position, mainstream nationalism in Kahnawake exhibits a flexible interpretation which favours the adaptation of some traditional principles to respond to current socio-political demands. Alfred's conclusion after studying the rise of nationalism among the Mohawks of Kahnawake is to confirm the existence of 'a stable core which forms the basis of the political culture and nationalist ideology'.[42] He does also acknowledge the existence of peripheral elements within the culture which are malleable and subject to change according to a fluid political context and economic climate. It would follow from these assertions that those countries enjoying the existence of a well-preserved stable core will find it easier to construct a nationalist discourse based upon the elaboration of an alternative socio-political project to that inspired by a Western model.

Native communities which have suffered a deeper erosion of their cultures will, in turn, encounter more difficulties in re-creating the core values to be placed at the heart of their nationalist discourse, if one is to emerge. In most cases, assimilation and demands for further autonomy prevail over pro-independence nationalism.

The Native peoples' relationship with Canada

Kahnawake stands as a good example of a community which has managed to preserve its specific identity and is now witnessing the rise of an active nationalist movement. Kahnawake is located on the south shore of the St Lawrence River, 15 kilometres from Montreal. It has a land base of 12,000 acres which includes what is known as the Kahnawake Indian Reserve, supplemented by the Doncaster Indian Reserve, a territory near Ste-Agathe-des-Monts (Quebec) shared with the Mohawks of Kanehsatake. Kahnawake's territory is governed by the Mohawk Council of Kahnawake which has created institutions in the following sectors which remain under its control: justice (Court of Kahnawake and the Kahnawake Peacekeepers), education, social services, health and economic development.[43]

In Kahnawake, 'Mainstream nationalism is characterized by a selective revitalization of key elements within an existing culture, a self-conscious and syncretic reformation leading to the creation of an identity and institutional framework strongly rooted in tradition but adapted to modern political reality'.[44] Alfred's definition could easily be used to describe other nations without states such as Catalonia or Scotland in so far as their nationalist movements try to combine tradition, common culture, history, former experiences of independence, and attachment to a concrete territory with the need to adapt and respond to modern challenges. The re-appropriation of tradition and its selective actualization are necessary requirements if a nationalist movement is to succeed.

A further element which characterizes Kahnawake nationalism concerns its negative evaluation of the Canadian framework. In an analogous way, most Catalan nationalists are certainly dissatisfied with the Spanish framework which does not recognize Catalonia as a nation, but rather equalizes it to the other autonomous communities created to water down the Catalans' and Basques' nationalist claims after forty years of dictatorship. The strategies employed to assimilate Native and Western nations without states into the mainstream culture vary in a remarkable way, but it could be argued that, in both cases, these nations were confronted with states whose main objective was either to integrate them or at least to favour their extinction as distinct cultural communities putting forward secessionist claims.

Most Native nations were forced to abandon their territories and often suffered more than one relocation while living in isolation; only recently have Indians moved in large numbers to live in urban centres. In contrast, some Western nations have undergone the reduction of their traditional territory and in cases such as Catalonia witnessed the arrival of large numbers of people from other parts of the state, most of whom did not consider learning the Catalan language or integrating into Catalan culture as a priority. On the contrary, during Franco's dictatorship, Catalan language and culture were not only discouraged but strictly forbidden.

In spite of these similarities, the most striking difference between Western nations without states such as Catalonia and Native nations such as the Mohawks of Kahnawake lies in the radically different tradition and culture embodied in Native nations in contrast with the newcomer societies. In the case of Catalonia, differences in language and culture did not amount to the radically diverse universe encountered by Native communities meeting Western colonizers. Native peoples have also suffered racial discrimination. In cases such as Catalonia we can point to ethnic discrimination directly linked with language and culture, but there are no distinctive physical features to be employed as a basis for racial discrimination.

When analysing the pattern of interaction between Native people and the newcomer societies, Alfred distinguishes three phases. In his view, early interactions took place in an atmosphere of respect stemming from the political and economic status of the Natives. Their condition as trading partners and military allies put them in a relation of cooperation with Westerners. Phase I corresponds to a 'cooptive relation' defined by the internal colonialism imposed upon Native people and the newcomer's construction of independent nation-states which immediately began a nation-building process. Phase II is characterized by confrontation provoked by the Euro-American appropriation of Native lands, and Phase III encompasses a crisis in the relationship between Native peoples and the colonizers which could lead to the assimilation of Natives, the enhancement of self-determination, or their eventual independence.[45]

During this process of interaction, Native identity was redefined to react to internal colonialism. Thus, from a traditional identity, some Native communities such as the Mohawk adopted a 'latent nationalism' owing to the generally insulated nature of their existence and the lack of a coordinated threat to their integrity. Later on, a negative evaluation of the Euro-American institutions imposed upon them prompted a 'revival nationalism'. In Alfred's view, 'The various permutations of the collective identity are understood as forms of nationalism because they maintain traditional cultural boundaries and create group self-identification as a political community distinct from the state, and consistently committed to the right to self-determination'.[46]

Such a perspective confirms the possibility of referring to Native peoples as nations without states and comparing them with Western nations lacking a state of their own since they all share the following attributes:

1 consciousness of forming a group with a collective proper name
2 the existence of a common culture which includes a myth of common ancestry
3 attachment to a specific 'homeland'
4 the shared remembrance (and oblivion) of some historical events which often involve memories of a time when the community enjoyed its own independent institutions
5 the will to decide upon their common political future.

But, there are at least two major aspects which acquire a specific form among Native peoples. These are their conception of self-determination, and the political framework within which they are aiming to live.

Native peoples have been forced to compromise their concept of nationhood to accommodate one emanating from the Western perspective. Throughout the process of colonization, states without nations were created in America, Asia and Africa.[47] The nation was constructed once the political institution was established and had the power and resources to engage in a nation-building project. Native peoples were forced to comply with Western norms and regulations while their indigenous governing bodies were emptied of power. In Kahnawake we are currently witnessing the abandonment of the conventional use of the term sovereignty. Mohawk sovereignty 'is conceived not only in terms of interests and boundaries but in terms of land relationships and spirituality'.[48] Harmony is portrayed as the essence of a Mohawk sovereignty which aims at a balanced relationship with other communities which should be based on respect for differences, and lead to a harmonious ideal state of affairs.

Most Mohawks reject integration into Canada, or at least they reject the idea of integration into Canada conceived as a nation, while some might accept the concept of Canada as a political framework for cooperation between nations. The Mohawk establish a distinction between participating in an administrative association with Canada, an option they currently accept, and a political linkage with Canada implying a surrender of sovereignty.

> Thus for the Mohawks, cooperating with Canada at the present time to maintain their community implies no surrender of sovereignty. And the prospect of Canada continuing to occupy a prominent place on that political landscape means only that they will have to continue relating with Canada in the future. There is no internalization of the idea of Canada, no supplanting Kahnawake's sovereignty caused by partici- pating in an administrative association with Canadian authorities.[49]

The Mohawks are in principle hostile to an eventual independent Quebec. They question Quebec's claims and point to the lack of legal mechanisms to permit secession within the Canadian Constitution.[50] They deny Quebec's authority over their territory since all treaties were signed with the Canadian government and not with Quebec, and reject the possible future creation of Quebec as a territorial unit including Mohawk lands. Quebec's nationalism has failed so far to accommodate the demands of Mohawk nationalism and has often portrayed them as 'Anglos'. The majority of French Quebeckers per- ceive the Mohawk's hostility towards their demands for sovereignty as a sign of an implicit alliance with the minority of English-speaking people within Quebec who oppose independence.

When discussing identity, Alfred attributes to the Mohawks a sort of multiple identity which includes being a Mohawk, an Iroquois and a pan-Native. The Mohawks regard the Iroquois cultural complex and the continuing existence of the Iroquois Confederacy as an alternative to the Canadian state. However, we should note that at a basic level the radically nationalist Iroquoian position contrasts with the type of nationalism which has emerged in most other Native communities seeking an enhanced autonomy within federal Canada. Numerous attempts to establish a pan-Indian organization have failed, while

Native communities have been quite successful in advancing their own goals towards further autonomy.

The most serious recent attempt to redefine the Native peoples' relationship with Canada from an institutional perspective is represented by *The Royal Commission Report on Aboriginal Peoples in Canada* (1996). The Report advocates the need to establish a modern partnership between the Native peoples and Canada correcting the present situation and opening the way for fruitful collaboration between the two. For this to become a reality, Canada has to recognize its Native peoples as nations. Such recognition does not threaten the political nor the territorial integrity of Canada since, according to the Report, Native peoples have almost always sought peaceful coexistence, collaboration and harmony in their relationships with other people. Three main elements are mentioned as a source of legitimacy for the Natives peoples' right to self-government:

1 The International law accepted by Canada acknowledges the right of peoples to self-determination. This, according to the Report, entails Native peoples choosing their own form of government within existing states. Note that the Report offers a restricted interpretation of self-determination which excludes the right to independence or secession while stressing Native people's right to autonomy without altering the shape of the nation-state within which they are included.

2 Canadian history shows that no 'right of conquest' could be invoked since North America had its own Native nations with which the first inhabitants of what later was to become Canada signed treaties.

3 The Canadian Constitution recognizes and protects the right to autonomy of Native peoples within Canada.

Native peoples have accepted the need to share power with Canada, in return they assert their right to self-determination as an inherent right and not as a gift conferred upon them by Canada. The Report recommends that Native peoples be treated as partners and that power is shared at three separate levels, federal, provincial and Native. The Royal Commission points to the great diversity within Native peoples, some of whom form very small communities and defines a Native nation as a significant number of natives sharing a national identity and forming a majority within a particular territory or set of territories.[51]

The Royal Commission advances the need to rebuild Native nations which are not defined by race but are generally constituted by political communities including people from different origins and traditions sharing a common culture, history, sentiment of belonging and identity.

The replacement of paternalistic policies by a partnership will be a crucial step in the rebuilding of Native nations. The Report suggests the issue of a new Royal Declaration in which Canada manifests its commitment to engage in a new relationship with Native peoples based upon recognition, responsibility and partnership. New legislation should be created to give shape to the intentions manifested in the Royal Address. It should involve: the modernization of treaties; the creation of a tribunal specifically dealing with treaties and native lands; a law concerned with the recognition and government of Native nations; and a fair redistribution of land and resources so that Native nations can achieve financial responsibility over their own government and services. The Commission notes that while in the United States 3 per cent of the territory (excluding Alaska) is allocated to Native peoples, in Canada, Native lands south of the 60th parallel represent less than 0.5 per cent of Canada's territory. The new partnership with Canada should aim at ending Native dependence, poverty and exclusion by contributing to stimulate Native nations' economic development.

The radical nationalism exemplified by Alfred's account of the Mohawk of Kahnawake sharply contrasts with the 'new partnership' put forward by the Royal Commission on Aboriginal Peoples of Canada. Both positions acknowledge the status of Native peoples as nations, are critical of the way in which Canada has treated them and denounce the successive policies which have violated the treaties signed at the time of first contact while aiming to assimilate Indians into mainstream Western society. The rejection of Canada as a political framework distinguishes radical Native nationalism from the enhanced autonomy advocated by the Royal Commission's Report. Their recommendation to generate a new relationship between Native nations and Canada stands as an attempt to redress an unfair situation based upon the long term discrimination suffered by Native peoples, in which Canada will have to modify some of its principles. It also appears as a strategy to appease a rising Native nationalism which is not content with the promise of further autonomy within Canada.

The Commission endorses the idea that 'First Nations' in Canada should be viewed as nations, and treated on a 'nation-to-nation' basis, but recognizes that this will require dramatic changes in the self-identities and institutions of Indian peoples in Canada. Autonomy within the Canadian federation and not independence is offered as a response to the Native peoples' claims for self-determination. The Commission argues that Native peoples should engage in a comprehensive programme of nation-building, but recognizes that many Indian communities may not wish to pursue this 'national' route, and insists that these communities should be free to reject it. This confirms the existence of substantial ambiguities and difficulties involved in adopting the national model.

The changes advocated by the Royal Commission require a Canadian reversal of attitudes and policies, but they also necessitate the trust and will to cooperate of Native nations sceptical about new initiatives which in the past have almost invariably failed them. The strength of the Native movement, the publicity given to its actions, and the will of Canada to protect its image as a democratic state may all contribute to a successful new partnership between Native nations and Canada.

On a broader level the struggle of Native Americans to defend their distinctive identity has to be linked with the struggle of indigenous peoples elsewhere. Globalization has contributed to the spread of their message and to the possibility of establishing links with communities living in other parts of the world. The Indian movement has created a supra-tribal consciousness unprecedented in Indian history. Globalization favours the creation of an indigenous consciousness based upon traditional ethnic values cutting across state boundaries. At the same time it questions how social cohesion within a single nation-state can be reconciled with respect for different identities sometimes based upon opposing values.

As I have already mentioned, the very different nature of the traditions, culture and written history which characterize Native Americans and differentiate them from nations without states in Europe is crucial when considering the two. Nevertheless, by including the study of Native American nationalism in a book about nations without states, I have sought to stress that there are enough common features between both types of movements emerging within Western industrialized states.

4

Nationalism as a Social Movement

This chapter explores how successful nationalisms turn from minority into mass movements. It is crucial to note that the agents, the strategies, the historical and the socio-political circumstances in which the nationalism of nations without states becomes prominent are fundamentally different from those of nation-state formation witnessed by most Western countries during the nineteenth and early twentieth centuries.

The cultural roots of most contemporary nationalist movements in nations without states can be traced back to the nineteenth century and linked in one way or another to the spread of Romanticism and its insistence upon the intrinsic value of cultural and linguistic diversity. The political awakening of these nationalisms, however, dates from the twentieth century and gains unprecedented salience in the second half of this century due to a set of changes affecting the traditional nature of the nation-state and prompting its rapid transformation. The intensification of globalization processes, the quest for individual as well as collective identity and the need to recover a sense of community and social coherence, principles damaged by years of increasing individualism, are among them.

In this chapter I analyse the particular role of elites in the creation of nationalist movements in nations without states focusing upon the relationship between nationalism, intellectuals and culture. I also study the different phases which lead to the emergence of the nationalist movement, and explore the main elements used by intellectuals in the construction of nationalist discourses. The text then moves on to consider the role of the media in the dissemination of the nationalist ideology. The impact of the media represents a completely new and extremely potent factor which radically transforms the nature of the messages transmitted. Communication technology permits the instantaneous transmission of images and messages which are now capable of reaching vast numbers of people who are subject to their influence. Nationalist leaders, symbols, ideals and projects are presented in a novel and unprecedented fashion.

Elites

For a nationalism to be successful it has to attract people from different social classes. Interest in the history, culture, language – if it exists – of a particular community linked to a concrete territory usually begins with the activities of a small group of intellectuals. If this elite movement is successful, then it spreads to large sectors of the population. The study of the emergence of nationalist movements in nations without states requires a specific approach different from that demanded by the analysis of nation-state formation in nineteenth-century Europe.

First, the nationalism of nations without states emerges within already established nation-states with their own national education system, a specific media structure, their elites and intellectuals, and a set of institutions representing the country and giving it a particular territorial, political, social and economic framework. The mere existence of a community which considers itself to be a nation other than the one the state seeks to promote poses a threat to and questions the legitimacy of the state whenever this is defined as a unitary political institution. For this reason, the state is likely to regard minority nationalisms as dangerous, or, at least, as an uncomfortable phenomenon to deal with. As I have already shown, the ways in which the state responds to the demands of the national minorities included within its territory depends upon the state's own nature, the specific character of the nationalist movement and the international support it is able to secure.

Second, the emergence of a nationalist movement in a nation without state requires the existence of some intellectuals prepared to build up a nationalist discourse different from and often opposed to that of the state. Here, as Anthony D. Smith suggests, it is necessary to distinguish between 'intellectuals who create artistic works and produce ideas from the wider intelligentsia or professionals who transmit and disseminate those ideas and creations from a still wider educated public that "consumes" ideas and works of art',[1] although in practice, the same individual may fulfil all these different roles.

A further element to be taken into account concerns the position occupied by the 'potential intelligentsia'. By this I refer to those educated individuals who, if the nationalist movement succeeds, are likely to become its leaders. The 'potential intelligentsia' is formed by individuals who feel dissatisfied with the state's treatment of their community. It also includes some individuals who have been excluded from the state's 'official' elite because of their regional origin or allegiance. This could be exemplified by the widespread adverse attitude among Castilians towards Catalans which led to the latter's exclusion from influential positions in the Spanish economic and political power structure during the nineteenth and most of the twentieth century, a trend that many would argue still continues to apply. The same point could be made about many French Quebeckers who feel marginalized within Canadian institutions unless they 'renounce' their condition as Quebecois, or manage to emphasize their Canadian identity above their regional identity.

In other cases, the potential intelligentsia emerges out of the decision of some individuals to prioritize their regional allegiance. This involves their commitment to the advancement of a national cause which often translates itself into their automatic exclusion from the state's selected elite. It has been argued that this is a strategy by means of which some educated people who would otherwise be unlikely to achieve a prominent position within the state's elite – because of fierce competition – can easily obtain a prominent position within a nation which is smaller and where competition is bound to be less intense. This argument emphasizes the self-interest of some individuals in promoting regional forms of nationalism in order to gain access to privileged positions.

In my view, although self-interest may in some cases play a substantial part, it is misleading to explain all nationalist feelings through economic motivation and the desire for power. A genuine love for the nation and a desire for its flourishing is a potent force guiding most nationalists in nations without states, especially in those cases when the nation feels culturally, politically or economically oppressed by the state. Devoting one's life to the defence and enhancement of the specific character of one's own nation can be an extremely fulfilling task. It provides meaning to the individual's life whilst setting a concrete and clear-cut objective to his or her actions. Because individuals usually embark upon nationalist projects as part of a group, they are bound to experience some kind of moral support and solidarity as members of a movement with a common goal. The sense of belonging to a nation can somehow be lived through the experience of comradeship arising within the nationalist movement or party. Differences amongst party members are not to be ignored, fierce confrontation between them is a common phenomenon, but this is not to deny the consciousness of forming a group with a common aim and the emotional closeness which often originates in such circumstances.

Once the nationalist movement gets under way and enjoys substantial support, or when it manages to transform the state's structure and secures a certain degree of political autonomy for the nation it represents, a greater number of educated people may feel tempted to join it. These 'newcomers', whilst in principle being welcomed by the traditional leaders of the nationalist movement, some of whom have by now turned into politicians, are nevertheless regarded by them with a certain degree of suspicion: 'Is he or she genuinely one of us? Where were they when we fought and suffered hardship and risked our lives to defend the nation we believe in?' These are some of the qualms which hang around the minds of those who stood for the nationalist project from its very beginning, qualms whose intensity may vary according to the length of the period during which the nationalist movement has been active, the magnitude of the repression suffered at the time when the movement first emerged, and the treatment it received from the state.

Current changes in the ranks of Catalan nationalist parties exemplify this. In Catalonia, the people who actively fought the Francoist dictatorship (1939–75) and participated in the crucial years of the Spanish transition to democracy and the creation of the Autonomous Communities System which confers considerable powers onto the re-established Catalan government – the *Generalitat* – are progressively being replaced by a younger generation brought up within the new democratic Spain; a generation which did not experience the repression which the Franco regime imposed upon Catalans and Basques. A generation for whom it is easier to be a Catalan nationalist than it was for their forefathers.

Quebec's nationalism came to light in the 1960s with the so-called 'Quiet Revolution'. Since then, the status and powers devolved to Quebec have increased dramatically and with them, as in Catalonia since 1979, the possibility of, but also the need for, an autochthonous intelligentsia. Love of country and/or self-interest are again mobilizing factors operating in the minds of the emerging intelligentsia aiming to advance Quebecois or Catalan nationalism, and the same undoubtedly applies to other cases.

Nations and nationalisms need intellectuals who will provide the tools to reconstruct a sense of a nation by studying, re-interpreting, and disseminating the nation's history, culture, language and all those other factors which make up national identity. A certain degree of coherence among the intelligentsia is essential if the nationalist movement is to prosper. Often the intelligentsia shows an internal cultural disunity which needs to be turned into a commonly accepted and constructed nationalist discourse. Such discourse tends to rely heavily upon the idea of a shared culture as a key element in the configuration of the group as a distinctive community with a set of characteristics, values, and a name which distinguishes it from other such communities. The nationalist movement's main objective is the mobilization of large sectors of the population by spreading a sentiment of dissatisfaction with the current status of the national minority. A critical attitude toward the *status quo* is combined with an appeal to awaken, recover or promote – this varies in each case – the common history, culture, territory, and language of the nation. Parallel to this, the nationalist movement seeks to encourage the re-emergence and strengthening of a sense of solidarity, and a feeling of forming some sort of extended family among the members of the nation. When referring to the task of nationalist historians, Hutchinson argues that they are 'not just scholars but encyclopaedic "myth-making" intellectuals who combine a romantic search for meaning with a scientific zeal to establish on authoritative foundations the nation's honour as a distinctive people with a high civilization and the laws of its development'.[2]

Rational and emotional arguments become intertwined in this process. Rationality stems from the objective reasons invoked by the nationalists when defending their case. Independence may mean a better economy, a higher quality of life, freedom from a series of constraints imposed by the state, and even a deepening of democracy by favouring decentralization and self-determination. Emotions are aroused when the nation is presented as a community which transcends the limited lives of particular individuals and provides them with a collective identity. Belonging to a nation which is real in the minds of its members, provides them with a sense of continuity grounded upon the sentiment of being part of a group presented by nationalists as an extended family. Individuals are born into particular families in the same way as they are placed within specific nations which act as major socializing agents. Individuals are brought up within particular cultures which define the way in which they relate to themselves, others and nature. The use of a particular language increases the sentiment of belonging to a community sharing a common set of values and practices. As in a family, membership of the nation implies a certain solidarity with the other members. It demands sacrifices and offers love and affection which generally become more prominent in situations of danger affecting the integrity and well-being of the group. Belonging to a nation assumes the need and will to defend it from external aggression, in the same way as members of a family protect it from 'outsiders' and when necessary fight them in numerous and strikingly diverse circumstances. As in a family, members of the nation can play different roles and adjust to different internal structures.

The distinctive character of the nation's intelligentsia may lead to a modernist, traditionalist or revivalist nationalist discourse, or to a combination or succession of discourses. In Smith's words 'in each case the intelligentsia attempts to provide new communal self-definitions and goals, involving the mobilization of formerly passive communities'.[3]

Nationalism and class

The social composition of the nationalist movement varies according to the socio-economic, political and historical circumstances in which nationalism emerges. There are substantial differences between the social composition of nationalist movements originating within industrialized nation-states, underdeveloped countries, colonial and post-colonial societies. In the West, we encounter prosperous nations without states such as Catalonia, the Basque Country, Quebec or Flanders which stand in sharp contrast with less industrialized and less economically successful ones such as Corsica, Wales or Occitany. A common feature shared by these nations without states, rich and poor, is the fact that they are all situated within the boundaries of industrialized nation-states and enjoy most of the advantages deriving from this.

Middle class people predominate in the social composition of nationalist movements in Western nations without states. In its initial stages, nationalism tends to be an elite movement which recruits most of its supporters from the educated classes; the eventual incorporation of the proletariat and the peasants is something which may or may not occur. But obviously for a nationalist movement to achieve power within a democratic political system, it requires cross-class support. It is also important to stress that nationalism may be defended by people belonging to different social classes at different historical moments.

For instance, in Catalonia during the nineteenth and early twentieth centuries, nationalism was primarily endorsed by a conservative bourgeois intelligentsia. It was not until the 1920s that nationalism was initially incorporated into the political discourse of the left, and we have to wait until after the Spanish Civil War (1936–39) to see the assimilation of Catalan nationalism into the communist and socialist discourses of the Catalan Socialist Unified Party of Catalonia (PSUC or *Partit Socialista Unificat de Catalunya*) and the Catalan Socialist Party (PSC or *Partit Socialista de Catalunya*).[4] Since 1979 the Convergence and Unity coalition (CiU, or *Convergència i Unió*) a centre nationalist coalition, has managed to attract cross-class support; however, most of its cadres have a bourgeois or a middle class background.

A further aspect of the relationship between nationalism and class concerns the impact which knowledge about the relative deprivation of a national minority may provoke. Awareness of being deprived and marginalized may contribute to the emergence of a nationalist movement representing those who are being discriminated against. The rise of Quebec nationalism illustrates this.

In Quebec up to the 1960s, nationalism was mainly represented by a Catholic conservative minority. Perin argues that 'the distinct society that we know today was primarily the creation, not of the state, but of the church'. In his view, 'the ultramontane thinkers provided intellectual justification for a movement that led to the consolidation and expansion of French-Canadian culture'.[5]

In Juteau's view, the expansion of Anglo-American capitalism prompted the replacement of the Catholic Church 'as the apparatus defining and controlling' Quebec identity; as a consequence of this, the nationalist ideology turned from a past-oriented, static and essentialist discourse into an ideology emphasizing control over one's destiny and modernity.[6] Quebec's new nationalism defined itself as a democratic and secular movement aiming to modernize Quebec. This new discourse attracted many middle and working class people who saw in it a way forward from a cultural and linguistic point of view, and who highly approved of the outspoken denunciation of the discrimination suffered by French-speaking people living in Quebec. In 1969, the Royal Commission on Bilingualism and Biculturalism (or '*B and B commission*'), set up in 1963, published the third volume of its study of Canadian society which focused on 'The Work World'. They offered a detailed account of the privileged position enjoyed by the English-speaking minority in Quebec. Conway writes: 'the gap between French and English [had] never been so clearly set out. When the cultural and linguistic privileges enjoyed by the English minority were combined with their considerable economic benefits, the political impact was incendiary.' The English were over-represented in better occupations, the upper management of most firms was English, while the francophones took the lower and poorly paid jobs. The B and B Commission concluded that 'the most privileged group in all of Canada was located in Quebec: unilingual anglophone males. The aptness of the colonial analogy struck a now deeper chord – you did not even have to speak the language of the majority, to hold, enjoy, and retain your privileges'.[7] Violent incidents followed such revelations, the Quiet Revolution ended, and in the years to come Quebecois nationalism would enter a phase of mass support which has provoked dramatic changes in the status of Quebec within Canada.

We may conclude that the ranks of nationalist movements in nations without states are primarily filled with individuals of a middle-class background. Many of them display what Hroch calls 'a patriotism of the Enlightenment type, which combines an active affection for the region with a thirst for knowledge of every new and insufficiently investigated phenomenon',[8] which once the movement gets under way, offers them the possibility of self-promotion. As Hroch emphasizes, high social mobility forms a favourable condition for the acceptance of the patriotic programme in the period of patriotic agitation.[9] The better educated and more mobile sections of the national minority adopt a more receptive attitude toward the nationalist movement. A significant number of supporters are bound to be recruited among them.

Phases of the nationalist movement

Hroch distinguishes three phases in the development of national movements: (a) the period of scholarly interest; (b) the period of patriotic agitation; and (c) the rise of a mass national movement.[10] He points out that in a number of cases the transition from (b) to (c) does not take place, and argues that participation in the national movement is not conditioned a priori by membership of particular classes or social groups.[11] Phase (a) is marked by 'a passionate concern on the part of a group of individuals, usually intellectuals, for the study of the language, the culture, and the history of the oppressed nationality'. In trying to adapt Hroch's typology to nations without states, we should stress that in phase (a) the nation may or may not be oppressed, but should certainly feel a considerable degree of dissatisfaction about its present situation.

Phase (b) comes into being when 'a group of patriots' decide to denounce what they consider as the nation's disadvantaged situation and see as their mission the spreading of national consciousness among their fellow countrymen and women. Hroch argues that in the cases he has studied, neither the richest nor the poorest strata are present in phase (b). He stresses that '*the more wealthy the social stratum the larger the section of it which was assimilated to or already belonged to the ruling nation*; the poorer the social stratum, the larger the section of it which belonged to the oppressed nationality'.[12] He argues that the later the opening of phase (b), the greater the role of 'the richer of the poor', and maintains that no class or professional group is an irreplaceable component of this phase of the national movement.[13]

Phase (c) does not always take place, but wherever it does, it signals the success of the nationalist movement. The participation of the bourgeoisie and the peasantry are considered by Hroch as an indispensable condition if the nation is to attain a fully rounded class structure. In my view, when considering contemporary nationalist movements in nations without states, higher importance needs to be placed upon the participation of the working class. If nationalism is to be successful in places such as Catalonia, the Basque Country, Quebec or Scotland, a large section of the working class has to feel engaged with the nationalist project, otherwise there is a danger of creating a nationalist movement which is primarily concerned with the bourgeoisie's aims and interests.

Hroch places great emphasis on the incorporation of the peasantry into the nationalist movement. He refers to them 'as the natural repositories of the nation's linguistic and cultural tradition'.[14] I do not dispute Hroch's argument, but the constant shrinking of the peasantry and the enlargement of the working and middle classes leads us to place greater emphasis on their incorporation into phase (c) if nationalism is to turn into a mass movement. A further element neglected by Hroch, and which I consider extremely relevant, concerns the need to integrate immigrants and encourage them to participate in the nationalist project. This can only be done if nationalism adopts a civic approach and operates as an 'inclusion' mechanism capable of welcoming all those who are prepared to stand for the nation's culture and language in an environment of respect for diversity.

Two factors are regarded by Hroch as the main contributors to the speedy success of national movements, these are high social mobility, and the existence of a strong communications system understood 'as a process of transmitting information and data about reality, and implanting attitudes and instinctive reactions'.[15] A further and crucial aspect concerns the use and definition of the 'national interest' which, in his view, corresponds to the 'transformed and sublimated image of the material interests of definite concrete classes and groups, whose members took an active part in the national movement (or had to be won over to participation in it)'.[16] In his opinion, *'where the national movement in Phase B was not capable of introducing into national agitation, and articulating in national terms, the interests of the specific classes and groups which constituted the small nation, it was not capable of attaining success'.*[17]

The task of intellectuals

Intellectuals have the capacity to create ideologies which can contribute to legitimizing particular regimes or social structures, but they can also provide challenge and criticism to those regimes and structures. When confronted with the task of intellectuals in nations without states we need to distinguish between their role in the early stages of the nationalist movement, and their task once the movement has attained considerable success and possibly turned itself into one or more political parties which may or may not rule the nation which, as a result of the nationalist movement's action, may have achieved a certain degree of political autonomy.

At the outset of the nationalist movement, intellectuals study the history, culture, myths, language and specific traits of the group and construct a picture of it as a distinct community. They emphasize the main differences between the national minority and the culture and language of the nation which dominates the state within which they are included. Hence, Catalans stress their specific identity as different from a Spanish identity primarily based upon Castilian culture. Scots emphasize their distinctiveness when related to a British identity basically moulded according to England's culture in the same way that the Quebeckers distance themselves from a Canadian identity primarily shaped by English culture and language.

At this stage, however, the intellectuals' function is not restricted to a re-creation of a sense of community among group members by investigating the cultural and political history of the community. One of the pressing matters facing them is the construction of a discourse critical and subversive of the current order, a discourse which delegitimizes the state and its policies as a threat to the existence or development of the nation they represent. The radicality of their statements depends upon the aims of the nationalist movement and the treatment their community receives from the state. Seeking cultural recognition, political autonomy or independence are likely to produce disparate discourses concerning the state's portrayal and the definition of its relation with the national minority. Thus, intellectuals play a double role.

On the one hand, they act as architects of the nationalist movement by providing cultural, historical, political and economic arguments to sustain the distinctive character of the nation and a legitimation of its will to decide upon its political future. Intellectuals, as Martin writes when analysing their role in revolutionary institutions, are seen as fulfilling a special function of social initiative, creativeness, and leadership in the pre-revolutionary and revolutionary situation. The intellectual is the creator of the common myth that guides the revolution.[18] The same could be said about the intellectual's position at the dawn of a nationalist movement.

On the other hand, as we have already mentioned, intellectuals are subversive and construct a discourse which undermines the legitimacy of the current order of things. They denounce the nation's present situation within the state and offer an alternative to it by promoting the conditions and processes of conflict. In so doing they become 'creators and leaders in the production of new state structures, new Gestalts of power and ideology'.[19]

When the nationalist movement is still incipient, a certain degree of altruism and love of country act as potent forces informing the intellectuals' actions. These sentiments are bound to emerge with greater intensity where a national minority suffers from repression exerted by the state. In these circumstances, backing the nationalism of the oppressed nation often involves not only radical exclusion from the state's elite, but a considerable risk to one's own life.

Intellectuals are to be considered as formulators of the nationalist ideology. Their task does not end here, however, since many of them also act as agitators and mobilizers of the nationalist movement. It has to be added that not all intellectuals perform both functions. In the case of a nation without a state of its own, its intellectuals' discourse is opposed by the state's intellectuals, some of whom will operate within the territory of the national minority defending the *status quo*, questioning its nationalist ideology and displaying a clear 'pro-state nationalist' attitude. It should be noted that within a democratic state, political disagreement about its legitimacy together with the definition and aims of the national minority's movement are at least permissible. In other circumstances, force is employed to prevent the rise of any social movement which could potentially pose a threat to the state's unitary structure.

Albeit that intellectuals play a vital role in the initial stages of the nationalist movement, Smith warns us 'to be careful not to exaggerate that role in the later stages or even in the organization of more regular nationalist movements'.[20] This poses a serious question: can nationalist movements once they get under way dispense with intellectuals? I think not. Once the nationalist movement achieves power it needs to select which parts of the history and culture of the community are to become prominent and turned into essential elements of the national identity they have to forge. A large section of the nation's population may for various reasons support the nationalist movement but they often remain divided. If the nationalist movement is to succeed it should promote a sense of community among the members of the nation. To do so the dissemination of a unified common culture and language becomes a priority and intellectuals are likely to play a key part in this process. Furthermore, the nation is an entity subjected to constant change and forced to respond to different influences and pressures to constantly adapt to the new circumstances surrounding it. The task of intellectuals is to grasp these changes and offer suggestions as to how the nation can better respond to them. The absence of intellectuals in any nationalist movement is bound to affect the strength of the movement by limiting its ability to react to social, political and economic challenges. Any nationalist movement needs a medium and long term programme of action which exceeds short term political strategies. The task of intellectuals involves the constant actualization of the nationalist ideology to respond to the community's needs. His or her job is one of service to society.

The preservation of culture Gellner argues that in industrialized societies 'only high cultures in the end effectively survive. Folk cultures and little traditions survive only artificially, kept going by language and folklore preservation societies'.[21] He adds, 'culture cannot survive without is own political shell, the state'.[22] In his view, the two major tasks of the educational system created by the state are to instil the culture, and to ensure adequate standards of literacy and technical competence for the employability and rapid redeployment of personnel. In this context 'culture is now the necessary shared medium, the life-blood or perhaps rather the minimal shared atmosphere, within which alone the members of the society can breathe and survive and produce. The culture chosen by accident of history as the medium of homogeneity, then defines the political "pool" and becomes the object and symbol of loyalty, rhetoric, and devotions'.[23]

When a nationalist movement is set in motion in a nation without state, it confers great importance on the preservation and enhancement of its own culture as different from that of the state within which the nation is included. According to Gellner's theory of nationalism, only high cultures survive in industrialized societies and they can only do so if the state protects them. From this we could infer that the main objective of a nationalist movement in a nation without state should be the transformation of the low folk culture into a high culture since low cultures are not functional in industrial societies. Only high cultures have a place in a world of national cultures which are already engaged in a ruthless struggle for survival. Globalization processes have toughened up the rules of the game. Today it is impossible to preserve the purity of a single culture and maintain it free from global influences, which in the area of language means the threat of Anglicization against which some nation-states have already started to implement some measures of dubious efficiency. France is a case in point.

To lead the process of transformation from a low to a high culture, the state requires the work of some intellectuals able to select, transform and create the new culture which in most cases will have deep roots to the community's folk culture. This is not to deny the incorporation of some new elements in the high culture's make up; however, and against those who sustain the so-called 'invention of tradition' thesis, I argue that some kind of connection between the new high and the old low culture is necessary. The high culture, to be easily assimilated, needs to be recognized as springing from the folk culture, or at least presented in a convincing manner as stemming from it, otherwise people will not identify with it. It might contain some 'invented' elements, but they are to be portrayed as a part of a larger corpus rooted in the nation's folk culture. The task of intellectuals consists in creating these new elements and connecting them to the folk culture, a task which is extremely complicated and requires, according to Gellner, the backing of the state. But, does it imply that the only way forward for nations without states if they want to protect their own cultures and place them in an equal footing with other cultures at the global scale is to achieve a state of their own? In Gellner's view, the answer is positive. Although he does not establish an explicit distinction between nation-states and nations without states, he strongly argues that 'a culture cannot survive without the state'.[24] He writes, 'But some organism must ensure that this literate and unified culture is indeed being effectively produced, that the educational product is not shoddy and sub-standard. Only the state can do this, . . . the state does take over quality control in this most important of industries, the manufacture of viable and usable human beings'.[25]

We must then conclude that for their cultures to survive, nations require either a state of their own or a set of institutions able to function as a state. I argue that independence is not the only way forward for nations without states. Alternative political arrangements may be satisfactory if they attain a sufficient degree of autonomy and are grounded upon the acceptance of the nation's right to self-determination.

Two key systems need to be controlled by the nationalist movement in the process leading to the consolidation of a specific national culture and identity, these are the education system and the media. They are both in charge of the unique task of socializing individuals through the use of a particular language and the dissemination of a set of values, traditions and ways of life. Nationalist political leaders and intellectuals need to be particularly aware of this and seek to control them. The education system and the media are generally in the hands of the state which employs them to propagate its own values and ideology. The strengthening of nationalism and specially its mutation from a minority into a mass movement makes a shift concerning the control, organization and structure of the education system and the media indispensable. Otherwise, the nationalist movement is bound to find impossible the achievement of a situation in which the language and culture of the nation are employed and cultivated by a large majority of the population on a day-to-day basis.

The processes leading to the spread and vitality of the nation without state's culture and language are crucial in generating sentiments of solidarity among the members of the community and play a key part in the construction of civic coherence. If the nationalist movement is successful, a new solidarity between the members of the nation without state emerges and the nation's language and culture become set to replace those of the state in most aspects of the community's public sphere. The state's resistance to this process cannot be downplayed since even democratic states fiercely oppose any attempts to question their legitimacy and unitary structure.

As I have already discussed, nationalism in nations without states requires the participation of some intellectuals who are confronted with the state's elite and a generally well established and state controlled education and media systems. The intellectuals' task is not confined to the transformation of a low into a high culture, it also involves a harsh and sustained struggle to dismantle the state's cultural influence to a point in which it allows the free evolution of the national minority. The degree and intensity of this struggle depends upon the objectives set up by the nationalist movement. If they seek independence, then they will tend to adopt measures leading to the eradication of the state's influence, but if biculturalism and bilingualism (wherever relevant) are embraced, a more complex equilibrium between both cultures and languages is to be sought.

Key elements of the nationalist discourse

The nationalism of nations without states is articulated around a set of principles different from those which inspired the classical nationalisms of the nineteenth and early twentieth centuries. As I have already mentioned, the fact that nations without states are included within the boundaries of states which rule them and often do not acknowledge their specificity as nations is crucial in understanding the demands and particular content of a new brand of nationalism which becomes salient at the turn of the century. A basic starting point shared by all nationalist movements is dissatisfaction with the current status of the nation they represent. However, it is necessary to be more precise and establish the specific terms of such disagreement. I distinguish between three major aspects which constitute the core of the nationalist discourse in nations without states. These are: moral, economic and political reasons.

Moral reasons All nationalist movements seek to legitimize their existence and their particular claims by appealing to moral reasons which are generally grounded upon the affirmation of democracy and popular sovereignty. The right of peoples to self-determination is invoked as a key principle defending the idea that each people has the intrinsic right to cultivate its own culture, develop its specific national identity and decide upon its political future. Moral reasons include the idea that individual rights cannot be fully enjoyed if they are not conceived in a context of respect for collective rights. Thus, for an individual to be able to develop all his or her potentialities, he or she cannot be considered in isolation but as a member of a larger group. Two sets of different rights which complement each other need to be taken into account, those concerning the individual as a free agent, and those related to the social dimension of individuals who live within specific communities. In late modernity, these communities tend to be nations.

Kymlicka points at the striking diversity of views on the rights of minority cultures which are contained in the liberal tradition. He argues that in the last two centuries, there have been times when the defence of minority rights was considered as a clear sign of one's liberal credentials. He writes:

> For example, it was a common tenet of nineteenth-century liberalism that national minorities were treated unjustly by the multinational empires of Europe, such as the Habsburg, Ottoman, and Tsarist empires. The injustice was not simply the fact that the minorities were members of the dominant nation in each empire as well. The injustice was rather the denial of their national rights to self-government, which were seen as an essential complement to individual rights, since 'the cause of liberty finds its basis, and secures its roots, in the autonomy of national groups'.[26]

Part of the success of contemporary nationalism in nations without states is due to the renewed emphasis it places upon the idea of forming a community. After years of developing and promoting individual rights, we are now confronted with the socio-political need to counteract an exceedingly individualistic society threatened by a fragmentation which stems from its growing lack of civic coherence. Nationalist movements in nations without states reject the current situations in which those nations find themselves as unfair, undemocratic, limiting and imposed upon them from the outside. Lack of collective freedom to develop one's own culture and decide about the future of the group is presented as a major element which legitimizes the nationalist discourse. Let us consider some examples that illustrate it.

For Jacques Parizeau, former Quebec Prime Minister, the Parti Québécois' main objective is 'the construction of a sovereign Quebec'.[27] In the Parti Québécois' (PQ) view, only sovereignty can guarantee the full development of Quebec's culture. The Quebec group *Intellectuals for sovereignty* (*Intellectuels pour la souveraineté*, or IPSO) has issued a document in which they list four main moral justifications to legitimize Quebec's aspirations for self-determination: (1) Canada's refusal to consider itself a multinational state; (2) Canada's refusal to grant Quebec full power over cultural (language, culture, communications) and economic (manpower training, unemployment insurance, regional development) matters; (3) the federal government refusal to limit its own spending power while continuing to interfere, most notably by imposing so-called 'national standards', in sectors which are under exclusive provincial control, such as education and health; and (4) the Canadian government's refusal to explicitly recognize a genuine asymmetry in the sharing of powers which would reflect the fact that Quebec is one of the founding peoples of the country.[28] In IPSO's view, 'These constitutional, political and administrative impasses occur because Canada refuses to recognize the existence of the Quebec people and its own wide-ranging diversity.'[29] Since the October 30 1995 referendum, dialogue between Quebec and the federal government has become more strained. Michel Seymour, president of the IPSO board of Directors, in his 'A letter to Canadians' appeals to the democratic sense of English Canadian intellectuals and invites them to denounce what he considers 'the federal government's increasingly authoritarian attitude'. In his view, 'the federal government can do nothing against the democratically expressed will of the Quebec people'.[30] Emphasis upon the people as depositories of sovereignty is employed throughout the text as the main legitimating argument in favour of sovereignty-partnership with Canada.

The Scottish National Party (SNP) also stresses the Scots' desire to feel represented and recognized as a separate community distinct from England: 'For almost 300 years Scotland has been without a Parliament and without a government that can truly *represent* and serve the people . . . Successive UK Governments have shown their *indifference* to Scotland. They have been *blind to Scotland's needs and deaf to Scotland's demands*. Yet, the demands for change grow even louder (italics mine)'.[31] The SNP explicitly mentions some moral reasons for Scotland's independence: 'An Independent Scotland will be a society where genuine democracy is upheld, and the rights and liberties of the citizens protected. Popular sovereignty will prevail . . . The people of an Independent Scotland will be citizens of a modern democratic state, not subjects of an archaic system'.[32]

Plaid Cymru, the main Welsh nationalist party, stresses the difference between Wales and England, 'Wales is not England. Wales is a nation with its own identity, culture, traditions and history. Above all, it has its own distinct political values, which are in marked contrast to the political values of England and particularly of the ruling classes of East England'.[33] They also invoke popular sovereignty and democracy as main principles underlying their nationalist claims:

In our model, sovereignty must be enshrined in the Welsh people, not in a Westminster Parliament nor in the English Crown. We want the

Welsh Parliament to be a Parliament of sovereign people – and for every individual permanently resident in Wales, irrespective of colour, race, language or creed, to be a sovereign citizen of our country. We wish to put behind us that outdated and derogatory concept that our citizens are, in any shape or form, 'subjects' of any institution – whether in London or in Wales. In the Wales we are trying to build, they will be citizens of Wales, of Europe, and of the world, and institutions of government will be there to serve them and to be answerable to them in a modern democracy.[34]

Plaid Cymru's appeal to democracy involves a redefinition of the people as a political subject and seeks to confer sovereignty upon the Welsh. Wales is no longer considered as a part of Britain, but as an independent nation which, as such, should be able to decide upon its political destiny. The nationalism defended by Plaid Cymru could be referred to as a 'civic' since it bases citizenship not on ethnic but on social factors such as permanent residence in Wales.

The Catalan nationalist party Democratic Convergence of Catalonia (*Convergència Democràtica de Catalunya*, or CDC) defines a Catalan as a person who lives and works in Catalonia and wants to be one. CDC in its Tenth Congress celebrated in November 1997 put forward two main claims, that Spain should acknowledge the existence of Catalonia as a nation, and that the Spanish state should define itself as multi-national. CDC understands Catalan nationalism as an integrative force which promotes 'the democratization of society by building up an alternative to bureaucracy and the impersonal tendencies favoured by globalization and the internationalization of culture'.[35]

Economic reasons   Moral reasons are sufficient to convince those who feel as members of the nation and have a substantial degree of national consciousness. But, as I have already shown, nationalist movements usually start as minority movements and their success depends upon the capacity of a small group of patriots to spread the message and obtain a mass following. Economic arguments usually play a pivotal role in the configuration of the nationalist discourse and can be employed as an effective weapon to attract new followers. The basic argument of most nationalisms emerging in nations without states links moral and economics factors: 'we don't feel represented', 'we are being neglected', and 'this is why our economy is not working'. This reasoning is employed by nationalist movements in poor nations without states such as Wales, Corsica or Galicia. In wealthy ones, such as Catalonia, Scotland or Flanders the discourse is slightly different, 'we are a prosperous nation but most of our revenue is taken away from us by the state', 'we need autonomy to exploit our own resources' or 'we will do better on our own'. Yet, where moral reasons do not satisfy some sectors of the population, the promise of a better standard of living, the end to unemployment and a better management of resources may prove strong arguments and convince them of the need to support the nationalist cause.

The Parti Québécois argues, 'only nations able to freely use all their resources can guarantee social and economic progress'.[36] The Scottish National Party's *1996 Programme for Government* starts with an address by its president Alex Salmond. He writes, 'An Independent Scottish Government must enable business to flourish, jobs to be created and services to be provided. Our exciting and forward looking programme shows how we can create that new environment for Scotland'.[37] Economic reasons are emphasized time and again. The promise to turn Scotland into a better place to live in is clearly spelt out: 'The SNP wants to eradicate poverty; regenerate the economy; encourage business and industry; achieve full employment; redress inequality; . . . [The SNP seeks to] voice the concerns of the Scottish people and Scottish industries, neglected for too long by Britain's representatives . . . Only Independence brings the power to make these goals a reality'.[38] Independence is presented as a condition *sine qua non* for Scotland's economic take-off.

In Catalonia, Jordi Pujol, leader of the Democratic Convergence of Catalonia Party, stresses the need to turn Catalonia into a 'country of quality'. He suggests that quality, once achieved, will bring about collective and individual respect, self-esteem and freedom. Identity, competitiveness, a sense of community and cultural projection are the four key ideas that Pujol introduces in the service of building up Catalonia.[39] He presents nationalism as an instrument for the modernization and internationalization of Catalonia. In defending the welfare state, he points to economic growth as a main condition.[40]

The plea for self-determination in nations without states has to be understood in a context of increasing globalization affecting not only the economy but also culture. The fact that nation-states are no longer able to control their own national economies and are subject to international forces opens up some scope for the generation of smaller units capable of competing in a global world. Being a nationalist is portrayed as the best solution if one is concerned with the fulfilment of collective as well as individual rights within a particular society. Economic reasons for self-determination are based on the idea of redressing a situation which is considered as unfair and even damaging for the nation. The main arguments employed by nationalists refer to the urgency to modernize the nation, decide upon its political and economic future and achieve a better quality of life.

Political reasons The main distinction between a nation-state and a nation without a state of its own lies in the different access to power and resources they enjoy. Although the nation-state is facing a profound process of transformation which is in many ways weakening its traditional power, it still remains the chief political actor. Minority nationalist movements are aware of the transformations which are currently affecting the nation-state. Most of these movements are not deterred by such changes and consider statehood as their final objective.

The plea for self-determination is a plea for *power* and reflects the desire to be considered an equal partner with other nation-states and thus able to participate in international organizations and act as a fully fledged world political actor.

The Parti Québécois stresses this point by arguing that, 'in our world there is only room for countries, since the treaties and agreements which determine the world's development are exclusively signed by nation-states and not by peoples'.[41] Nationalist parties in Wales, Catalonia, the so-called Padania, and Scotland manifest a strong desire to have their own representatives within European Union institutions. They lay strong claims for a EU structure based upon decentralization and subsidiarity. In this line, the SNP argues that 'it is time for Scotland to regain its place in the world' and cease to be an 'invisible nation'.[42] Plaid Cymru presents itself as 'the only party offering Wales a system of full self-government within the European Union'.[43] The Northern League (*Lega Nord*) refers to Europe as an alternative *patria* in the place of Italy.[44] Pujol insists on the European character of Catalonia, a feature that in his view allows the CDC to combine tradition and the cultivation of Catalan identity with a desire to overcome parochialism and appear as a modern European political party. He regards the European integration of Catalonia as a major challenge that requires constant modernization.[45]

Nationalism and the media

The resources of the nationalist movement in question and the freedom it enjoys within the state are decisive factors when considering how mass communication affects the dissemination of nationalism in nations without states. Thus, while some states restrict their national minorities' access to the media, other states may allow them to set up their own newspapers, radio stations and TV channels. The latter is usually the case where the minority nation is granted some form of political autonomy within the state. In a federation, access to the media is easier since the different nations forming the state should, in principle, be considered equal; unfortunately, experience shows that one nation tends to dominate the others and enjoy an easier access to the media.

In cases where the national minority is not even recognized as such, and where its representatives and organizations are clandestine, access to the media is practically impossible; the state controls them. In such circumstances, national minorities try to create their own media channels which are always under threat. They also attempt to use other countries' media to put forward their particular claims. As I have already mentioned, during the Francoist regime (1939–75), Catalan nationalism was banned and Catalan culture and language were proscribed from the public sphere. Nationalist groups created their own pamphlets and journals, which, once discovered by state agents, were closed down and their representatives severely punished. Some nationalist messages involving a critique of the regime were occasionally broadcast from foreign locations. Thus, the state's attitude towards its nations determines to a large extent their access to the media, and the possibilities they have to disseminate their particular nationalist messages.

In what follows I consider how the new technical media impinge upon the dissemination of nationalism in nations without states through the analysis of two main aspects. First, I study the nationalist leaders' use of the media and their particular relation with the audience. Second, I consider the process of appropriation of and reaction to mediated nationalist messages. The role of nationalist intellectuals in the production of ideas as a constitutive element in social reproduction, and the analysis of the media's contribution to the construction of national identity once the national minority has established its own media channels are beyond the scope of this section.

On nationalist leaders and the media   In modern societies, it could be argued that democracy depends on the free access of all groups in a population to the media. Many of the features I shall examine when discussing the use of the media in the advancement of nationalism in nations without states could be applied to nationalism in general. One of the characteristics that distinguishes the nationalism of nations without states from other nationalisms is its capacity to challenge the concept of a centralized state and offer a radical alternative to it. This explains the tension which pervades all dimensions of the relationship between the media, the state and the promotion of regional nationalism.

Nationalist leaders in nations without states which enjoy various degrees of political autonomy seek to convince the population of the need to support the political programmes they represent. Above all, this involves defending the distinct character of their nation and demanding further autonomy which should eventually lead to the state's acceptance of the nation's right to self-determination. This primary objective has to be understood against the backcloth of a powerful state always reluctant to give away any aspects of its sovereignty. Even democratic states strongly resist the idea of defining themselves as multinational, since this might be regarded as containing an implicit acknowledgement of equal rights for all nations or parts of nations integrated within the same state.

The strengthening of mass communication has given unprecedented visibility to political leaders. This can be an asset to them provided that they manage to present themselves in such a way as to inspire trust, loyalty or affection, but visibility can also turn sour and generate hostility. Visibility provokes a new kind of fragility; political leaders are exposed and even if they try hard to control their own image, this can be easily damaged by 'an emotional outburst, an impromptu or an ill-judged action. The fall from power can be breathtakingly quick'.[46] Honesty, hard work, genuine concern for the people, the ability to speak in a clear and convincing manner, are some of the qualities which political leaders try to attach to their own images. Further to all these characteristics, nationalist leaders in Western nations without states struggle to avoid being presented as 'tribal' and 'backward'. The cause they endorse is often portrayed by the defenders of the nation-state's hegemony, as a threat to the state's integrity which could unleash atavistic forces which are impossible to control. Nationalist leaders require high skills and expert communication advisers to help them to counteract such accusations and project a positive self-image in which their commitment to modernization and democracy is a crucial element.

Leaders need to manage visibility. In so doing they seek to appear as engaged in the advancement of the nation and its people and strong enough to denounce the current situation and face the state from which they expect to gain further recognition. A significant factor to bear in mind when studying the public face of regional nationalist leaders is the much more limited power they enjoy compared with state leaders. The leader of a nation without a state is in many ways a 'dependent' leader whose power is often determined by state leaders who represent the nation-state's government. The serious implementation of subsidiarity within a single state could increase the power of regional leaders. There are also special occasions in which a regional leader may acquire considerable power due to particular circumstances. For instance, the Catalan nationalist coalition CiU (Convergence and Union) supported the Spanish Socialist Workers Party (PSOE) when it lost the majority in the Spanish parliament (1993–5), and is currently backing the Conservative Popular Party (PP) which did not obtain the majority in the 1996 general election. During both periods, the Catalan president Jordi Pujol managed to attain a substantial development of the Catalan statute of autonomy which included retaining 30 per cent of the taxes collected in Catalonia. This unprecedented political scenario has enhanced the image of the Catalan leader and increased his power to negotiate a better settlement for Catalonia within Spain while stressing the fact that not all Spanish Autonomous Communities' presidents enjoy the same prestige and power.

The greater the power enjoyed by a regional nationalist leader, the easier it becomes for him or her to develop an 'aura' which the media has the capacity to enhance. Leaders become available to the audience in a mediated form, they turn into familiar faces and people even notice it when they change their hair-style, but the media also generate a certain distance between the leaders and the audience. There is no direct dialogue and co-presence is relegated to special occasions when leaders are able to send specific messages which might be of interest to a particular audience. Electronically mediated messages are usually concerned with matters of general interest, although on some occasions, they can have a high relevance for a single sector of society.

A fundamental quality for a nationalist leader is to be perceived by the audience as 'one of us'. This is the only way people can identify with the leader. The process of identification is a complex one, it entails radically different individuals being able to identify with a single person who has to be seen as embodying a manifold set of characteristics. Leaders play a crucial role in the articulation and success of nationalist movements. The media adds an unprecedented and intricate dimension to it.

On those who receive mediated nationalist messages   When addressing the members of a nation without state, nationalist leaders are set
face to face with an heterogeneous audience which displays radically
different attitudes with regard to the nationalist message. Among
them there are those who already support the nationalist cause, people
who are sensitive to it but need to be turned into active supporters,
people who are indifferent to the whole thing, and others who are
hostile to any nationalist claims implying state decentralization. The
audience is largely unknown to the leaders who demand a response,
and seek to mobilize them in the defence of the nationalist cause. This
may involve obtaining their support in a referendum or election
campaign; often it requires people to vote for a particular nationalist
party.

The audience's response is difficult to predict, this is why the
population is often monitored through opinion polls. The leaders'
popularity is constantly tested during election campaigns, or after
particularly controversial events. It has become a routine to commission opinion polls to find out not only the, to a certain extent,
unpredictable reaction of the audience but also to know what are their
main wishes and concerns.

The socio-historical circumstances in which nationalist messages are
to be disseminated play a key part in the ways in which the appropriation of such mediated messages takes place. Individuals are exposed
to specific messages, which contain ideas, images and information
about particular events. The call to defend the nation and the appeal
for solidarity among the members of a group sharing a common
culture is experienced in the intimacy of the home. Nationalist leaders
summon political, moral and economic reasons in the construction of
their discourses, but they also touch upon the people's sentiments and
emotions. Love of country is invoked as the ultimate justification of
nationalism, one which has to be revived or seeded in the hearts of
the nation's members.

The appropriation of nationalist mediated messages is a continuing
process that usually involves other individuals, contexts and messages
interwoven with those initially received.[47] After a discursive elaboration, the initial appropriation of nationalist messages may be transformed. For example, during an election campaign, the nationalist
leaders' discourse initially experienced by potential voters in a private
setting may become affected by other media reports, opinion polls,
public events involving the nationalist leaders in conditions of co-
presence, comments, discussions and other people's interpretations of
the initial message. Yet, it can be argued that nationalist messages are

subject to a constant and unprecedented scrutiny stemming from the public dimension they have acquired as a result of an extensive use of mass communication.

Nationalist leaders cannot be reduced to mere transmitters, they need to be sensitive to the people's reaction to their messages. They are leading the people, but for leadership to be successful an active dialogue between them and their audience has to be established and maintained. Otherwise there is the danger of building up elaborate political discourses which are not in tune with the people's sentiments, needs and wishes. Leaders try to capitalize on ideas and feelings which might be latent in people's minds and hearts – memories of past splendours, shared victories and defeats, myths and culture – while denouncing the nation's current situation and promising a better future. Many factors contribute to the success or demise of these alternative nationalist messages which defend the right to self-determination of nations lacking a state of their own. As we have seen, the media open up unprecedented possibilities and risks to the dissemination of such messages. The nationalist leaders' chances to implement a particular programme and, what is even more important, acquire legitimacy depend upon the explicit support they are able to attain. National minorities' access to the media is determined by the state's attitude, the power and resources available to them, and the support they might receive from diasporic communities and other pressure groups living outside their territory.

It is crucial to acknowledge that the advent of mass communications has radically transformed the nature of social interaction and the modes of experience in modern societies. Such transformations have impacted upon the mechanisms employed to disseminate different forms of ideology.[48] As this chapter has shown, by specifically referring to the impact of the media in the construction, dissemination and reception of nationalist messages, mass communications have fundamentally transformed Western politics. I shall now move on and consider what are the main strategies which are generally used by nationalist movements resisting the homogenizing tendencies of the state within which their nation is included. Cultural resistance is commonly employed by national minorities to defend their specificity by peaceful means. There are other instances in which some nationalist groups turn to violence. In the following chapter I shall consider 'total war' and 'political terrorism' as examples of situations in which nationalism is associated with the use of violence.

5

Cultural Resistance and Political Violence

National minorities respond in a myriad ways to the homogenizing tendencies of the states within which they are included. The state's objective is the creation, or wherever it already exists, the strengthening of the nation. To achieve this, the state seeks to favour the emergence of a sense of community and to reinforce feelings of solidarity among its citizens. As I have already shown in Chapter Two, nations without states of their own find themselves in extremely different political scenarios mainly determined by: the nature of the state containing them; the strength of the national minority's movement struggling for cultural recognition, political autonomy, federation or independence; and the different processes of state formation which have resulted in various nation-state structures.

In what follows I shall consider cultural resistance and armed struggle as the two major strategies employed by nations without states to resist the homogenizing policies generally implemented by the state. Their use depends on the specific socio-political and historical circumstances existing in each particular case. The linkage between strategies and outcomes is an extremely complex one which among other factors depends on the support received by the nationalist movement, the will of the state to accommodate its demands, the pressure exerted by international bodies and the strength of diasporas living outside the nation's territory.

Cultural resistance and armed struggle are the result of, and have the capacity to increase, the national awareness of a given group, they challenge the *status quo* sponsored by the state, and seek to attract outside attention to the minority's demands. The success of these counter-strategies is by no means homogeneous and a proper assessment would require a specific analysis of each case. However, a more theoretical and general approach to these matters could shed some light onto the common mechanisms utilized by the nationalist movements of nations without states in their quest for recognition.

A fundamental difference between democratic and totalitarian or fascist regimes should be taken into account when considering not only the resistance strategies chosen by national minorities, but also the consequences of their use for the individuals who carry them out. While in a totalitarian state peaceful activities to preserve a particular language and culture entail the risk of severe punishment, in democratic societies similar activities are tolerated and sometimes may even be encouraged by the state. As I have already mentioned when examining how nationalist movements come into existence, in their initial stages only a small group of intellectuals engaged in activities oriented toward the preservation of the vernacular culture struggle to obtain some state support. It should be noted, though, that most democratic states are resistant to the idea of promoting internal difference.

Cultural resistance

This section focuses upon Catalan and Welsh nationalism as examples of primarily non-violent forms of nationalism, the former taking place within the totalitarian Francoist state, the latter within democratic Britain. First, I consider the cultural resistance activities carried out in Catalonia to confront the Franco regime (1939–75) and offer a typology of the different counter-strategies Catalans employed to oppose the homogenizing policies implemented by the state. Although it is impossible to offer an exhaustive typology which could be applied to all nations without states seeking to redress their situation by peaceful means, I think that the analysis of Catalonia during the Franco regime might contribute to the study of this particular type of action and allow us to draw some parallels with other cases. Second, I study the re-emergence of Welsh nationalism as a movement based upon the promotion of the Welsh language and consider whether the arson attacks on 'second homes' belonging to English people could be interpreted as a challenge to the traditionally non-violent character of Welsh nationalism.

Cultural resistance refers to the cultivation of a particular culture and language, where there is one, and to the use of all sorts of symbols of a national minority's identity in the public as well as in the private sphere. Its objective is to preserve and, whenever possible, to develop a specific language and culture which are under threat by the homogenizing policies implemented by a state which does not acknowledge or encourage internal difference. In a situation of repression, such actions symbolically break the state's control of the public arena and challenge the unitary and homogeneous image put forward by the state.

Catalonia During the Franco dictatorship, Catalan language and culture were learned at home and could only be put into practice within restricted groups determined by family or friendship ties. But, in spite of the extreme repression exerted by the regime, there were still some small groups ready to take the risk of speaking out in a different language.[1]

I distinguish four major forms of opposition within the public domain: 'symbolic actions', 'interference actions', 'elite actions' and 'solidarity actions'. By 'symbolic action' I mean a single and usually isolated action carried out by a small group or even a single individual whose main objective is to break the control of the public space in the hands of the oppressive regime. In this category I include, among others, graffiti and flag displaying. Symbolic actions are usually performed in the street and other public places, and addressed to all occasional witnesses.

By 'interference actions' I refer to single actions executed by small groups during the course of public events. The task of such actions is to challenge the regime at its core by disrupting rituals and ceremonies whose aim is precisely to prove that homogeneity and control have been achieved. 'Interference actions' imply a high degree of risk, since security measures designed to prevent any sort of disturbance are strongly implemented on such occasions. 'Interference actions' envisage a double reception: on the one hand, they are addressed to those attending the public event, but on the other, they seek the attention of 'alien' observers, such as the international press or foreign representatives, partially or completely unaware of the national minority's situation. In studying the Catalan state of affairs during Francoism we find many examples of 'interference actions'. In 1960 during Franco's visit to Barcelona, a concert to commemorate the centenary of the Catalan poet Joan Maragall was organized in the *Palau de la Música Catalana* (Catalan Music Palace). Franco did not attend the concert himself, but four members of his cabinet did. Included in the programme was *El cant de la senyera* (Song of the

Catalan Flag), a masterpiece by Maragall with nationalist overtones, that was cancelled at the last minute. Around two hundred Catalan nationalists, mainly members of the Catalan Language Academy (*Academia de la Llengua Catalana*) and the parapolitical group CC (*Crist Catalunya*), demanded the performance of *El Cant* and they finally began to sing it themselves.[2]

By 'elite actions' I refer to actions and activities carried out by a small but devoted intelligentsia. Their objective is the maintenance and, when at all possible, the development of the nation without state's high culture. 'Elite actions' are primarily concerned with the protection of the language. The Institute for Catalan Studies (*Institut d'Estudis Catalans*), dismantled in 1939, was reorganized in 1942 by Josep Puig i Cadafalch and Ramon Aramon. Their clandestine activities involved the publication of books and articles on medicine, science and other subjects in Catalan. *Omnium Cultural*, a semi-clandestine institution from 1964, was legally recognized in 1967 and then saw a dramatic increase in membership (from 639 members in 1968 to 11,000 in 1971). Among the activities of *Omnium Cultural* were the teaching of Catalan and the sponsoring of the Prize of Honour of Catalan Belles Lettres (*Premi d'honor de les lletres catalanes*).[3]

In the late sixties and early seventies the influence of the 1968 student uprisings in France and the 'Prague spring' favoured the proliferation of radical organizations within the university, and nationalist claims were perceived as bourgeois. Nationalist groups disappeared from the university arena to return only after Franco's death.

The Francoist regime went through different stages, and whilst it is true that it never changed its character as a dictatorship and its conservative ideology, it did certainly modify some of its practices in order to appear more acceptable to the Western democracies. The opposition movement took advantage of all possible openings to actively advance its resistance. The later stages of the regime saw an increase in the number of 'solidarity actions'. By 'solidarity action' I mean an action that is usually prepared or instilled by a small elite but whose aim is to mobilize a larger number of people, to achieve mass participation. The objective of a 'solidarity action' is to show the strength of the opposition by focusing upon a particular demand and presenting it as something that cannot be denied due to the massive support it receives. A fundamental change concerning the context in which actions are performed distinguishes 'solidarity actions' from both 'symbolic' and 'interference actions'. The latter attempt to break the control of the public sphere in the context of a highly repressive discipline surrounding all public activities. The former can only take place when a relative attenuation of the oppressive nature of the regime allows some breaches to materialize and the population then dares to gather together challenging the power of the state.

An eroded dictatorship striving to present itself as democratic has to use force in a carefully calculated way. A demonstration cannot be dealt with by shooting people. 'Solidarity actions' are addressed to the officials of the regime who are forced to acknowledge the power of the 'different' but at the same time such actions are designed to appeal to the media and to foreign observers who will be attracted by their magnitude. An example of a 'solidarity action' is the one million strong mass demonstration in Barcelona on 11 September 1977 in an attempt to claim a statute of autonomy for Catalonia. Franco was already dead and an overwhelming majority had ratified the political reform presented by the Prime minister Adolfo Suárez. However, the status that Catalonia might achieve within the new democratic Spanish state was not yet clear. The massive demonstration of 1977 reinforced the Catalan rejection of a simple administrative decentralization of the state, compelling the government to consider the promulgation of a new Statute of Autonomy for Catalonia.

Cultural resistance within the private domain was, in some cases, a fully conscious activity particularly among middle classes and some sectors of the bourgeoisie who were responding to the political repression exerted by the regime. I want to suggest that among the working class and the peasantry the maintenance of the Catalan language and culture was perceived not so much as a specifically resistance activity encouraged by the clandestine circulation of Catalan literature, literary prizes and clandestine Catalan lessons to which these people had no access, but as something much more elemental and less conscious. The working classes and peasants continued to speak Catalan because it was the language they had learned from their parents, the language they used in day-to-day life to express emotions and to describe and talk about their most intimate feelings. They had to learn to use Castilian (Spanish) at work, at school, when shopping or going to court, but once at home they would describe their experiences using their mother tongue. When repeating the 'other's' words they would always use Castilian, the language of the 'alien', the language of power.

The *Nova Cançó* (New Folk Song) movement of the sixties played a key role in the regeneration of the public sphere in Catalonia. As Giner argues, it encompassed a number of different strands: the generational confrontations of the age, the international cultural climate – it was part and parcel of the 'protest' and pacifist Western popular culture of the time – anti-fascism, nationalist revivalism and pan-Catalanism.[4]

Wales The peaceful strategies employed by Catalans to defend their national specificity during Franco's dictatorship may be compared with similar actions carried out by national minorities which are under threat in other parts of the world. In contrast, the emergence of Welsh nationalism took place within an already democratic polity, Britain. Therefore the means employed by the Welsh and the responses to their nationalism have been somewhat different from those applied and obtained by Catalans under Francoism. Before examining the strategies that contemporary Welsh nationalism employs in the advancement of its goals, it might be worth considering a brief summary of the processes which led to the creation of the Welsh nation.

Wales: an historical overview Wales was initially inhabited by Celtic-speaking clans of shepherds, farmers and forest dwellers who came from continental Europe and originally even further east. They settled in Wales in successive waves between the seventh century BC and the period immediately before the arrival of the Romans from whom they had to defend themselves (the Romans invaded Britain in AD 43).[5] The Welsh were converted to Christianity by Celtic monks, notably St. David.[6] In the late fifth century, border wars between the Welsh and the seven English kingdoms known as the heptarchy were chronic. Contact with Ireland and the wider Christian communion of the North Atlantic seaboard continued. The trade relation with the Norse people also persisted, however commercial activity was quite often replaced by Norse raids and the Welsh people needed to defend themselves. The country was first united under Rhodri Mawr (844–78) and divided again after his death.

Hywel Dda, king of Wales in the mid-tenth century collected Welsh law and custom in a unified code. At the same time the position of the *bard* was formalized to yield a wealth of poetry, music, and learning. Border wars continued and Gruffudd ap Llywelyn was successful in bringing Gwynedd, Beheubarth and finally (though briefly) the whole of Wales under his dominion. He maintained Welsh independence until his death in 1063. Welsh culture blossomed in the twelfth century. The flowering of the literary tradition was exemplified in prose and eulogistic poetry. The *History of Gruffudd ap Cynan*, probably written in the reign of his son Owain Gwynedd, provides a classic statement of the political and cultural values of independent Wales.

Wales was made up of the three kingdoms of Gwynedd, Powys and Deheubarth, which by the third quarter of the twelfth century formed a well-defined sphere of Welsh political influence (*Wallia* or *Pura Wallia*) in contradistinction to the sphere of Norman influence (*Marchia Wallie*).[7] Norman control was established in the thirteenth century when Edward I provided for the security of his conquests by means of a programme of castle building, initiated after the war of 1277 and subsequently extended to include the great structures of Conway, Caernarfon, Harlech, and, later, Beaumaris. Each castle sheltered a borough where English colonists were settled.[8]

In 1282 Edward I conquered Wales. The Statute of Rhuddlan (or Statute of Wales, 1284) established English rule. The conquest did not involve the assimilation of the Welsh by the English, rather 'a colonial system was established in those parts of Llywelyn's Principality which were by 1284 in the hands of the king'.[9] Thus Welsh people did not become subjects of the crown on the same terms as the inhabitants of England. To placate Welsh sentiment, Edward had his son (later Edward II), who had been born at Caernarfon Castle, made Prince of Wales in 1301 thus originating the English custom of entitling the oldest son of the monarch of England as Prince of Wales. A gradual cultural decline took place after conquest.

In 1400, Owain Glyndwr led the most outstanding rising in Wales against the new order and the tyranny of the border barons. This rising, which is often considered as an early example of a national movement for freedom, resulted in the English losing government control. In 1404 Glyndwr was holding a separate parliament. He sought to create an independent Wales under prince and parliament which would have its own independent Church and educational structure through the creation of a system of Welsh universities. His ideas did not prosper after his death, but he undoubtedly contributed to generating a somehow unspecified sense of Welsh national identity.

The accession of the Welsh Tudor dynasty to the English throne, after Henry Tudor's victory at the battle of Bosworth Field in 1485, encouraged Welsh assimilation on the basis of equality. In this period, Wales was territorially structured according to the English model of shires; leading Welsh families held their land from the king while the others became lease-holders and tenants after the English pattern. The feudal aristocracy was received at the English court. A deep breach, fostered by economic inequality, opened between landlord and tenant and remained unhealed for centuries.

The Act of Union (1536) enshrined Henry VIII's wish to incorporate Wales within his realm. It meant the complete administrative assimilation of Wales into the English system. Welsh customary law was abolished and English was established as the sole language of legal proceedings.

In 1543 the Courts of Great Sessions were created, modelled on the practice already used in the three counties which since 1284 had formed the municipality of North Wales. The Great Sessions remained the higher courts of Wales until 1830, when, against considerable opposition, they were abolished.

Catholic tradition died slowly under Elizabeth I and James I; Puritanism was strongly resisted and Oliver Cromwell had to use oppressive measures to impose it. In the eighteenth century Wales turned rapidly from the Established Church to dissent with strong Calvinist leanings. In 1735 the Calvinist Methodist Church gathered large numbers of followers from the Church of England and contributed to the rise of an incipient Welsh nationalism. The desire to protect Welsh native culture from progressive Anglicization rose in the eighteenth century.

The Industrial Revolution transformed Wales and threatened rural life, the protests known as the Rebecca Riots (1843) are an example of this. The mineral wealth of Wales was opened to exploitation and radically transformed the life of Welsh people. Large numbers of Welshmen emigrated to the US. Chronic poverty and increasing unemployment intensified in Wales after the First World War and continued almost unchecked until the Second World War. After the war the Labour government, which drew substantial support from the socialist stronghold of South Wales, undertook a full-scale programme of industrial development.

Plaid Cymru was founded in 1925 as the Welsh Nationalist Party which since then has sought the protection and promotion of Welsh culture and language. In 1964, the Labour government appointed a Secretary of State for Wales, a ministerial post of cabinet rank, and subsequent Labour and Conservative administrations promoted the transfer of functions to the Welsh Office. A Royal Commission on the Constitution was appointed to consider increasing demands for an elected assembly in Wales. In 1973, the Commission recommended devolution for Wales. An Act giving Wales some devolved powers was passed at Westminster in 1978, but rejected by the Welsh people in the 1979 Referendum. Finally, in September 1997, the Welsh voted for the establishment of a Welsh Assembly and elections for it took place in 1999.

Contemporary Welsh nationalism   One of the main features of Welsh nationalism is the rejection of violence. Wales was politically united with England in 1536 by the Act of Union and can be considered as part of the ancient kingdom of Great Britain. In the nineteenth century Welsh culture and language, as was the case in Catalonia and other small European nations, experienced a revival prompted by the influence of Romanticism. Nationalism as a political movement emerged in the early twentieth century, slightly later than in Catalonia. The Welsh Nationalist Party was founded in 1925, and renamed Plaid Cymru in 1945. In contemporary Wales, Plaid Cymru and the Welsh Language Society (*Cymdeithas yr Iaith Gymraeg*) are the main representatives of Welsh nationalism. The two major achievements of Welsh nationalism in recent times have been the 1967 Welsh Language Act, which was the outcome of a sustained and controversial campaign of non-violent direct action and disruption, and the establishment of the Welsh language television station, S4C, *Sianel Pedwar Cymru* or Channel Four Wales which had to confront, among other things, the opposition of the then Prime Minister, Margaret Thatcher.[10]

The long-standing commitment of Welsh nationalism to peaceful means has been to some extent altered by arson attacks on 'second homes' belonging to English people. In the 1980s the Sons of Glyndwr (*Meibion Glyndwr*) organized an incendiary campaign focused on absentee-owned second homes and the estate agents who sell them. The focus was on property rather than on people. When the Anglican cleric and poet R. S. Thomas called for a campaign of 'non-violent night attacks' upon the homes of English people in Welsh-speaking districts, very few people backed it. Plaid Cymru and the Welsh Language Society reject the use of any kind of violence, but the issue of 'second homes' is an extremely sensitive one and this is why a certain ambiguity could be detected about the *Meibion Glyndwr* campaign. As Jenkins argues, 'this reflects a perceived increasing shortage of homes for local young people due to distortions in the housing market caused by affluent – and non-Welsh – absentee home owners'.[11] In his view, the increase in house prices together with rural unemployment produces emigration and a loss to the area of Welsh speakers. The demographic structure of whole areas is altered leading to conflict about Welsh-language education, a questioning of the use of Welsh as a medium for education in areas which were traditionally Welsh-speaking and are now mainly English-speaking. In Dyfed this was one of the main arguments which caused confrontation between the Labour Party and Plaid Cymru at a local level.[12] Jenkins emphasizes the crucial role of language in the construction of Welsh identity, and points at second homes, immigration and education as three sensitive issues perceived as a threat to Welsh culture and language.

Only about 20 per cent of the population of Wales are Welsh-speakers and this poses serious questions to the definition of Welsh national identity if this is to be based upon language. To turn nationalism into a mass movement it has to include the majority who do not speak Welsh, even if, parallel to this, an active Welsh language campaign is to continue. The biggest question, of course, concerns how to attract English-speaking people who may or may not define themselves as Welsh into a common project for the preservation and development of the Welsh language and culture. So far, Welsh nationalism has employed cultural resistance to the threat of further Anglicization and violence has been explicitly rejected. The 'second homes' arson campaign has introduced a novel dimension to the resistance strategies employed by Welsh nationalists by advocating the use of violence against property; but, to a large degree, Welsh nationalism remains a peaceful movement and, at the moment, it seems unlikely that it will turn to political violence.

Armed struggle

Nations without states have a manifold relationship to violence. The nation-state claims the monopoly of the legitimate use of force within its territory, but often, it sees its legitimacy claims challenged by national and ethnic minorities who do not accept its monopoly. Political terrorism, ranging from isolated target attacks to civil war, exemplifies the readiness of some national minorities to claim for themselves one of the most important features of the traditional state.

Some nations without states may become new political actors as a result of their economic performance, cultural strength or the emergence of substantial changes in their relations with both the state containing them and with some further supranational institutions. Others set out to put pressure on the state and the international community to recognize them by means of armed struggle. Liberation movements and intra-state wars sometimes lead to the creation of new nation-states (Slovenia, Croatia and Bosnia are cases in point). Such movements are often successful in persuading the state to confer some autonomy upon them, although independence is harder to achieve. The proliferation of supranational institutions containing several nation-states will facilitate the devolution of power to their national minorities since they are all likely to be included within the same political framework. For this to happen, supranational institutions need to be founded upon rigorously and imaginatively applied democratic principles, giving great prominence to subsidiarity and the principle of consent, and they also need to be perceived as legitimate institutions accountable to their citizens. If this were not to be the case, then supranational bodies would be repeating the same mistakes once committed by nation-states anxious to attain the cultural homogenization of their citizens. To become truly democratic, the supranational organizations which are currently being consolidated have to respect cultural diversity and seek to find some common principles and values able to hold together an otherwise diverse population.

Nations without states may claim some kind of internal policing within their territories. In the meantime, the post-traditional nation-state's armies will be integrated into multinational defence organizations such as NATO, to which in the future nations without states will probably be able to send their own contributions. Internal policing will be one of the main areas in which nations without states will define their access to the means of violence. Catalonia and the Basque Country already possess their own separate police force, although the Spanish police force – the National Police and the *Guardia Civil* – are still present within these two areas. In Spain, regional police forces have limited functions concerning the maintenance of law and order within their territory. Similar arrangements are likely to be put in place in other regions enjoying substantial degrees of political autonomy.

There are some occasions in which certain groups engaged in the struggle for the recognition of the national minority they represent regard cultural resistance as insufficient. Negotiations with the state are either impossible because of its undemocratic nature, its unwillingness to consider the nationalist claims of the national minority involved or because an extremist group advocating violence against the state considers that this is the most effective tactic to speed up a process of dramatic change in the status of the minority and its relation with the state. The use of violence in the relation between the state and its national minority or minorities is double-edged since violence against the state is as common as violence performed by the state against its national minorities. The frequency and character of such violence leads us to distinguish between 'total war' and 'political terrorism'. 'State terrorism' will also be considered as a phenomenon which has the capacity to generate, and/or contribute to the intensification of political violence.

Total war

Total war is a civil war between members of the same state belonging to antagonistic national communities. The intensity of the conflict rules out the term terrorism and refers to a situation in which the state army fights recently formed or recently augmented militias composed of ordinary citizens. With no foreign intervention it is unlikely that the minority will take over and win the confrontation unless it faces an extremely weak state. Intra-state wars do not tend to use high-technology weapons and almost always involve deliberate, systematic attacks on civilians to weaken the military resources on which adversaries can draw. A significant feature of total war is that civilian populations of warring groups are often intermingled. When battle lines exist, they often cut through cities, towns, and even neighbourhoods. Control over particular pieces of territory is of major importance in a total war. To secure complete territorial control, militias seek to drive out civilians from other groups and force them to leave their homes and property. The recent war in former Yugoslavia exemplifies the horrific practices of ethnic cleansing involving forced expulsions and the systematic slaughter of civilians. The Chechnya struggle for independence (1996–7) also illustrates a case of total war, in this case against the Russian state. At the time of writing, NATO is keeping up the pressure on the Yugoslav president, Slobodan Milosevic, to pull back his forces in Kosovo. Milosevic abolished Kosovo's autonomy, since then, the ethnic Albanian majority of Kosovo have been claiming their right to self-determination. The Kosovo Liberation Army (KLA) has emerged to confront Serbian forces and has Kosovo's independence as its main objective. The repression carried out by Serbian troops and police has so far resulted in numerous civilian casualties, the systematic destruction of civilian homes, and thousands of ethnic Albanians being forced to flee their homes and turned into refugees.

Total wars often generate staggering numbers of refugees precisely because they are based on systematic attacks on civilian populations. Ethnic or national differences, if linked to class, religion or status, no doubt become explosive whenever political or economic stability is collapsing within a single nation-state. The break-up of Yugoslavia clearly illustrates how communities who lived together and intermarried for a considerable period of time are capable of becoming fierce enemies. They have emphasized to the extreme the features they do not share as opposed to those which in the past proved sufficient to make their coexistence as members of a single society possible. Minimal differences have been exaggerated, old as well as newly invented stories of hatred retold. In response to the xenophobic propaganda of their leaders, people have stripped others of their humanity or come to regard them simply as criminals. The war in former Yugoslavia stands as an example of something that should have never been allowed to happen. According to Bennett, events which had taken place during the Second World War and even during the four decades of Tito's rule ceased to matter. In his view,

> the Serbian media dredged up and distorted every conceivable event from Serb history. Yugoslavia's non-Serbs were simply scapegoats for the economic and political failings of communist society in the 1980s and a convenient tool which Milosevic was able to exploit to further his own political ambitions. However, the xenophobia cultivated by the Serbian media was very real and, in time, it destroyed Yugoslavia.[13]

Bennett compares the role played by the media in Milosevic's Serbia to that played by the Nazi media in Hitler's Germany while taking into account the technological advances which have taken place since the 1930s and which add a more pervasive and insidious dimension to their influence. He points to a war psychosis that set in in Serbia, not in the Serb communities of Croatia and Bosnia-Herzegovina, at least three years before hostilities began. He writes:

> Irrespective of whether or not Serbs were facing genocide in much of Yugoslavia, as the Serbian media alleged, Serbian society was already gripped by fear and ordinary people genuinely came to believe that they were under siege and, critically, began behaving as if they were surrounded by blood enemies determined to wipe them out.[14]

Political terrorism

Terrorism is calculated violence against a target population which may or may not directly suffer the effects of the act of violence, but which is terrorized by the prospect of becoming a victim. Fear is the intended effect of terrorism. The population must perceive themselves at risk and as the ultimate target of terrorist action. Shultz refers to political terrorism as 'goal directed violence employed in pursuit of political objectives. It is calculated violence directed at affecting the views and behaviour of specific groups'.[15]

Political terrorism is usually directed against the state, but there are occasions in which it is directed against other ethnic groups, opposing parties or classes. As Laqueur mentions, the aims of the terrorist may vary from the redress of specific grievances to concrete challenges to the *status quo* which may sometimes involve a demand for independence, better treatment for a particular group or the desire to overthrow the government.[16] The aim of terrorism is to force change by bringing about a solution to a situation in which fear pervades the day-to-day life of the target population. Violence is regarded as a valid tool in the pursuit of a particular outcome to a conflict situation.

According to Crenshaw, 'the argument that terrorism should be considered as "rational" is based on the assumption that radical organizations possess internally consistent sets of values and regularized procedures for making decisions'. As she writes, 'terrorism is seen collectively as a logical means to advance a desired end'.[17] A further and significant factor to be taken into account is the existence of outside support for the cause that the group using political violence seeks to advance. For instance, so far the backing of the North American Irish community has proven highly relevant in the process of finding a peaceful solution to conflict in Northern Ireland.

O'Brien challenges the view which confers a rational character on terrorism. He argues that 'liberal democracies are embodiments of rationality, while terrorists, being violent, are quintessentially irrational'.[18] It is paradoxical, in terms of the affirmation of the rationality of terrorism that terrorist action is often unsuccessful in the achievement of its political aims. But it should also be noted that whenever political violence is successful in achieving its aims, there is a certain reluctance to refer to it as 'terrorism'. A further point concerns the 'tendency in the West to treat any violent challenge to a liberal-democracy or even to any polity that meets the formal requirements of a liberal-democracy as illegitimate and hence an example of terrorism, even if the violence escalates to a level that points to a fundamental breakdown of political authority'.[19]

Terrorism is more likely to emerge in heterogeneous societies divided by sharp ethnic, or class boundaries. In Gurr's view, minority elites in highly stratified societies are likely to use violence routinely.[20] But to be considered as a source of conflict, internal boundaries need to be perceived as unfair, and as a source of discrimination.

Terrorism entails an open defiance of an established political system. It is impersonal, but if properly organized, it is never 'indiscriminate' or 'arbitrary', since this would fundamentally alter its character as calculated violence toward the achievement of a certain end. Wilkinson challenges this interpretation of terrorism. In his view, the elements which characterize political terrorism are: indiscriminate-ness, unpredictability, arbitrariness, ruthless destructiveness, and the implicit amoral, and antinomian nature of a terrorist's challenge.[21] The difference between these two interpretations of terrorism as goal directed or as arbitrary violence lies at the heart of a frequently quoted sentence in the literature about terrorism: 'one man's terrorist is another man's freedom-fighter'.

Crenshaw insists on the purpose-oriented character of terrorism. She distinguishes three main aims in terrorist action: to obtain the sympathy of a potential constituency; to provoke fear and hostility in an audience identified as the 'enemy', taking into account that intimi-dating the 'enemy' impresses both sympathizers and the uncommit-ted; and to provoke a counter-reaction from the government.[22] She points to weakness and impatience as the major driving forces in a terrorist organization.

Terrorism does not solely arise where a national minority is oppressed by the state and no democratic channels of participation exist, as was the case with the activities of the Basque paramilitary group ETA during the Francoist regime. The new democratic Spain has conferred a substantial degree of autonomy on the Basque Country which enjoys its own parliament while being entitled to a financial arrangement with the state which is far more advantageous than that of the rest of the Spanish autonomous communities. In spite of the availability of democratic channels of participation, ETA has continued its terrorist campaign for the independence of the Basque Country.

First, from Crenshaw's perspective, 'an extremist organization may reject non-violence and adopt terrorism because they are impatient with time-consuming legal methods of eliciting support or advertising their cause, because they distrust the regime or are not capable of, or interested in, mobilizing majority support'.[23] The continuation of terrorist activities after democratic channels have been established can also be related to the psychological consequences of engaging in an activity which requires high commitment both to political objectives and to a group. Crenshaw refers to the psychological relationships within the group in which shared risk, solidarity, loyalty, guilt, revenge and isolation may act as discouraging elements for the terrorists' decision to halt violence and alter their course of action. In her view, 'this may explain why opposition persists even after griev-ances are met or non-violent alternatives opened'.[24]

Second, there are those who reject the assumption that in a democ-racy there is always a peaceful method for a minority to have its grievances redressed, especially if that minority comprises or is included within a more or less permanently smaller group, since 'democracy tends to further the interests of the majority at the expense of the minority'.[25]

Definitions of terrorism are suspect, since they are often employed to denigrate the activities of political enemies. Edmund Leach in his lecture on *Custom, law and terrorist violence* stresses that a 'high proportion of today's violent criminals [are] political or religious fanatics who see themselves as potential martyrs in the cause of some highly bizarre and improbable political Utopia, and who certainly do not recognize themselves as criminals at all'.[26] The lack of shared moral values and principles between terrorists and the state whose *status quo* they seek to alter is so complete that as Leach puts it, 'the "other" comes to be categorized as a wild animal, then every imaginable form of terrorist atrocity is not only attributed to the other side but becomes permissible for oneself. Indeed, counter terrorism becomes, in a bizarre sense, a religiously sanctioned moral duty'.[27]

The state's labelling of certain opposition groups' activities as terrorism serves three major purposes. First, it explicitly establishes the illegitimacy of the opposition and all those related to it in the eyes of the majority of the population; easy access to the media facilitates the state's portrayal of terrorism as unjustified and illegal, thus reducing it to criminal activity and emptying terrorism of its political content. Second, it provides a justification for the severe punishment of dissent, ignoring Leach's advice that 'however incomprehensible the acts of the terrorist may seem to be, our judges, our policemen, and our politicians must never be allowed to forget that terrorism is an activity of fellow human beings and *not* of dog-headed cannibals'[28] because, as Schlesinger points out, 'the dehumanization of the state enemies endangers civil liberties'.[29] Third, it seeks to persuade the outside world of the marginal nature of internal political opposition and stress the stability of the established political system.[30] As Guelke emphasizes, 'judging violence inevitably involves interpretation, and differences of interpretation may be as important in accounting for conflicting reactions to particular episodes of violence as differences in basic norms about what is right or wrong'.[31]

But, is there a direct link between terrorism and the perception of grievances by a particular group? Or, as some scholars argue, should terrorism be treated as a form of pathological behaviour? Is the terrorist a criminal, a mad person, or a freedom fighter? There is a sharp division among those who study terrorism when considering its causes.

A first tradition points to the social, political or economic deprivation experienced by a certain community as the major element contributing to the emergence of terrorism. From this perspective, terrorist activities are oriented towards the redress of these grievances and are usually carried out by a small extremist faction within a broader movement. The use of violence is justified by its perpetrators as the only channel available to achieve a quick and radical response from the state leading to the end of unjust discrimination.

Against the school of thought which relates the emergence of terrorism to the existence of grievances which those discriminated against perceive as unjust, stands a second tradition which adamantly rejects the so called 'root causes' theory. Laqueur argues that 'there will always be disaffected, alienated, and highly aggressive people claiming that the present state of affairs is intolerable and that only violence will bring a change'.[32] Terrorism is then disconnected from unfair treatment and oppression of a particular group and defined as a 'pathological contagion' caused by the decision to employ violence against innocent people. Terrorists are portrayed as criminals who construct a rationality alien to that of the state. They frontally question the state's legitimacy and defy its power by challenging what has been traditionally acknowledged as one of the key attributes of the state, this is its claim to 'the monopoly of *the legitimate use of physical force* within a given territory'.[33]

Terrorism employs a wide variety of tactics which include the assassination of leading representatives of the system, indiscriminate terror, injuries, expropriation, kidnapping, car bombs and hijacking of airplanes, among other things. Terrorists justify their actions by arguing that they 'constitute an effective means to a legitimate end'. Guelke maintains that acts of violence will appear more legitimate if the ends are emphasized, and if the means employed in their advancement are somehow proportionate to the objectives sought. He stresses the difficulty in achieving a normative definition of terrorism which reflects the 'absence of a clear consensus among states or world opinion at large as to the content of such a norm, compounded by a problem of trying to judge means without reference to ends'.[34] In his view, the large distance that seems to exist between the means being used and the goals sought provides part of the explanation for the characterization of terrorism as a strategy of desperation and as the weapon of the weak.[35] Following this line of argument, Lawrence Freedman argues that dependence on terrorism tends to be a sign of strategic failure. It could be argued that relying on a terrorist strategy for a considerable period of time during which no signs of substantial change take place amounts to terrorist failure.

In a situation of extreme repression, however, the terrorists' inability to promote a mass movement backing their demands could be attributed to the pervasive surveillance and repressive methods employed by the state in an attempt to crush opposition. Harsh repression against the community which the terrorists claim to be fighting for may be regarded as evidence of the effectiveness of their campaign and a reason to persist. Terrorist action is often aimed at provoking a violent state response, yet the rough treatment of the group in question is likely to be employed by terrorists as a justification for their continued activity, and might generate sympathy for their actions. The image of the state as an oppressor is emphasized and people may come to adopt a more tolerant if not positive attitude towards armed struggle. Again this could be illustrated by referring to the highly repressive nature of the Franco regime against Basque people and its immediate response to ETA activities in the sixties and early seventies when significant sections of the native population accepted or at least showed an ambiguous attitude towards them.

The making of the Basques   The Basques constitute the only surviving pre-Aryan race in Europe, and their language, Basque (or *Euskera*) is the only pre-indoeuropean language which is alive in Europe. Basques called themselves *Euskaldunak* (those who speak *Euskera*) and their land is referred to as *Euskalherria* (*Euskera*-speaking people's land).

The Basques had little contact with the Romans when they invaded the Iberian peninsula, only the Southern part of *Euskalherria* received their influence. Pamplona was founded by the Romans on the old Basque city or Iruña. In the fifth century the Basques fought against Barbarian invaders crossing the Pyrenees towards the Iberian peninsula. In the sixth century they were defeated by the Visigoths (AD 581). The Basques did not constitute a political unit until the early seventh century when the Duchy of Vasconia was created. It comprised lands both North and South of the Pyrenees currently included within both France and Spain. In its initial stages the Franks appointed the Duke of Vasconia, later on the Basques achieved independence from the Franks and had to confront the Visigoths who invaded the Duchy of Vasconia.

The Moors' invasion of the Iberian peninsula (AD 711) created the opportunity for the Basques to defeat the Visigoths. In the ninth century, the Basques were fighting the Franks in the North and the Moors in the South. At this point the kingdom of Navarra emerged from the Duchy of Vasconia as an independent state; Eneko Aritza of

Pamplona was its first king. His greatest achievement was to defeat the Franks at Roncesvalles (728).

The kingdom of Navarra was subject to constant pressure from neighbouring kingdoms. It reached its maximum splendour in the eleventh century during the reign of Sancho III *el Mayor* (Sancho the Great). After his death in 1035 the kingdom was divided. In 1234 the Basque monarch had no successor and the crown went to a French dynasty. At this point Alava, Guipúzkoa, and Bizkaia separated from the kingdom of Navarra. Various crises affected the Basque Country during the fourteenth century and reduced its population. Social tensions between peasants and landlords prompted violent confrontations in the fifteenth century.

In 1512 amid the war between Castile and France, the Castilian army with the support of the Holy Alliance invaded Navarra. In 1513 the Castilian–French war ended, however, Castilian domination continued. King Fernando el Católico swore to respect Navarra's sovereignty and its laws (*Fueros*). Thus the union between Castile and Navarra was to preserve the separate territory, institutions and laws of both kingdoms.

The Basques ruled themselves according to the *Fueros* (local statutes and charters) first established between the Basque regions North of the Pyrenees and the Foix of Occitany, and later on between the kingdom of Castile and Basque regions south of the Pyrenees. Most of the *Fueros* were codified in the seventeenth and eighteenth centuries, although some of them date back to the seventh century. They exempted the local population from both military service and taxation, and allowed the provincial assemblies the right to veto royal edicts, a privilege rarely employed. The *Fueros* were conceived as reflecting the rights of the Basque people, rather than as concessions granted to them. The Basques throughout history defended the *Fueros* which granted their autonomous status within the Spanish state.[36]

Centralist attempts to abolish the *Fueros* were contested in the Basque regions. The Basque support for the Carlist movement was connected to their objective of opposing centralism and defending the *Fueros* which were finally abolished in 1876 after two long civil wars (*Guerras Carlistas*).

The rapid industrialization of the Basque Country took place immediately after the abolition of the *Fueros*. Modernization transformed all spheres of social life. The emergence of a Basque working class, the displacement of Basque youth from the rural areas to the countryside, the arrival of large numbers of immigrants from Castile – thought of as the oppressor's country which had finally managed to abolish the *Fueros* – all contributed to the emergence of Basque nationalism. It first took shape in the form of a small cultural revival, soon after that Sabino Arana Goiri emerged as the ideologist of Basque nationalism and founded the Basque Nationalist Party in 1894.

A similar movement led by Arturo Campión and Juan Iturralde y Suit took place in Navarra which did not participate in the dramatic changes brought about by early industrialization affecting Bizkaia and Guipúzkoa. Navarra remained a primarily rural country and nationalists there moved no further than regionalism and were often monarchists.

The Basque Nationalist Party espoused a strong Catholic and nationalist ideology and gained the support of significant sectors of the population. In 1932 a referendum on political autonomy for the Basque country obtained overwhelming support in the provinces of Alava, Guipúzkoa and Bizkaia, but was defeated in Navarra. A draft Statute of Autonomy for the Basque Country was finally sanctioned by the Spanish Courts during the Second Spanish Republic in October 1936. However, Franco's insurrection against the democratic government of the Republic and his subsequent victory resulted in the Statute never being implemented.

The Spanish transition to democracy was initiated after Franco's death in 1975. The 1978 Spanish Constitution was ratified by the majority of Spaniards, but in the Basque country most nationalist forces opposed it arguing that it was ambiguous about Basque rights. In the Constitution referendum, the abstention rate reached 56 per cent in Guipúzkoa and Bizkaia.[37] The Basque Statute of Autonomy was ratified in a referendum in 1979, 61 per cent voting and 89 per cent casting a positive vote. The president of the Basque parliament in exile, Jesús María de Leizaola (1896–1980)[38] returned from France, and elections to the new Parliament took place in 1980, Carlos Garaikoetxea leader of the Basque Nationalist Party became the first *lehendakari* (head of the Basque government) in the new democratic period.

Basque nationalism and violence It can be argued that both communities, Catalonia and the Basque Country, were equally discriminated against by a totalitarian regime determined to crush intra-state difference. The reasons which could explain why violence emerged in one community and not in the other are to be found in a deeper analysis of the content of Catalan and Basque nationalist doctrine as well as in the different socio-political structures of both societies. While Catalan nationalism has a predominantly civic character and has traditionally sought to participate in Spanish politics, allusions to the uniqueness of the Basque race and blood are to be found in early formulations of the Basque nationalist doctrine.[39] Sabino Arana, the main ideologist of Basque nationalism, put forward the idea of *Euskadi* (the Basque Country) as a country occupied by a foreign power, Spain, primarily identified with Castile. The Francoist regime and its obsession with persecuting all symbols of Basque culture gave plausibility to Arana's theory of occupation.

A further reason concerns the different, although in both regions precarious, situation of their vernacular languages and cultures. Catalan as well as Basque were proscribed from the public sphere; but, the number of people who could understand and speak Catalan greatly outnumbered those who could understand and speak *Euskera* (the Basque vernacular language).[40] Profound social and economic transformations affected the Basque Country in the 1950s. The uncontrolled industrial expansion around the main Basque cities was accompanied by a large inflow of Castilian-speaking immigrants from other parts of Spain. The Castilian language is often referred to as Spanish; a feature which responds to the dominant role played by Castile over the other peoples of Spain. At the same time, the Basque language and culture were suffering a high degree of erosion, their use being restricted to increasingly reduced circles of native Basque people. In Jáuregui's view, this encouraged the rejection of Castilian culture and favoured the spreading of anti-immigrant attitudes. The presence of a strategic elite of Castilian origin acting as an agent of linguistic as well as cultural oppression contributed to enhancing feelings of hostility against Castilian migrants.[41]

Fear of complete assimilation into mainstream Castilian culture was linked to the idea of the Basque Country as a colonized country which should use all means available to free itself from foreign (Castilian) domination. In this context, ETA emerged as a paramilitary organization embracing a radical nationalism whose main aim was to expel the colonial power through the use of force and the creation of an autochthonous government. ETA understood its activities as part of a revolutionary war, a war of liberation which they compared to that of Cuba, Algeria or Angola. They justified armed struggle as the only available strategy since, in their view, all possibilities of dialogue had been exhausted. ETA's main concern was to find the most effective means to achieve its goals in the shortest possible time.

The Francoist state responded to ETA's violence by increasing its repressive measures in the Basque Country, thus unwittingly becoming the most efficient agent in awakening Basque national consciousness and publicizing ETA.[42] Francoism symbolized the 'foreign' occupation of the Basque Country and armed struggle was portrayed as the only alternative if independence was to be achieved. In this context, powerful feelings of a mystical and messianic cast were linked to a blind conviction of the effectiveness of violence in the process of freeing the Basque Country. These sentiments, when combined with an awareness of the extremely precarious condition of the Basque culture and language, acquired romantic, irrational and tragic over-tones closely connected with ideas of self-sacrifice and death as necessary conditions if the 'future happiness and re-emergence of the Basque patria' were to be achieved.

The Spanish Popular Party government has up to now employed a radically different strategy to end terrorist violence in the Basque Country from that implemented by the Labour government in Northern Ireland. So far, the Spanish Conservative government has relied on the implementation of tougher measures to fight terrorism and has promoted the organization of cross-party mass demon-strations against ETA. The latter were initiated in Summer 1997 as a response to the ETA's new strategy of killing Conservative MPs and local councillors. In Spain, the government advocates the 'social exclusion' of all those who sympathize with the terrorists, and specially the Herri Batasuna, the political branch of ETA. Dialogue with ETA is discarded as an alternative, since, in the state's view, there is nothing to discuss with criminals. The government argues that the 1978 Spanish Constitution and the Basque autonomous insti-tutions provide a democratic framework for Basques to exercise their right to self-determination. ETA objects to that; it does not accept a concept of self-determination which excludes the right to indepen-dence of the Basque Country. The state's attitude ignores the exist-ence of any political claims related to ETA's activity and has so far proved unsuccessful in halting terrorism. ETA's ceasefire declared in September 1998 opens up a possibility for a peaceful solution for the Basque Country. The ceasefire was announced shortly before the Basque Country regional election campaign began. Then the Euskal Herritarrok (EH), a nationalist left wing coalition containing Herri Batasuna was created, and it became the third political force in the 25 October 1998 regional election after the Basque Nationalist Party (PNV) and the Popular Party (PP).[43] At present it is still unclear how the Spanish government will react to ETA's ceasefire.[44]

Catalonia   As I have mentioned above, not all deprived communities turn to terrorism, nor does terrorism always reflect deprivation. The comparison between Catalan and Basque nationalism during the

Francoist regime illustrates this point. Thus while the Basque Country witnessed the rise of ETA in the 1960s as a paramilitary organization whose main objective was to fight the dictatorship and demand independence, Catalonia did not experience the emerging of any significant resistance movement based upon the use of violence.

During Francoism's late stages and at a time when the transition to democracy was initiated, Catalan nationalism was split into two major movements; one opted to comply with the newly created democratic channels of participation, and the other turned to armed struggle. The latter, made up of a small number of people, was badly organized and lacked a stable structure. Between 1977 and 1978 two major terrorist actions took place, these were the killings of a Catalan businessman and of a former mayor of Barcelona (Bulto and Viola). In 1979, after such actions, a very small paramilitary organization called *Terra Lliure* (Free Land) was created. The strength and resources of *Terra Lliure* as well as its members' skills were extremely limited. The group was eventually dissolved and most of its members joined the Catalan Republican Left Party (*Esquerra Republicana de Catalunya*) which stands for the creation of a Catalan independent republic obtained by peaceful means.

Quebec In other, cases, political violence has been short-lived and managed or at least contributed to the emergence of wide social movements keen to achieve their objectives by participation in the democratic system. The Front de Libération du Québec (FLQ) is the only political movement which has used violence for political purposes in Quebec's recent history. Like ETA and the IRA, it started its activities in the early 1960s, its ideology was a mixture of leftist nationalism and the decolonization theories of Fanon and Memmi, from whom they borrowed the idea of violence as a legitimate tool in the struggle for self-determination. The 1970 October Crisis proved crucial in the development of Quebec nationalism. The FLQ kidnapped the British diplomat James Richard Cross and Quebec Labour Minister Pierre Laporte. The federal government declared the 16 October War Measures Act (WMA) and suspended civil liberties. Under the Act, over 450 people were arrested, of whom 403 people were freed without charge and only 18 were convicted of minor offences.[45] The democratic path towards further autonomy chosen by the Quebec people in voting for René Lévesque as leader of the Party Québécois, was crucial in the FLQ's disappearance from the political arena.[46]

Northern Ireland   The Third World theory was fashionable at a time when many colonial countries were struggling for independence and slowly being accepted into the international system of nation-states. The rise of ETA can also be related to the emergence of similar paramilitary groups elsewhere in Europe, and in particular, to the emergence of the IRA who employed a similar terminology to that of ETA in describing the situation of Northern Ireland as one of illegitimate occupation by a foreign power. Northern Ireland was presented, and still is in contemporary nationalist circles, as the last remnant of the British empire.

Northern Ireland: historical background   In the early Christian times what today is known as Northern Ireland was an area with its own distinctive Celtic culture known as *Ulaid* (in English: Ulster).[47] The region was converted to Christianity by Saint Patrick (fifth century), a missionary based in the north. By the second half of the sixth century, monastic foundations were evident in all regions of Ireland.[48] St Columba's foundation of the monastery of Iona (563) provided the best known base for the Celtic Christianization of Scotland. The Irish monasteries became notable centres of learning and remained influential until the late eleventh century. The *Book of Kells*, a copy of the Four Gospels, dating from about the eighth or ninth century is one of the most outstanding examples of Irish manuscripts produced by the monks.

The most famous composition of early Irish literature, the epic saga *Táin Bó Cuailnge* contains the best known account of Ulster's mythic history. The oldest manuscript of the *Táin* was compiled in the twelfth century and contains language dated to the eighth century. The *Táin* is mythic regarding events and its protagonists but has a great value as a source for the Celtic history of Ireland.[49]

The Norsemen first arrived in Ireland in 795. They made frequent raids and seized two ports Annagassan and Dublin (838). A large scale invasion in the North of Ireland took place from 862 to 879 when the Norse ruler of Dublin reached maximum power. By the end of the tenth century, Norse power was declining. The Cenél nEogain of the Northern Uí Néill and the Clan Cholmáin of the Southern Uí Néill, both descendants of Niall of the Nine Hostages (fifth century) alternated as kings of Ireland between 734 and 1002. Then the king of Munster, Brian Boru challenged them and defeated their Scandinavian allies at the Battle of Clontarf (1014) and ruled for a short period.

In the eleventh and twelfth centuries the ecclesiastical reform movement which had originated in Western Europe was extended to

Ireland. By the mid-twelfth century, the Irish Church had been reformed and modernized considerably without English influence. 'In the light of this', Richter argues, 'Pope Adrian IV was not justified in 1155 in granting the English king Henry II permission to go to Ireland in order to reform the church, which he did in the Bull *Laudabiliter'*.[50] In Ireland this has often been interpreted as an 'English plot' against the Irish. The Normans first came into Ulster in the mid-twelfth century and conquered the northeast coast while the hinterland remained Gaelic. The English divided Ireland into counties for administrative purposes, English law was introduced and Parliament started in England and Ireland in 1297. Only Anglo-Irish were represented in the Parliament.

In the fourteenth century, Irish discrimination brought about protest and Gaels recovered large parts of Ulster. Irish language, law and civilization experienced a revival. English power diminished. The recognition of Henry VIII as king of Ireland (1541) involved the confiscation of monastic property, as well as the lands of the rebels. At that time a pronounced migration of Scots to Ulster took place.

The English defeated Hugh O'Neill (1603) and the lords of the north in the early seventeenth century. It was then that James I decided to 'plant' six of Ulster's nine counties with immigrant English and Scottish colonists. Ulster became a province dominated by Protestant and Scottish planters. The native Irish claimed allegiance to the proscribed Catholic Church. They became landless and displaced by the colonizers. The Ulster Plantation can be considered as the starting point of an historical process which has resulted in the present 'troubles'. The strength of Irish culture in the Northern part of the island was to be challenged by the physical removal of most of the native Irish population from the most fertile areas and their replacement with immigrant Protestant Scots and English settlers. The plantation temporarily collapsed, but only to be reinforced in the 1650s when Oliver Cromwell led the reconquest of Ireland. A union of the three kingdoms of England, Scotland, and Ireland was effected in 1653. By an Act of Settlement, Ireland was regarded as a conquered territory. By this time Ulster had become the most British and most Protestant part of Ireland, although a large Irish Catholic population was also living in Ulster. The rest of Ireland remained Catholic. James II, a Catholic king of England, sought to reverse discrimination against Roman Catholics, but he was challenged by William III, a Protestant, who defeated him and his Catholic supporters at the Battle of the Boyne (1690) – an event still commemorated by Unionists in contemporary Ulster.

At the beginning of the eighteenth century, the Williamite wars reinforced Catholic discrimination by imposing the Penal Laws which excluded Catholics from the army, banned them from politics at both local and national levels, and deprived them of access to education.[51] At that time a deep cleavage existed between the Protestant English and Scottish elites – landowners and commercial elites – and the lower classes divided by religion – Catholic and Protestant – who were competing for jobs. Protestant elites favoured lower-class Protestants.

Exacerbated conditions in County Armagh gave rise to bitter sectarian strife. The 1795 battle between Catholics and Protestants at the Diamond favoured the creation of the Orange Society (later known as Orange Order) to protect Protestant interests and perpetuate dominance over Catholics. The Act of Union of 1800 put Protestants under the formal protection of the British (now Union) Parliament. In the 1830s attempts at dissolving the Orange Order, which had spread to Scotland, England and the Irish diasporas, did not succeed.

In 1828–9 the British Test Act was repealed and Roman Catholics were emancipated, this provided political equality for most purposes. The dramatic success of Roman Catholic Daniel O'Connell's emancipation movement aroused Protestant hostility and it was violently suppressed in 1843. The nineteenth century brought a succession of Irish crises among them the Great Famine of the 1840s[52] which brought desolation to the countryside and favoured a population transfer to the recently industrialized Belfast area. A large number of Irish people migrated to the British mainland, North America, Australia and New Zealand, among other destinations.[53] In the Belfast area, Protestants held the monopoly of skilled jobs, particularly in engineering, and they also controlled trade and industry. Catholics were to be mostly found in non-skilled jobs, a divide which still holds in contemporary Northern Ireland which currently has one of the highest regional percentages of unemployment in the European Union.

Discussion about Irish self-government led to the Liberals' attempt to introduce a Home Rule bill for Ireland in 1886, 1893 and 1912. The first two were defeated in the House of Commons and when the third managed to get through the government postponed its implementation because war broke out in Europe. During this period, the Orange Order re-emerged, associated itself with the Conservative party and placed the defence of the Union of Ireland with England as its main objective. Violent confrontations took place between Catholics and Protestants. An Irish cultural nationalist movement led by Douglas Hyde and Eoin MacNeill developed in the late nineteenth century.

The harsh repression of the 1916 Easter Rising had explosive consequences in Ireland. The escalation of violence led to an unsustainable situation. The 1920 Government of Ireland Act divided Ireland into two self-governing parts: Northern Ireland formed by six of the nine counties of Ulster which remained as part of the British state primarily due to the opposition of Protestants in this area who feared the possibility of becoming a minority within a largely Catholic Irish state; and the three remaining counties of Ulster together with the 23 counties of the rest of Ireland considered as a dominion of the British Empire and known as the Irish Free State. Éamon de Valera became its first president.

In 1937 De Valera introduced proposals for a new constitution ending the power of the crown, the new constitution did not proclaim an independent republic, but it replaced the title of the Irish Free State with the word Éire (Ireland). The new constitution was ratified by a plebiscite in 1937. Britain recognized the status of Ireland as an independent republic in 1949 and consolidated the position of Northern Ireland as united with England.

Irish nationalism and violence Sectarianism against Catholic Irish people has pervaded the history of Northern Ireland since the partition of Ireland (1921). Protestants controlled the economy and politics, skilled jobs were systematically reserved for them. Conflict intensified in the mid 1960s when Catholic civil rights protests set the scene for violent confrontations. The Irish Republican Army (IRA) was reactivated (Provisional IRA) and took as its mission to protect Catholics from 'official and unofficial' assault, and fight for the liberation of Northern Ireland from Protestant domination and the creation of a united Ireland. Paramilitary organizations were also created among Protestants.

British forces came to Northern Ireland in the early 1970s to keep the peace. However, they were soon perceived by Catholics as an oppressive foreign force defending Protestant interests. Bloody Sunday in 1972 stands as a landmark in a history of violence, discrimination and poverty.[54]

Northern Ireland stands as another example of a society in which political violence is often linked to a long story of deprivation and discrimination. Northern Ireland is a highly heterogeneous society divided along sharp ethnic boundaries which translate into a deep economic cleavage.

The history of the native Catholic Irish is one of discrimination initiated by the abolition of their customary rights to land and property. In the mid seventeenth century they witness the confiscation of most of their remaining land in response to the 1641 revolt.

British government support for the Province's place within the UK was made conditional upon a majority of the Northern Ireland population wishing to maintain this *status quo*. The Anglo-Irish Agreement (1985) conferred upon the government of the Republic of Ireland a formal consultative role in the internal affairs and administration of Northern Ireland. Protestants strongly opposed the Agreement. Catholics adopted a more cautious attitude since they were obviously pleased about the introduction of the Republic's Government into the governing process of Northern Ireland, but wanted to wait and see in order to assess the impact of such a measure.

The Social Democratic and Labour Party (SDLP), which represents constitutional nationalism and rejects the use of violence as a means to achieve Irish independence, and the republican Sinn Fein mainly represent Catholics in Northern Ireland. The Provisional IRA (Irish Republican Army) is a paramilitary organization which advocates the use of violence 'as a legitimate means of forcing British withdrawal from the Province and as a defensive strategy for protecting the Catholic population from the security forces and from the attacks of Protestant paramilitary organizations'.[55] Bowyer Bell defines the IRA ideology as driven by the dream of a united Ireland, free and Gaelic.[56] The IRA's use of violence does not imply the existence of a wide consensus upon its practice. Jenkins' explanation of political violence in Northern Ireland relates it to a long story of grievances suffered by the Catholic population. He writes:

> Nationalism does *not* necessarily translate into either acceptance of, or support for, violence (in much the same way that support for the union with Britain does not necessarily translate into sectarianism). Nor should it be forgotten that the context within which Catholic support for violence must be understood is the violence of the state security forces and Protestant paramilitary organizations. With the benefit of hindsight, the present conflict in Northern Ireland has its immediate historical roots in the violent and inept repression of the (largely Catholic) Civil Rights Movement by the (Protestant) Stormont regime in the late 1960s.[57]

Conflict resolution: the 1998 Belfast Agreement

The emergence of a large social movement advancing the goals of the national minority, the systematic destruction of the paramilitary organization and the opening of negotiations with the state are crucial and radically different factors which can determine the end of terrorism within a particular society. The emergence of a large social movement willing to engage in a dialogue with the state in order to achieve radical changes may act as a deterrent force for terrorism. A mass following is generally more powerful and effective than a minority movement engaged in political violence. It is also easier for the state to dismiss political opponents who rely on the use of violence by referring to them as criminals and violent people thus stripping their actions of any political content, than to dismiss massive state opposition.

The rise of a large movement against a particular state has the capacity to question its legitimacy and might prompt foreign governments and other organizations to challenge its legitimacy. Horowitz stresses the relevance of international support for the minorities' claims as a key feature in deciding the outcome of a secessionist movement. He writes, 'whether and when a secessionist movement will emerge is determined mainly by domestic politics, by the relations of groups and regions within the state. Whether a secessionist movement will achieve its aims, however, is determined largely by international politics, by the balance of interests and forces that extend beyond the state.'[58]

The elimination of state dissidents by force is another of the possible reasons for the end of terrorism in a particular country. I shall elaborate on this point later on when considering state terrorism. The opening of negotiations with the state stands as a further alternative when considering methods to halt political violence. States are usually disinclined to 'give up' and negotiate with terrorists, since negotiations, whether conditional on the abandonment of violence or not, presuppose the existence of a political conflict as the root of terrorist activities.

The Labour government from its appointment on 1 May 1997 has given priority to the initiation of all-party talks in Northern Ireland which include Sinn Fein. The government managed to obtain a renewed ceasefire from the IRA and invited Senator Robert Mitchell from the United States to act as a chairman in the peace process talks. The decommissioning of arms by the IRA was made into a condition to be met during the talks, but no specific date for its accomplishment was ever given. This position underlines the government's stance on the illegitimacy of the use of violence for political ends but it also stresses the role of negotiations as a means to attain political aims which, for a long time, had been pursued through the use of violence.

As Guelke argues, 'seeking the inclusion of the political representatives of the paramilitaries was an acknowledgement of the link between their violence and the long-standing conflict between the Protestant and the Catholic communities in Northern Ireland'.[59]

An extremely tense negotiating process was initiated. The British Prime Minister Tony Blair, the Irish Prime Minister Bertie Ahern, the Secretary of State for Northern Ireland Mo Mowlam, and the President of the US Bill Clinton intervened in the process and put pressure on all sides to continue the talks. The *Belfast Agreement* (also known as the *Good Friday Agreement*) was finally signed on 10 April 1998. The Agreement represents a major breakthrough in conflict resolution strategies. It seeks to reconcile the unionist desire that Ulster remain as a province of Britain, and the republican claim for an independent united Ireland free from English domination. The two objectives are opposed, and have provoked years of intense violence and suffering for the people of Northern Ireland. The *Belfast Agreement* acknowledges this, and states that, 'we must never forget those who have died or been injured, and their families'. It adds, 'But we can best honour them through a fresh start, in which we firmly dedicate ourselves to the achievement of reconciliation, tolerance, and mutual trust, and to the protection and vindication of the human rights of all'.[60]

The major conditions for peace set up in the Agreement are 'the total and absolute commitment to exclusively democratic and peaceful means of resolving differences on political issues' and the endorsement of *consent* as a principle on the basis of which the people of Northern Ireland should decide upon their future. The participants in the drafting of the *Belfast Agreement* endorse the commitment made by the British and Irish Governments that, in a new British-Irish Agreement replacing the Anglo-Irish Agreement, they will, 'recognize the legitimacy of whatever choice is freely exercised by a majority of the people of Northern Ireland with regard to its status, whether they prefer to continue to support the Union with Great Britain or a sovereign united Ireland'.[61]

The Agreement provides for a democratically elected *Assembly* in Northern Ireland which is inclusive in its membership, capable of exercising executive and legislative authority, and subject to safeguards to protect the rights and interests of all sides of the community. It also envisages the creation of a *North/South Ministerial Council* to develop consultation, cooperation and action between Northern Ireland and the Irish Government on matters of mutual interest within the competence of the Administrations, North and South. A further new institution to be created is the *British-Irish Council* (BIC) whose aim would be to promote the harmonious and mutually beneficial development of the totality of relationships among the peoples of these islands. It will comprise representatives of the British and Irish Governments, devolved institutions in Northern Ireland, Scotland and Wales and, if appropriate, elsewhere in the UK, together with the representatives of the Isle of Man and the Channel Islands.

The Agreement should be placed within the context of a wider constitutional reform initiated by the Labour Government, one that involves the decentralization of the UK and the setting up of devolved institutions in Scotland, Wales and Northern Ireland.

The most controversial and delicate matters covered by the Agreement have to do with the provisions for an accelerated programme for the release of prisoners whose organizations maintain a 'complete and unequivocal ceasefire', and 'the decommissioning of all paramilitary arms within two years following the endorsement in referendums North and South of the agreement and in the context of the implementation of the overall settlement'.[62] These two points recognize the political character of terrorist activities carried out by Northern Ireland paramilitary forces, and it emphasizes the great determination of the British and the Irish Governments to achieve a peaceful solution. The quasi-war Ulster political scenario is revealed in the content of the Agreement where provisions for the release of prisoners, decommissioning and changes in security arrangements on the part of the British state stand as major items in the agenda for peace. The British state accepts the compromise to 'make progress towards the objective of as early a return as possible to normal security arrangements in Northern Ireland consistent with the level of threat and with a published overall strategy'.[63] Aspects of this strategy are to involve: the reduction of the numbers and role of the Armed Forces deployed in Northern Ireland to levels compatible with a normal peaceful society, the removal of security installations, the removal of emergency powers in Northern Ireland, and other measures appropriate to and compatible with a normal peaceful society.

During the Agreement Referendum campaign (22 May 1998) and the first election to the Northern Ireland Assembly (25 June 1998) most Unionist as well as Republican political leaders insisted on the need to make the Agreement work. The Referendum endorsed by 71 per cent of the population of Ulster (turn-out 80.98 per cent) and 94 per cent of the population of the Irish Republic (turn-out 55.59 per cent) provided strong support for the peace process. In Ulster, however, these results revealed a profound split within the ranks of Unionism. Catholic voters supported the deal almost unanimously, while Protestant voters were divided. For those who voted 'no' in the Referendum, the *Belfast Agreement* signified a sell-out, a clear first step towards what they hate most, the prospect of a united Ireland in which Protestants would lose their privileged status and become a minority. As Senator Tom Hayden writes, 'Unionism continues as the political identity of the threatened majority which fears change. Their choice of British identity must be honoured even while its scaffolds of privilege are taken down'. In his view, 'loss of power to a green Catholic tide is the terror plaguing Unionism which must be addressed'.[64]

The Agreement contains specific provisions for a new economic development for Northern Ireland, something which is badly needed. Peace will undoubtedly bring investments to Ulster which has one of the lowest standards of living within the EU. Further to this, the British Government will pursue policies to promote the Irish language. It will 'facilitate and encourage the use of the language in speech and writing in public and private life where there is appropriate demand'.[65] It will also facilitate Irish-medium education, and encourage and provide financial support for Irish language film and television production in Northern Ireland.

At the time of writing, the peace process has just received two big blows. First, an arson attack on a Catholic woman's house in a Protestant area in Ballymoney which resulted in her three young children being burned alive (11 July 1998), an action which took place amid rising tension at Drumcree where members of the Orange Order wishing to march over the Catholic Garvaghy Road (Portadown) had been confronting the RUC for over a week. A second, and equally appalling action was the Omagh bombing (15 August 1998) which killed twenty-eight people and left 220 injured. It is still uncertain how these two events will influence the peace process; what is becoming clear is that the road towards peace is an extremely difficult one.

State terrorism

The use of violence to achieve a certain response from a target population through the creation of extreme fear is not an exclusive activity of groups fighting against the state such as national minorities resisting oppressive regimes, struggling for cultural recognition, demanding further autonomy or wishing to secede. There are occasions on which the state itself engages in terrorist practices against some groups living within its territory. State terrorism is a strategy commonly used by weak states which attempt to retain power and control their population by creating an environment in which some individuals are victimized through membership of a particular group, primarily defined in terms of ethnicity and class. Violence is often employed by elites who have secured and maintained power by the use of force, as is usually the case with authoritarian regimes which have risen to power after a military uprising, a *coup d'état* or a civil war. Francoist Spain and Stalin's Soviet Union are cases in point. Wherever violence is perceived as a useful resource in suppressing challenges to the state and maintaining the *status quo* there is a high probability that its use will be regarded as an acceptable tactic in future conflicts.

By contrast, as Gurr argues, 'democratic principles and institutions inhibit political elites from using state violence in general and terror specifically'.[66] The acceptance of democracy by the state elites and the creation of institutions based upon the implementation of democratic rule acts as a deterrent to the state's use of terrorism. However, the state whose own nature involves the monopoly of violence has all the available means to establish a surveillance regime involving the use of intensified policing which might rapidly descend into terror unless it is efficiently monitored and organized according to democratic principles. Giddens claims that totalitarianism is a tendencial property of the modern state.[67] This statement requires careful consideration against the backcloth of state practices to defend and protect democracy, since there are occasions when, in the name of democracy, nation-states have effectively demolished opposition minority groups living within their territory. Democratic political norms emphasize compromise in conflict and appeal to dialogue as a means of communication between the state and its citizens. In many instances of state terrorism, state representatives break or ignore their own laws, this is why an independent and democratic judicial system remains a key feature of democratic polities. The use of violence by a democratic state, if made public, may automatically condemn the politicians and officials responsible for it. Their actions are to be considered illegitimate and if credibility for the democratic character of the state's institutions is to be preserved, they have to be excluded from office and severely punished. But there are also moments in which the state invokes 'temporary' or 'emergency' legislation to provide legal support for 'security actions'.[68]

A fundamental obstacle to studying state terrorism as opposed to terrorism against the state lies in the scarcity of available information about state-organized terror. While the media tend to concentrate on terrorism against the state and the defence of the *status quo*, the disclosure of state terrorism is often portrayed as subversive unless extremely powerful arguments can be employed to prove the existence of this type of terrorism.

Information on internal repression is completely banned in undemocratic regimes, although it is sometimes made partially available through clandestine channels of communication, foreign media, which may have access to opposition groups in exile reporting on their country's situation, or through the work of organizations such as Amnesty International.

State authorities can hardly be expected to admit the use of repressive measures against its minorities. The documents proving state terrorist practices are systematically destroyed or kept secret and journalistic investigation restricted. Inquiries into state terrorism by foreign agencies are often rejected on the grounds that they represent an interference with state sovereignty. In spite of that, monitoring the incidence of state terrorism is not impossible. The accuracy of the information may vary but it is still feasible to obtain a fair amount of data illustrating state terrorist actions.

'In contemporary states', Gurr writes, 'the necessary condition for state terrorism is the existence of a group, class or party that is regarded by ruling elites as an active threat to their continued rule'.[69] In his view, if the group in question launches a campaign of revolutionary violence against the state, then by the proportionality principle, regimes are justified if they respond with whatever coercive measures they regard as appropriate to halt it. But this principle requires the regime to carefully consider internal standards of political morality as an element which may constrain the state's action. Questions about other possible alternatives to violence need to be examined, since the use of excessive violence may risk a loss of the state's legitimacy in the eyes of its own supporters.

Repressive measures against national and ethnic minorities within some nation-states have been and still are a common practice. Three major strategies have been implemented by the state in accomplishing its ideal objective of creating a single unified nation coextensive with the state. National minorities have been either eliminated, assimilated or repressed. (1) Genocide is the annihilation of a national minority or any target group within the state by means of premeditated large-scale murder. (2) Assimilation is the outcome of voluntary or involuntary renunciation of one's culture and language to adopt the state's national identity. This process is involuntary when individuals are forced into the mainstream language and culture because the state actively discourages, forbids or punishes the use and development of a set of cultural values, habits and language other than those promoted by itself as the only and compulsory option. As a result, individuals are socialized within the state's culture which is portrayed as the only legitimate culture, while all the others are pictured as a challenge and a threat. (3) McCamant defines repression as a technique of domination, he points out that 'most attempts to dominate involve non-coercive means, and only by seeing repression in this larger context can we begin to analyse how and why rulers attack domestic enemies'.[70] Schmid offers a more subtle distinction between 'oppression', referring to a continuing situation of involuntary subordination characterized by acts of omission against a particular group of citizens, and 'repression', understood as a more active process of social control aiming at the elimination of actual and potential opponents by a variety of coercive sanctions.[71]

In this chapter I have explored the different strategies which are often employed by nationalist movements seeking to oppose the state and defend their right to self-determination. Cultural resistance involves the defence of the nation's culture and language by peaceful means and has proved instrumental in numerous cases. In the case of Catalonia, peaceful resistance during Francoism and dialogue with the new democratic Spanish state have delivered the longest period of political autonomy for Catalonia and contributed to its cultural and economic success.

In other instances, nationalist groups turn to violence ranging from civil war to political terrorism and challenge the state's monopoly of violence over the territory of the nation they claim to represent. Violence has pervaded Northern Ireland's politics during most of the twentieth century and brought suffering to both the Republican and the Unionist communities. The Belfast Agreement (1998) has opened up a new future for Northern Ireland in which differences will hopefully be dealt with through dialogue. In the Basque Country, ETA's ceasefire of 1998 may contribute to an eventual opening of negotiations between the Basque nationalist left (*izquierda abertzale*), other Basque nationalist parties and the Spanish state. ETA's renunciation of violence, if it holds, also signals a fundamental twist in favour of dialogue.

In my view, the future of nations without states as political actors depends on their nationalist movements openly endorsing democratic principles. Only by defending democracy and applying democratic means to defend their right to exist and develop within larger political institutions in which they feel represented, can nations without states legitimize their right to self-determination.

6

Nations without States as New Global Political Actors

Whilst much has been written about the profound transformations which the nation-state is currently undergoing, few writers have sought to address how such transformations impinge upon the renewed strength of regional forms of economic and political organization. It therefore seems timely and instructive to examine how the elements which are now forcing radical changes affecting the nation-state system contribute to the generation of a new economic and socio-political environment which favours the emergence of new political actors. It is within this political climate and context that the present chapter is located. In particular, I wish to argue that if nations without states are able to instil a strong sense of identity among their members and prove economically viable, then they are likely to come onto the scene as political actors in the twenty-first century. Their relevance is directly tied up with the functionality of smaller units which: (1) are economically efficient; (2) enjoy a substantial degree of civic coherence derived from the idea of sharing a national identity based upon democratic principles and practices and; (3) are able to function within larger political and economic institutions of an international or supranational character. Throughout this chapter I focus upon the European Union (EU) as a living laboratory in which experiments about new ways to understand sovereignty, territoriality and identity are currently being tested.

In the first section of this chapter, I examine how some of the main features of the traditional nation-state are being altered under the influence of globalization processes. Here I introduce the concept of the post-traditional nation-state to refer to a nation-state which has been forced to make substantial modifications to its traditional concepts of sovereignty, territoriality, control of the means of violence and the administration. In this section, the tensions and demands faced by some EU members when responding to pressure for further European integration are employed to illustrate some of the major challenges which are currently bringing about the end of the traditional nation-state. Questions about national identity and geopolitics, as well as economic issues are discussed here.

The second section focuses upon the study of national identity in post-traditional nation-states. It considers the links between national identity and citizenship and studies current changes affecting the construction of British identity in the light of devolution being applied to Scotland, Wales and Northern Ireland. In the third section, I consider the reasons which permit us to envisage a medium term future in which nations without states could gain political relevance as novel political actors at a global level.

The post-traditional nation-state

Held and McGrew refer to the growing disjunctures between formal and conventional authority claimed by the nation-state.[1] Ohmae speaks of the nation-state as an institution which in terms of real flows of activity has already lost its role as a meaningful unit of participation in the global economy of today's borderless world.[2] He refers to it as a 'nostalgic fiction'. On the other hand, scholars such as Ruggie and Krasner are reluctant to dismiss the importance of the nation-state and emphasize its continuing power.[3] Whatever the positions defended, what all approaches acknowledge is the need to rethink the nation-state in the light of current changes affecting its nature.

The traditional nation-state as a locus of political decision-making, as an economic unit, and as a self-contained cultural recipient has, to a considerable extent, been superseded by regional and supranational institutions. In late eighteenth-century France, a long and contested process shifting loyalty away from kings and lords, and placing it upon the nation was initiated. Then, the nation, personified through symbols and rituals which symbolically recreated a sense of 'people', became the focus of a new kind of attachment. Throughout this process, nationalism proved to be exceedingly useful for refocusing a people's loyalty away from the monarch. The replacement of kingdoms, fiefs and counties by a nation-state system covering the entire globe was not fully accomplished until the twentieth century, when the autonomy and the territorial borders of the nation-state were formally recognized in the treaties following the First World War. Then, the nation-state's authenticity as arbiter of its own 'internal affairs' was recognized, however, it was not until after the Second World War that a nation-state system covering the world was consolidated. Soon after this moment, and as a result of the technological revolution and the emergence of a global economy, the traditional nature of the nation-state was to be questioned. This inaugurated a path fraught with novel challenges and profound transformations destined not only to bring about the post-traditional nation-state, but also to infuse the nation-state system with new institutional patterns and structures.

Nationalism has remained as the major legitimating doctrine employed by the nation-state since its foundational moment. It basically argues that peoples should be ruled by members of their own communities who manage to attain their consent. From the late eighteenth century onwards, the nation was identified with the people living within the state's territory. A common culture destined to encourage the emergence of sentiments of solidarity among them was to be instilled through more or less pervasive national education programmes. Minority cultures and regional ways of life faded away within states which had the skills and resources to be efficient in their homogenizing policies. France is a case in point. Weaker and ill-organized states such as Spain were less successful in their attempts.

In the eighteenth century, when the revolutionaries stated that the principle of sovereignty resides essentially in the nation, they may be taken to have asserted that the nation was more than the king and the aristocracy. To distinguish between those who belonged to the nation and foreigners, strangers and enemies, citizenship was created. Citizenship was the badge identifying those who could enjoy rights conferred upon them by the state, and who also had duties towards the state and their fellow countrymen and women. Citizenship acted at the same time as an inclusion and exclusion mechanism. It had to be struggled for, and it stood as the main feature defining membership of a state.

At present, we are witnessing a process of profound transformation which has a proven capacity to alter the nature of the traditional nation-state in a fundamental and unprecedented way. 'The nation-state which exists in a complex of other nation-states', Giddens argues, 'is a set of institutional forms of governance maintaining an administrative monopoly over a territory with demarcated boundaries (Borders), its rule being sanctioned by law and direct control of the means of internal and external violence'.[4] This definition encompasses four dimensions of the nation-state which are currently being modified: its existence within a nation-state system, its capacity to exert administrative control, its power to claim the legitimate monopoly of the means of violence, and its territoriality. The EU decision to further the political integration of its members provides an invaluable example of how nation-states are reacting to globalizing forces. In what follows I shall draw on EU legislation and practices to illustrate how European states are rapidly adjusting to the new political scenario in which they now have to live.

The nation-state system

The nation-state is defined as existing within a system of nation-states which has traditionally been based upon the mutual recognition of sovereignty which simultaneously provides an ordering principle for what is 'internal' to states and what is 'external' to them.[5] In this context, the relation between sovereignty and the principle of equality of states becomes very close, since 'a state cannot become sovereign except within a system of other sovereign states, its sovereignty being acknowledged by them; in this there is a strong pressure towards mutual recognition as equals, whatever the factual situation in respect of differential power'.[6]

The nation-state system is now confronted with an unprecedented rise in the number of international and supranational organizations ranging from the United Nations (UN), to the European Union (EU), including also non-governmental organizations such as Greenpeace or Amnesty International. Some of these organizations are emerging as a result of an increasing sense of weakness experienced by nation-states and the desire to avoid war. As Giner argues when referring to the creation of the European Community (EC), it was state weakness, not strength, which forced many politicians, economic interest groups and social movements to move in the direction of unity.[7] The longing for peace after the massive destruction brought about by the Second World War was also crucial in the creation of the EC. Yet the nation-state system is still a highly operative body owing to the fact that nation-states are the only officially visible entities within institutions such as the UN, NATO, ASEAN and other international organizations. An exception to this is the recent creation of the Committee of the Regions which the Maastricht Treaty (1991) introduced to the EU structure. Its establishment has opened up a space, although an extremely limited one, for the presence of sub-state entities within an institution initially created by some European nation-states concerned to protect and enhance their own economies and prevent war.

Ohmae argues that, increasingly, the questions requiring international attention do not fall within the borders of established nation-states. Rather, in his view:

> they are for the most part, problems having to do not with *realpolitik* or the balance of power, but with the daily lives – and the daily quality of life – of ordinary people in ordinary settings. The lens associated with nation-states tends to filter such problems out. As a practical matter, people do not live and work in countries. Day to day, their relevant sphere of life is local or regional.[8]

Nation-states are the subjects and creators of a global network which for the most part disregards regions and national or ethnic minorities as political actors. The nation-state system often ignores the emotional bonds which unite citizens of particular nation-states to some of the sub-state national communities to which they belong.

The political integration of independent nation-states forming supranational institutions such as the EU, if successful, holds the potential to alter the nation-state system itself. If nation-states freely surrender aspects of their sovereignty and approve of the creation of supranational bodies having legislative as well as executive and judicial powers, which the EU seems to be day by day acquiring, then a point could be reached when the representatives of the nation-states could be replaced by those of larger political institutions, such as the EU, in international forums, such as the UN, to discuss global issues affecting their policies. At the moment the EU is a pioneering political institution based on multi-nation-state collaboration, but it represents more than this, since its objective of becoming a political union could, in time, provoke the break-up of the nation-states forming it.

Only some of the numerous territorial political units into which medieval Europe was divided turned into nation-states; most of them disappeared, others were absorbed into larger political units.[9] In a similar manner, only some nation-states are to be expected to survive in their present territorial form. The creation of supranational institutions such as the EU will lessen the relevance of preserving the territorial integrity of current nation-states, since control over key areas such as the economy, social policy, the environment or immigration will be centrally monitored by EU institutions. In this context it will be easier for smaller cultural communities which prove economically viable to claim a space to make their representatives heard within EU institutions.

The nation-state's relevance and continuity depends upon its ability to adapt to a changing economic and political environment in which nations without states such as Catalonia, Scotland or the Basque Country seem to be achieving greater significance than ever before. They flourish with a thriving cultural and economic dynamism. The issue is not one of turning into independent states – not at a time when the traditional nation-state model is becoming outdated and proves unable to fulfil the needs of its citizens who often find themselves turning either to supranational bodies or sub-state institutions. Rather, it consists of thinking and creating new efficient bodies functional in the new circumstances in which we are expected to live at the start of a new millennium.

Ohmae's vision of the nation-state's future is far more radical than the one I espouse. For him, the nation-state corresponds to 'a much earlier stage of industrial history, it has neither the will nor the incentive nor the credibility nor the tools nor the political base to play an effective role in a genuinely borderless economy'.[10] As I have already argued, I hold a much more cautious approach towards the nation-state's resilience. In spite of that, I agree with Ohmae that nation-states, to restore sustainable and self-reinforcing vitality, ought to 'cede operational autonomy to the wealth-generating region states that lie within or across their borders, to catalyse the efforts of those region states to seek out global solutions, and to harness their distinctive ability to put global logic first and to function as posts of entry to the global economy'.[11] The granting of further political autonomy to sub-state units and the setting-up of federalist structures to deal with the nationalist claims of nations without states shows a way forward in the state's recognition of internal national diversity and provides new mechanisms to increase the cultural, political and economic dynamism of nations without states. Furthermore, decentralization is based on sound democratic arguments.

Administrative control

A second feature which characterizes the traditional nation-state is its capacity to exert administrative control within a limited territory. This involves the power to legislate and to penalize those who break the law. Nation-states are faced by an ongoing process involving the increasing intrusion of external bodies in their legislative as well as their judicial functions. The Maastricht Treaty (1991), for instance, comprising the Economic and Monetary Union as well as the Political Union Treaties presents a fresh example of nation-states, freely agreeing to surrender some aspects of their sovereignty. It also illustrates the resistance offered by some nation-states, such as Britain when it decided to opt out of implementing common social policies – though this position was partially reversed after the Labour government decided to sign the European Social Charter (1997).

The main feature of Maastricht was its determination to turn the European Community into a politically united Europe. Maastricht utilized the existing offices of the EC and added new intergovernmental offices on home affairs, justice, and foreign and security policy. A common European citizenship was also established allowing citizens of one EU country who live and work in another EU country to vote in the local and European Parliament elections of their country of residence. Only recently the European Court of Justice has, for the first time, overruled a decision taken by the British courts (1998).

Probably the most ambitious step towards further European integration is the introduction of the Euro as a stable currency in the EU. Not all EU members have agreed to the Monetary Union, for instance Britain remains outside the group of nation-states which have opted to joint the EMU (European Monetary Union). The first step of EMU is to irrevocably fix the exchange rates for the currencies of the countries participating, so that each national currency is simply an expression of the common currency. Monetary policy will be determined by the European Central Bank (ECB) modelled on the *Deutsche Bundesbank* as regards its structure and orientation. The ECB will be politically independent and will have the prime objective of maintaining currency stability. The loss of direct control over the national economy is one of the main factors invoked by those opposing Monetary Union. Arguments about the loss of national identity are often connected to financial arguments against EMU. It is expected that on 1 January 2002 European notes and coins will be issued, then, after six months, national currencies will disappear and the Euro will be the only tender in the countries participating in EMU. And through participating these nation-states will have surrendered one of the major symbolic features of their identity.

But this is by no means the hardest dilemma faced by EU members seeking further economic and political integration. The attempt to coordinate the social policies of all member states means that EU institutions will intervene in the member countries' internal policies and overcome the strong resistance of some countries such as Britain. Monetary Union and the coordination of social policies stand as two examples which reveal the unprecedented degree of intrusion into what for a long time were regarded as inalienable powers of traditional nation-states. It is worth bearing in mind that the governments of these nation-states have freely decided to follow the path towards further European integration as a strategy to guarantee their own survival and strengthen their position within the world economy.

The post-traditional nation-state is aware of its own limitations and attempts to supersede them by adopting a set of policies which radically distance it from the classical nation-state. What some European nation-states find unpalatable is the realization that the changes prompted by further political integration have led to a completely different political scenario in which their traditional power and status are being challenged in a radical way. There is no route back to the old days when some nation-states could dream of closing their borders and living in isolation. Political, economic and social interdependence are becoming more acute than ever before. The post-traditional nation-state is a political institution able to work in partnership with other states within the framework of larger institutions of which it is so far the main player and engineer, but progressively these institutions are opening up some space for new political actors to emerge and be represented within them.

Territoriality

Max Weber's definition of the state includes territoriality as one of its main defining features. He refers to it as the space within which the state's regularized administrative staff is able to sustain the claim to the legitimate monopoly of control of the means of violence.[12]

From the late eighteenth century onwards, a process was initiated by means of which the chronically disputed and loosely managed frontiers characteristic of feudalism turned into clearly delimited borders demarcating the territory within which the nation-state could claim its sovereignty. Borders became carefully monitored, and they had to be agreed between different nation-states. In some cases, borders became contested, this happened when more than one state put forward separate claims upon a single territory. War and diplomacy have been consistently employed to solve this type of dispute. State borders have traditionally been regarded as an expression of state power, and strong states have sought to expand their territory by conquest, annexation, or other diplomatic means. We need to bear in mind that the map of Europe has been redrawn numerous times after intra-state conflicts and external confrontation with other states. The two World Wars, the independence achieved by some former Soviet Republics after 1989, and the recent break-up of Yugoslavia and the separation of Czechoslovakia stand as examples of an almost constant redrawing of borders among states.

But it should be stressed that the validity of such territorial alterations has to be sanctioned by the international community. This is a feature which highlights a key issue in international politics; the constitution of a new sovereign state is not a purely internal affair, rather it requires the approval of the reflexively monitored state system. The decision to acknowledge, for example, the independence of the Baltic Republics, or the new states emerging from the break-up of the former Yugoslavia, or the peaceful separation of Czechoslovakia required the sanction of the international community, which responded with different speed in each particular case. Concepts of sovereignty and popular representation were at the heart of the arguments invoked by those who sought to create independent states when applying for international recognition.

The increasing porousness of the nation-state's borders signals the end of its monopoly over the state's economy and stands as a distinctive feature of the post-traditional nation-state within which cultural homogeneity is no longer attainable. As Martin Albrow argues, 'the categories, structures and boundaries of the old modern state appear now as problematical or alien to the organization of daily life for increasing numbers of people'.[13]

The nation-state's territory is steadily losing its relevance as a frame for political, economic, social and cultural life. In such a context, some nations without states, understood as cultural communities able and happy to live and develop within larger institutional frameworks, are beginning to establish quite a distinctive relationship with their territory. For them, territory is becoming a quasi-sacred component of their identity. Territory is turned into a symbolic space containing memories of the communities' history, sacred shrines, holy places, battlefields, and specific geographical features endowed with a highly emotional charge. Furthermore, territory also contains a strong political dimension since the nation's territory defines the limits within which self-government is to be exercised.

The territoriality of the nation-state is being challenged by the displacement of its own borders. EU member states are already witnessing the break-up of their own traditional frontiers, and seeing them replaced by new frontiers delimiting the EU territorial borders. The displacement of frontiers alters the meaning of geopolitics. Frontiers acquire great significance for stability. For instance, the potential admission of Turkey into the EU raises questions about how to control what would become the EU's eastern frontier with volatile countries such as Iraq, Syria, Georgia and Armenia, and how to deal with the Kurdish people's claim for an autonomous land.

At the same time, political decentralization, and with it the transfer of power to regional bodies, emphasizes once more the need to redefine territoriality as a key element in the post-traditional nation-state. Through it the state's territory is subdivided into regions, some of them endowed with a strong sense of shared identity and struggling to become economically competitive within an environment which extends well beyond the state's borders.

The demise of the traditional nation-state involves the partial loss of control over its territory, some matters being dealt with at a supranational level, while others are devolved to regional institutions which often put forward specific claims based upon cultural and historical claims over their territory.

In Ohmae's view, the nation-state has lost its role as a meaningful unit of participation in the global economy of today's borderless world. Both its ability and its freedom to contribute to the global economy have been seriously undermined by the genuinely global capital markets which restrict its capacity to control exchange rates or protect its currency.[14] My point here is that the intensity and scope of the transformations affecting the nation-state make it impossible to continue to refer to it as such, this is why I employ the term post-traditional nation-state to describe the new entity born out of the erosion suffered by the traditional nation-state.

Furthermore, it is impossible for the state to base its education system upon the transmission of a series of values and principles without accounting in some unspecified way for cultural and linguistic diversity not only within but also beyond its borders. Education has to include some notion of the concept of multiculturalism in an attempt to grasp the increasing cultural plurality pervading most contemporary societies. Capital and products are not the only things that travel fast. Large numbers of people have migrated to societies culturally distinct from those they originally came from. At the same time rising numbers of migrants and refugees from Africa, Asia and Eastern Europe are seeking entrance to the EU.

The media have also undergone a radical transformation in the last few years due to the technological revolution which has resulted in a shrinking of time and space. Simultaneous communication is now available and nation-states are unable to control the waves of information to which their own citizens have access.

The post-traditional nation-state is aware of these changes and responds to them by at one and the same time attempting to adapt to and resist the new conditions in which it is forced to operate. Again, the process of European integration offers a valuable example of this. The single European Act (1985) developed by the 1992 Programme sought, according to the European Commission, to create a 'Europe without frontiers'[15] based upon the development of the principles informing the Treaty of Rome which implied 'commitment to the free movement of both capital and Labour, a common investment policy, and the coordination and rationalization of social welfare goals'.[16] Some of the territorial barriers existing between EU states were knocked down. The non-tariff barriers to trade embedded in health, safety and industrial standards, professional and trades qualifications, descriptions of goods and administrative procedures were dismantled. The 1992 Programme required the reinforcement of the EU external barrier while internal barriers were progressively dismantled.

The Schengen Agreement (1985 and 1990, implemented in March 1995) signed by Austria, Belgium, France, Italy, Germany, Luxembourg, the Netherlands, Portugal and Spain – Britain, Ireland and Denmark remained outside – resulted in the abolition of frontiers between the signing parties. The nation-state's traditional concept of sovereignty over its particular territory was altered after it decided to enter an agreement with other nation-states and surrender this emblematic aspect of its sovereignty. But, to what extent do post-traditional nation-states still retain sovereignty over their territories? Can we refer to EU states as sovereign bodies? Conventionally, states are assumed to exercise sovereignty with unrestricted scope. However, the set of changes we have been analysing show not only that the scope of sovereignty may vary, but also that nowadays the post-traditional nation-state is submerged in a process of transference of its traditional powers upwards as the European Union exemplifies, and also downwards to the regions it contains. But, as Miller argues, 'such transfers must in the last resort be regarded as provisional, in the sense that nations have a residual claim to re-appropriate rights of decision where they believe that vital national interests are at stake'.[17] This is reflected in the doubts and resistance against the abolition of internal frontier controls manifested by some EU members.

A recurrent topic when considering territoriality is the ingrained distrust of northern countries in respect of the efficiency and reliability of southern administrative and judicial authorities regarding the control over the external frontier of the EU. In January 1998 France sent police reinforcements to its Italian border to prevent Kurds from entering. At the same time Germany demanded tougher measures should be implemented by Italy to prevent the flood of Kurdish refugees from Turkey and other migrants and asylum-seekers from Albania, Sri Lanka, Egypt and Algeria, among many others. More than 3,000 migrants and asylum seekers have arrived by boat in Italy since July 1997.[18]

The factual unification of the Schengen countries' territory was to be strengthened by the development of some 'compensatory measures' to guarantee that non-Schengen borders would be closely policed. Schengen also sharply extended transnational police powers, involving the right of police forces to carry out pursuits and arrests across frontiers. As a result, a European internal security operation directed against organized crime, drugs and illegal migration was initiated.

Schengen contemplates the possibility of the unilateral re-imposition of systematic frontier controls on persons if a country feels that its security is threatened, if there is popular or electoral pressure, or if the controls on the external frontier are not satisfactory.[19] This particular clause acknowledges that ultimately sovereignty remains with the nation-state. Yet the degree of erosion of state frontiers established by Schengen illustrates the tremendous changes to which territoriality and sovereignty are being subjected in the post-traditional nation-state. It is to be expected that Schengen will be superseded by the full implementation of the Maastricht Treaty on the road toward further political integration.

Violence

The direct control of the means of internal and external violence is a further dimension which is being transformed in the post-traditional nation-state. The use of high technology in warfare and its high cost have prompted different pacts and alliances between independent nation-states. The most significant of the alliances concerned with Western security is the North Atlantic Treaty Organization (NATO) created in 1949 when eleven European countries joined with the United States. This entailed the return of American forces to Western Europe after the Second World War was over and the division of Europe into two armed camps. The Soviet threat both unified Western

Europe and strengthened its relation with the US. NATO has considerably expanded since its foundation, especially after the dissolution of the USSR and the Warsaw Pact.

The Maastricht Treaty contains a Common Foreign and Security Pillar (CFSP) which, according to Article J.4 of the Treaty, 'shall include all questions related to the security of the Union, including the eventual framing of a common defence policy which might in time lead to a common defence'.[20] As Gummett argues, the Treaty further requests the Western European Union (WEU), as an integral part of the development of the EU, to elaborate and implement decisions and actions of the Union which have defence implications, while respecting and not prejudicing the obligations and commitments of certain member states under NATO.[21]

The shared control over the means of violence among NATO members and the reliance upon the US military forces are the main features which distinguish European security. The sheer capacity for mass destruction of modern warfare has induced states to seek protection and organize defence through a complex system of alliances. The reluctance of most European countries to develop a solely European defence system has strengthened the presence of the US in NATO, and confirmed its superiority.

The end of the Cold War is the most important event influencing how security is conceived, defended and promoted in the West. From a liberal perspective, the end of the confrontation between the Soviet Union and the United States and the introduction of capitalism and liberal democracy in Russia should contribute to activating the development of the Conference on Security and Cooperation in Europe (CSCE) which originated in 1972. The CSCE sought to reduce tension, including provisions for cultural, scientific and environmental cooperation and was one of the very few initiatives which spanned the West–East divide before 1989.

In 1990 the CSCE became a permanent organization and, since then, it has substantially increased its activities. The establishment of the Forum for Security Cooperation and the negotiation of the Conventional Armed Forces Agreement (CFE) are of enormous significance because in the future they could provide a basis for collective security across the whole of Europe. It is not clear how much impetus the CSCE will receive in the near future, and whether its development could at some point undermine NATO.

From a realist perspective, NATO is an indispensable organization when considering Western security. Russia is still a nuclear superpower whose economic and political future remains for the time being unstable. In this context NATO initiated a major review of its role in 1990 and while it committed itself to continued dialogue and further reductions in military forces, it decided to create an Allied Rapid Reaction Force (ARRC), operational in 1995.

NATO has been cautious in responding to applications for membership from countries in Central Europe. Full membership was rejected in 1994, although a programme for military cooperation with selected states of the former Soviet Union was launched. A complex and decisive debate about the future role of NATO and the eventual development of the WEU and whether it might be integrated into the EU is currently taking place among EU member states.

The strength of multi-nation-state security institutions such as NATO acts as a deterrent and has prevented large-scale military conflict in Europe since the end of the Second World War. The willingness of NATO to intervene in localized conflicts within European countries and its efficiency if it does intervene are a different matter. There is strong reluctance to intervene in nation-states' internal affairs since this is generally perceived as a violation of nation-state sovereignty. In most cases a higher international authority, the UN, is left to decide whether military intervention is a feasible option. It has often done so. Thus in cases in which specific regimes have been accused of oppressive and repressive practices against some sectors of their own population, the international community has challenged these particular states' monopoly over the means of internal violence.

Nevertheless, the UN intervention in the Yugoslav civil war is a clear example of how long-drawn-out the process of reaching a decision aimed at keeping peace between combatants and supplying humanitarian aid can be. The principle of non-intervention in foreign countries' internal affairs prevented an early response to Yugoslavia's civil war. It took EU diplomats a long time to decide to send peacekeeping forces to former Yugoslavia. It was only after news of genocide and real danger of a possible expansion of the conflict that the UN decided to intervene.

The former Yugoslavia formally ceased to exist in January 1992, about seven months after the outbreak of hostilities initiated in June 1991, when the twelve members of the EC officially recognized Slovenia and Croatia as independent states. Three months later, in an attempt to halt war in Bosnia-Herzegovina, the USA followed the EC in recognizing Slovene, Croatian and Bosnian independence. The EC set itself up as mediator, then the UN joined the diplomatic search for a peaceful solution to the conflict. Diplomacy failed and reports of atrocities continued to appear in the media. It was not until March 1992, after the seventeenth ceasefire of the Croatian war had held for two months, that teams of UN peace keepers began arriving in Croatia. The war went on irrespective of UN involvement.[22]

Discussion of NATO, the CSCE and the WEU points to a common experience faced by the post-traditional state, this is the tendency to form security alliances and create cooperation blocs which function at a political, economic as well as security level. The greatest challenge to the post-traditional state stems from the new and unfamiliar political scenario within which it lives. The absence of military-economic blocs opens up new possibilities for cooperation and radically transforms the political sphere, but, it is not clear whether the present situation will lead to a single world order characterized by peace and cooperation or whether new threats to stability will either emerge or be generated in order to justify the existence of an expensive military system.

The post-traditional nation-state is characterized by its need to abandon self-sufficiency. It represents a type of state which has surrendered some crucial aspects of its sovereignty in order to maintain a substantial degree of power and status. In doing so, the post-traditional nation-state allows for the emergence of new political actors which are forcing a reinterpretation and redefinition of the nation-state's traditional functions.

National identity

Max Weber's definition of the state does not include a systematic account of national identity. He did not grasp the relevance which this would achieve in the twentieth century, although he himself experienced the passion of nationalism, and displayed a German nationalist attitude during the First World War and after. Traditional nation-states have invariably sought to homogenize their population and instil in them a sense of community giving rise to feelings of solidarity among their citizens. The varying degrees of strength and access to power and resources enjoyed by different nation-states have determined the intensity with which they have attempted and more or less successfully accomplished national homogenization. Up to now, the nation-state has aimed at creating a sense of common national identity among its citizens. Control of the media and the education system have proved crucial in this task. Wherever it encountered resistance to its objective, the nation-state did not hesitate to apply tough measures which sometimes involved the active repression or even the annihilation of internal cultural difference.

The post-traditional nation-state, which accepts democracy as a guiding principle for its policies and institutions, is forced to acknowledge that these are unsustainable policies in a borderless world characterized by an increasingly global economy and the strengthening of different forms of national and ethnic identity. To maintain the correspondence between citizenship and a single national identity, the nation-state had to use forceful means, which in some cases entailed the use of violence. In the post-traditional nation-state, citizenship has to be understood as loyalty to a set of political principles able to hold together the culturally diverse population of the state. Often national identity does not coincide with citizenship. Thus some Spanish citizens may define their national identity as only Catalan, Basque or Galician. In a similar manner, some British citizens may claim a Scottish, English, Welsh or Irish identity.

In Western Europe, historically and culturally based sub-state national identities such as Catalan, Scottish or Welsh identity are gaining prominence. Simultaneously, we are witnessing how some long dormant identities are being awakened, while others are being invented. Occitan and Cornish identity fall into the first category; Rioja or Andalucian identity in the second. Hyphenated identities have grown popular in the US, where a common citizenship finds expression in a wide range of hyphenated descriptions which mix ethnic origin and allegiance to the United States. Jewish-American, Afro-American, Irish-American are some examples.[23]

In a similar way, in the EU, it is possible to envisage a future in which hyphenated identities may become fashionable. It is not clear though, if the hyphen will involve two or more elements. That is, will people define themselves as Catalan-European or Scottish-European for example? Or, would they add Spanish or British as a further source of their identity? Will it be the other way round and will regional identities disappear? In addition, will some hyphenated identities reflect a sense of belonging to a particular ethnic group while being a citizen of the EU? For instance, could we refer to a Afro-Caribbean-European, Romany-European or Jewish-European identity?

The post-traditional nation-state is faced with the need to accept the consolidation of, and where they did not previously exist, the emergence of multiple identities whose origins can be traced back, both upwards from the generation of new transnational or multinational identities, and downwards from the rise and reinforcement of regional and ethnic identities. The post-traditional nation-state reacts with a certain ambivalence to this process. Yet while at one level it accepts and, in some cases, it even promotes the consolidation of sub-state identities, at another, it displays a renewed state nationalism destined to counteract regional demands for further autonomy and even secessionist claims. Britain under the Labour government stands as a good example of this.

On British national identity

The Labour government's programme of constitutional reform involves, among other things, the creation of a Scottish Parliament and a Welsh Assembly. The Belfast Agreement (10 April 1998) envisages the establishment of a devolved parliament in Northern Ireland. These are constitutional changes based upon the decentralization of power and the opening up of government. An easily predictable but not specifically intended consequence of this will be the generation of greater regional awareness. Thus, Scottish, Welsh and Irish identity are most likely to be strengthened in the near future.

But, in the light of such processes, will British identity be reinforced or irreparably weakened? The Scottish, Welsh and Irish redefinition and invigoration of their identities will unquestionably alter the way in which British and English identities are to be constructed. The *Scotland's Parliament White Paper* (July 1997) states in chapter three: 'The Union will be strengthened by recognizing the claims of Scotland, Wales and the regions with strong identities of their own. The Government's devolution proposals, by meeting these aspirations, will not only safeguard but also enhance the Union'.[24] This interpretation assumes the possibility of people living with multiple identities. Being British and Scottish or Welsh is not regarded as inconvenient to political stability. On the contrary, respecting difference and promoting subsidiarity is presented as positive for Britain's future.

Yet, this is not the only possible scenario facing the UK, since regional autonomy could contain the seeds of further demands for autonomy or even independence. The potential victory of the pro-independence Scottish National Party in Scotland, and a majority achieved by the pro-independence republican Sinn Fein in Northern Ireland could at least put pressure on Westminster to contemplate a federal structure for the UK. Under such circumstances, the independence of Scotland or Northern Ireland from Britain and within the EU could become a reality.

In Britain, the decentralization of the state stands in parallel to the frequent use by the Prime Minister of a British nationalist vocabulary and discourse aimed at strengthening the Union while simultaneously seeking to redefine British identity. Tony Blair's address to the Labour Party Conference (September, 1997) illustrates this point. In it, Blair praised 'the richness of the British character', as 'creative, compassionate, outward looking. Old British values, but a new British confidence. We can never be the biggest, we may never again be the mightiest. But we can be the best'.[25] During his speech, Blair mentioned Britain or British 53 times, and employed the word 'nation' to refer to the UK 19 times. His vocabulary and expressions envisaged a single united Britain. He said: 'I believe in Britain. I believe in the British people. One cross on the ballot paper, one nation was reborn'. This refers to the May 1997 Labour victory in the British general election. Throughout his speech, Blair constantly refers to Britain as a nation, a nation which, if we are to acknowledge his own words in the Scottish White Paper when he also refers to Scotland as a nation, must be formed by other nations. That is, Britain is then probably a 'nation of nations'.

Blair's British nationalist tone is evident. Some people would call it patriotic. Most nationalists tend to define themselves as 'patriots' to avoid the possible connection between a certain type of nationalism and the exclusion, discrimination and even violence which are sometimes associated with it.

All traditional nationalist themes are present in the Prime Minister's address:

1 The wish for one's own nation to stand above others, as distinct from them, is reflected in the following sentence: 'Today I want to set an ambitious course for this country: to be nothing less than the model 21st century nation, a beacon to the world.'

2 The need for regeneration: 'Today I say to the British people: the chains of mediocrity have broken, the tired days are behind us, we are free to excel once more'. The Prime Minister, and with him the Government he represents, portrays himself as the saviour who will guide the nation away from its 'mediocre' existence, towards a better future: 'Our goal: to make Britain the best educated and skilled country in the world, a nation, not of a few talents, but of all the talents.'

3 Continuity with the past, 'Our new society will have the same values as ever.'

4 The call for people to participate and make sacrifices to achieve the goals which will turn Britain into a 'pivotal country, a leader in the world'. Blair said: 'Help us make Britain that beacon shining

throughout the world. Unite behind our mission to modernize our country.'

5 Emphasis upon the sentiment of forming a community with a shared project is clearly stated in the final paragraphs of his address where Tony Blair makes a pledge for a renewed Britain. He invites all citizens to participate in such a project thus encouraging a sense of community among the British people. The following sentences illustrate this point: 'Give to our country the gift of our energy, our ideas, our hopes, our talents. Britain, head and heart, can be unbeatable. That is the Britain I offer you. That is the Britain that together can be ours.'

6 A certain messianism. Blair's speech adopts a quasi-messianic tone when he says: 'Believe in us as much as we believe in you. Give just as much to our country as we intend to give. Give your all.' The ultimate sacrifice for one's country is to be ready to give up one's life, this is the paramount example of love of country and solidarity to one's fellow men and women.

Blair's discourse, as I have showed above, contains the main recurrent themes characteristic of any nationalist discourse. The crux of the matter with these types of discourse concerns the values, principles and objectives which are to be presented as national goals. Love of country when filled with democratic and moral objectives contains a powerful message to regenerate the nation. As Durkheim argues, each state becomes an organ of the 'human ideal' in so far as it assumes that its main task is not to expand by extending its borders, but to increase the level of its members' morality. Therefore, societies should place their pride in becoming the best organized, having the best moral constitution, rather than in being the biggest or richest of all societies.[26] The opposite applies whenever a nationalist discourse is filled with non-democratic principles and based upon the systematic exclusion and discrimination against those who do not belong.

The Prime Minister's address is a powerful example of a renewed state nationalism which most striking feature is the determination to combine it with the recognition of the existence of national minorities within the British state. The active decentralization policy pursued by the Labour government since it was elected in May 1997 has generated the creation of autonomous institutions in Scotland, Wales and Northern Ireland. The greatest challenge to this process of decentralization lies in whether the government will succeed in reformulating British national identity for it to contain sufficient elements to foster a shared sense of British civic coherence compatible with the respect for and encouragement of national diversity within the Union. This attempt exemplifies a new type of state nationalism which corresponds to the post-traditional nation-state as an institution conscious of its own limits and ready to respond to the democratic nationalist claims of its own minorities.

Blair's address also echoes the relevance of the European Union and stresses the need to 'lead in Europe again'. To achieve this aim, he points to Britain's need for a further engagement with the European project while protecting its national interest: 'We cannot shape Europe unless we matter in Europe. I know there will be a hard choice to come over a single currency, and our policy, based on the national interest, remains unchanged'. It is crucial to note that the decentralization of the UK takes place against the backcloth of the EU. This dramatically transforms the meaning of devolution and even independence, since all EU countries will eventually be ruled by the same institutions, laws and social policies. Further European integration, if it is to succeed, will bring about a political scenario in which the application of the principle of subsidiarity will inevitably encourage substantial regional autonomy.

The Prime Minister's address exemplifies the major challenges facing the nation-state and illustrates how even an advanced policy of internal decentralization is counterbalanced by the idea of a 'one nation's destiny and people', thus epitomizing the finest nationalist terminology, goals and principles.

Labour's recent initiative to put forward a new image of Britain – *Cool Britannia* – encompasses the wish to promote Britain as a modern country which should be a 'beacon to the world', but it also includes a desire to reshape British identity as more inclusive and ideally less circumscribed by the traditional attributes of Englishness.

The decentralization policy adopted by Westminster towards Scotland, Wales and Northern Ireland stands in sharp contrast with the reticence and caution with which the UK government has been responding to EU measures destined to speed up European integration. The UK has not joined the EMU, and is reluctant to accept a loss of national economic control to both the markets and to new European institutions – in particular the European Central Bank. In the case of Britain, there is fluid subsidiarity running downwards to the regions, but sheer reluctance to renounce some aspects of traditional forms of nation-state sovereignty. Therefore, while regional identities are revitalized and encouraged, the prospective emergence of a European identity in Britain remains feeble.

In contrast, other European countries such as Spain, Italy or

Germany display a much more favourable attitude towards the idea of defining themselves as 'European'. So far no real sense of a well constructed European identity able to match the influence most nation-states still hold when Europeans define their identities, is to be found. If we were to analyse which citizens of the EU display a more positive attitude towards European integration, we might be surprised to discover that members of nations without states such as Catalonia or Scotland are among those to show greatest enthusiasm. This can be explained by referring to the different historical processes which prompted the end of some of these nations without states as independent political units and the various degrees of force employed toward this end. It is common for nations without states such as Catalonia and Scotland to regard membership of the EU as a free option which creates a new socio-political and economic framework in which they expect to participate. In this sense, both Catalans and Scots, especially those seeking further autonomy or independence, regard the EU as holding an opportunity for them to weaken their ties with the nation-states within which they are included. Such ties may become unnecessary if the EU progresses towards political integration. Catalan and Scottish nationalists are also hopeful that the new EU structures which are currently being put into place will contemplate their existence and provide some space for them to feel directly and fully represented in the European institutions. The prospective emergence of a Europe of the Regions would undoubtedly be welcomed by them.

Nations without states

In the first part of this chapter, I have outlined the processes which lead to the emergence of the nation-state as a political institution and examined how some of its main attributes are currently being transformed giving rise to what I call the post-traditional nation-state. The changes I have just mentioned open up the way for the unfolding of new political institutions. Will they favour the rise of nations without states as new political actors in the near future? Do they announce the end of the nation-state, or are they to be regarded as engines of a reinvigorated and modified version of the traditional nation-state? It seems both timely and instructive to consider how these questions could be answered. Two central issues here include the feasibility of nations without states as new global political actors and the potential strengthening of supranational institutions.

The surrendering of crucial aspects of the nation-state's sovereignty to supranational institutions goes hand in hand with a process of devolution of power to sub-state units. Ohmae refers to region states as 'medium size economic units, not political ones, oriented toward the global economy, and willing to attract foreign investment to improve the quality of life of their people'.[27] Ohmae's definition of region states does not coincide with what I refer to as nations without states, since while the latter are based upon a common culture, history, consciousness of forming a distinctive community, attachment to a particular territory and the wish to decide upon their political future, the former are conceived as mere economic units which may or may not share further characteristics. Nations without states are distinctively different from region states in that they hold a specific national identity and assert the right to be considered as political units at the point when their very political nature is in the process of being redefined.

In my view, the main shortcoming of Ohmae's theory stems from its economic reductionist analysis. By emphasizing the significance of the emergence of a global economy in which region states are functional, he neglects cultural and moral aspects. He ignores the human need for identity, and the wish of most people to live and develop within a community to which they tend to be emotionally attached. Ohmae not only underestimates the force of non-economic factors when considering region states, but he undermines the need for social coherence. He writes: 'Where true economies of service exist, religious, ethnic and racial distinctions are not important – or at least, they are of as little importance as human nature allows'.[28] I wish to argue that this is only the case if we presuppose a situation of constant economic prosperity. Capitalism pervades the global economy, and it is based upon the accumulation of wealth. Making greater profit is only possible at the expense of some kind of exploitation taking place somewhere in the capitalist economic chain. Capitalism seems to be accompanied by striking differences which manifest themselves not only between areas of the world but also within single societies. Yet not all regions can be prosperous at the same time.

Ohmae's argument that 'Singapore is 70 per cent ethnic Chinese, but its 30 percent minority is no problem because commercial prosperity creates sufficient affluence to keep them contented'[29] has become ironically accurate in showing how economic instability generally favours the emergence of ethnic and national differences. The crisis now being faced by the Tiger economies is throwing millions out of work, wiping out years of progress against poverty and risking social unrest. Thailand and Malaysia aim to throw out at least 2.5 million labourers, while south Korea is likely to send back all its 270,000 guest workers. At the time of writing, violent protests and hostility against migrants are becoming acute and ethnic hatred is on the increase.[30]

Region states founded upon an economic basis may be functional in a global economy, but they lack the moral and cultural resources to create a sense of community among their members. Nations without states will undoubtedly benefit from situations of economic prosperity and suffer the effects of economic crisis as region states do, but what is distinctive about them is their capacity to generate a common identity among their members grounded upon a sentiment of belonging to a particular community which, in turn has the capacity to engender a bond of solidarity among them.

Furthermore, it seems to me that, to define region states as mere economic units while simultaneously defending the urgency that the state cedes operational autonomy to them, as Ohmae suggests, contains some kind of internal contradiction. In my view, the demand of operational autonomy for region states to organize and promote their economies will necessarily involve the need to adopt certain policies which might differ from those implemented by the state. In so doing, region states will inevitably become political units since the running of the economy requires the freedom to legislate in a way which promotes and supports specific economic policies. Ohmae's point about the economic character of region states seems to neglect this fact, and this could be interpreted as an attempt to account for and defend the economic dynamization of some areas (region states) without, in principle, challenging the nation-state's integrity and power. In his own words, 'nation-states should turn into effective catalysts for the activities of the regions'.[31] After examining what he describes as the failure of the Canadian state to catalyse its regional economies in a constructive way after the contentious debate over the status of Quebec he writes: 'What, then, holds Canada together as a country? If it has no mission to catalyse these regional economies [the Canadian regions]; what mission does it have?'[32]

I wish to go further and argue that besides becoming effective catalysts for the regions, nation-states have already entered an unstoppable process leading to their own fundamental transformation. At the same time, quite powerful regional governments are likely to be consolidated and to unite under the umbrella of common supranational institutions such as the EU. Nation-states will in time turn into nations without states themselves, since they are destined to surrender fundamental aspects of their sovereignty to an EU

Parliament and Government which, if political integration is to be successful, will to a great extent replace most national governments' traditional tasks.

The application of the principle of subsidiarity as envisaged by the Maastricht Treaty could lead to a future political scenario in which, for instance, Scotland, Wales, England, Catalonia, Castile and the Basque Country among other EU members could sit at the same table enjoying a similar degree of political autonomy – legitimized by economic prosperity and a common national identity – having most of their policies determined by a European Parliament in which they would all have their own representatives. Within this framework, the post-traditional nation-state will have lost some of the power the traditional nation-state once enjoyed; in contrast to this, some former national minorities will gain new devolved powers. They might still be considered as minorities, but if they achieve a status of equality with other EU members, this categorization will be automatically reversed.

Nation-states are destined to reduce their scope to that of the dominant national group within their territory. Yet, the post-traditional nation-state will either shrink to accommodate only its traditional dominant group, England in Britain and Castile in Spain, or endorse decentralization and be constituted by culturally different parts endowed with their own autonomous governments. The post-traditional nation-state will be forced to abandon dreams of cultural homogenization and economic and political dominion over a culturally heterogeneous citizenship. Transnational forms of citizenry are already being experimented with; European citizenship stands as a case in point.[33]

Europe of the Regions

A crucial question cutting across the potential creation of a Europe of the Regions concerns what regions, or what nations without states will acquire such a privileged status? At the time of writing, significant differences exist between various European nations without states. There are also striking differences between regions, thus while some of them have an economic basis but a feeble or absent cultural structure, others such as Catalonia, Flanders and Scotland have managed to maintain a powerful cultural distinctiveness. The EU does not distinguish between the two, and in what follows I shall employ the term region as containing both meanings. This will make it easier to refer to EU policies and attitudes; however, the reader should be aware of the crucial distinction which should be made between what I call nations without states and regions defined purely upon economic criteria.

Evidence of regional economic advantage began to emerge in the 1980s. The dynamics of a Single Market and the rising significance of European regional policy have encouraged the emergence of a new kind of innovative, specialized economic region oriented towards the global economy.

The 1988 reform of the Structural Funds, the new opportunities generated by the Single Act and the 1992 Programme have contributed to a general move towards reflexivity and indigenous growth at the regional level.[34] Poor regions have benefited from changes in the Structural Funds, while better-off regions have taken advantage of the new opportunities opened up by the implementation of the Single Act. The 'Four Motors of Europe' (a cross-frontier collaboration involving Baden-Württemberg, Rhône-Alps, Lombardy and Catalonia, which has recently been joined by Wales) has proved successful in attracting both European funds and foreign capital to a joint venture based upon the use of their combined strength. The outcome of this points to changes in the relationship between national and state level: 'The Europeanization of policy-making means that regions both can and have to take more responsibility for their socio-economic destiny, a trend that has been identified in most countries'.[35] In my view, this requires greater political autonomy at a regional level, a feature which both confirms the nation-state pressure to devolve powers to the region, and the need for regions to turn into political units of some sort.

The Committee of the Regions was set up in 1994 by the Treaty on European Union. It aims to represent the interests of the regional and local authorities in the EU. The Committee of the Regions is made up of 222 independent representatives of the regional and local authorities and the same number of alternates, who are appointed for four years by the Council of the Union, acting unanimously, on nomination from the member states. The mixture of regional and local representatives within the Committee undermines its character as a body representing the regions. This has sparked off great controversy among its potential and actual members, especially since there are no rules about how the fixed number of representatives from each country have to be distributed between the various levels of authority, regional and local.

The Committee of the Regions is an advisory body of the EU. Its opinions have no delaying effects and are in no way binding on decision-making bodies.[36] The policy areas in which the Committee must be consulted by the Council and the Commission are: health, culture, promotion of general and vocational training, trans-European networks, and structural and regional policy. It becomes evident that the Committee has a very limited scope and influence within the EU. The Europe of the Regions which many nationalists in nations without states defend is far from being represented by the Committee of the Regions. In spite of this, the Committee is a first step towards greater recognition of the significance of a regional Europe.

The process towards an eventual regionalization of the European Union is still in its early stages. There are striking differences between various European regions and it is unlikely that all of them obtain the same degree of political autonomy and recognition within the EU. What seems undeniable though, is that a new and unpredicted process through which selected nations without states are achieving cultural, economic and political relevance has already been initiated. A process which as I have showed in this chapter is closely tied up with the advent of globalization and profound changes affecting the nation-state traditional structure.

Conclusion

In this book I have sought to analyse the renewed significance acquired by nations without states in recent years and study the factors which contribute to envisage a medium term scenario in which they might become new global political actors. So far, I have argued that a clear-cut distinction between nation, state and nationalism should be established as a precondition for understanding the constant tension and interdependence between these three elements.

Since its establishment, the nation-state has enjoyed access to substantial power and resources which often have been employed to generate a single national identity within its boundaries. The intensification of globalization processes has weakened the traditional nation-state by breaking its monopoly over the economy, defence, the media and culture, among many other aspects and functions. Rising global interdependence and the emergence of transnational political and economic forces are shifting the locus of real decision-making elsewhere. At the same time, small political and economic units have become functional in a globalized world, and this in part accounts for the unexpected salience which nations without states are currently acquiring.

Globalization is bringing about a radical transformation of the nation-state and opens up the way for alternative political units to develop and consolidate. As a result, frontiers, international law, economic, environmental and social policies are already being reshaped in order to respond to new questions and dilemmas.

I consider the rise of nations without states as the product of a multidimensional process changing the relations of power in society. In my view these are the main elements of this process:

(1) The proliferation of supranational and international institutions initially created to deal with financial and security issues. Originally, most supranational institutions were formed by nation-state representatives. In the West, the number of such institutions rose after the First and Second World Wars. In recent years we have witnessed the proliferation and strengthening of some of these institutions; the European Union is a case in point. It stands as a unique attempt by already established Western and mostly prosperous nation-states to go beyond the economic community which they originally created after the Second World War. But we have also observed the emergence of the so-called non-governmental organizations as new political actors which cut across state boundaries. They unite otherwise diverse populations who happen to share a common socio-political objective, be it the protection of the environment, the defence of animal rights or the struggle against poverty and various other sources of discrimination. Non-governmental organizations denounce diverse forms of injustice and neglect by promoting a particular set of values which charge their claims with a highly ethical component. In this sense it could be argued that the legitimacy of their claims is based upon the defence of certain moral values which only sometimes possess a well defined religious component.

(2) The tendency of the nation-state, which is aware of its own increasing weakness, to surrender certain aspects of its sovereignty to supranational institutions in an attempt to maintain its power and influence. The increase in the number of transnational institutions dealing with matters traditionally reserved to the nation-state and the revitalization of sub-state nationalism are contributing to the weakening of the nation-state in a fundamental way. We are already observing some signs which point to a radicalization of state nationalism which not only seeks to undermine the democratic nationalism of some of the national minorities living within its territory (where they exist), but often involves a harsher treatment of the different ethnic groups it contains. The nation-state attempts to resist the pressure to surrender some crucial aspects of its traditional sovereignty to supranational and international institutions by actively pursuing the strengthening of its citizens' sense of national identity.

The nation-state is faced with a controversial dilemma. On the one hand, it has to favour the development and strengthening of the transnational organizations it belongs to, for example the European Union, as a necessary condition for its own survival as an economically, politically and socially competitive and viable unit. On the other, it struggles to retain its power and to resist further pressure to transform its traditional nature. Often this feeds a renewed 'state nationalism' hostile to supranational institutions, intra-state devolution, and to the acknowledgement of internal ethnic and national differences. Following this line of action, Western states are already implementing more rigorous asylum and immigration policies. In my view, even tougher regulations should be expected in the near future.

The radicalization of state nationalism should be understood as a response to the globalization processes which have irreversibly weakened the traditional nation-state. It also responds to pressure exerted by national and ethnic minorities living within the state's territory. The claims of such minorities have the capacity to challenge the state's legitimacy and may result in further autonomy being granted to them. Yet some people in democratic Western states fear that further decentralization and the recognition and encouragement of intra-state ethnic and national diversity might result in the irreversible disintegration of the state as a single homogeneous and cohesive unit, assuming that it ever was one.

(3) The erosion of frontiers turning the nation-state into a permeable unit unable to control external cultural and economic flows. Traditional frontiers are only kept in a symbolic manner; the nation-state is no longer, assuming that it ever managed to be, a self-contained self-sufficient unit, rather its own dependence and porousness are on the increase. The intensification of globalization processes generates an increasing interdependence between diverse peoples, cultures and markets.

The weakening of the state contrasts with the prominence achieved by the nation as a cultural community which is based upon attachment to a clearly demarcated territory, the sharing of a common set of values and traditions, and the wish to decide upon its political future. Globalization has undermined the state's aim to achieve cultural homogeneity within its borders by providing new channels of communication which not only reproduce images and messages originating outside the state, but also open up a possibility for minority cultures, enjoying enough power and resources, to access a global dimension.

(4) The, to a certain extent, global acceptance of democracy (without a necessary consensus on its definition) as a guiding principle for government. Nations without states have appropriated the concept of democracy and made it a crucial component of their nationalist discourses. Nations without states claim the right to self-determination as the ultimate consequence of democracy; however, there is no agreement about what self-determination means. As I have shown, there are different ways in which self-determination can be understood, they primarily depend upon who is to define it, the state or the national minorities themselves. But there are also substantial contrasts between the definitions that different nations without states offer depending on the intensity of their national consciousness and the radicalism of their demands. In some cases they view self-determination as enhanced political autonomy while in others, only independence fulfils their demands. In the West, for instance, the Mohawk of Kanahake concept of self-determination is substantially different from that espoused by other Native nations of North America, while different Quebec, Scottish and Catalan nationalist political parties also fill the word self-determination with slightly different meanings which only in some cases involve the right to secession.

(5) The rising disenchantment with traditional politics and the burgeoning of new social movements. An increasing passivity and alienation from politics seems to pervade the attitudes of a growing number of people in Western societies. Scandals revealing the improper behaviour of politicians who betray the trust of their voters seem to be on the increase. Furthermore, the utopian component which certain political ideologies used to espouse has mostly disappeared since the fall of the Soviet Union and the abandonment of socialism as a valid alternative to capitalism. The utopian component of politics has been replaced by a constant search for alternative ideologies able to encourage people to actively participate in the running of their own societies. In this sense, the soaring manifest apathy towards traditional politics heavily contrasts with the vitality enjoyed by new social movements whose main objective is to call attention to a particular issue and to mobilize people in order to redress a specific situation perceived as unjust. A new way of doing politics which seems to focus on finding alternatives to traditional well established and structured party-politics is emerging. The nationalism of nations without states is one of these new social movements in so far as it aims to redress a situation in which the nation has suffered some unspecified type of discrimination, be it cultural, political or economic, by using democratic means.

(6) The need for emotional closeness expressed through the quest for individual as well as collective forms of identity and the attempt

to re-create a sense of community. The extremely competitive and individualist society brought about by capitalism, together with the fragmentation which accompanies modernity in its late stages, have encouraged some individuals to identify with the nation as the most significant of several categorical identities that mediate between the autonomous but relatively weak individual and complex and powerful global forces. At a time when traditional sources of identity such as class are weakening or receding, national identity seems to acquire an unexpected and powerful significance. Individuals transcend their finite nature through identification with the nations they belong to. Nationalist movements in nations without states seek to generate a common consciousness among their members and to restore an endangered sense of community among them. The nation, portrayed as a community which transcends the life of the individuals who belong to it, encourages its members' emotional attachment and favours the emergence of a certain sentiment of solidarity among them. At present, there are a significant number of nationalist movements in Western nations without states which advocate modernization, openness and democracy as the main features informing their nationalist discourses and it is only in this sense that they may be referred to as new progressive social movements.

Nations without states: major questions and dilemmas

In the West, nations without states find themselves living within radically different political scenarios ranging from cultural recognition to political autonomy and federalism. In some extreme cases they are subject to repression and prevented from developing their own specific cultures and languages. The degree of national consciousness among different members of nations without states is also subject to substantial variations which have a direct influence on the strength and intensity of different nationalist movements. In addition, there are remarkable variations among the attitudes of different states towards the national minorities they contain. Yet the sanctioning of democracy as a guiding principle by a particular state should, in principle, favour some kind of recognition of its internal diversity, though we should bear in mind that democracy can be interpreted in a disparate manner which may lead to the implementation of substantially different policies with regard to intra-state cultural differences.

The existence of a committed 'potential intelligentsia' is crucial in the activation and consolidation of the nationalist movement. Its members should be able to construct a discourse critical of the state and be ready to search, cultivate and even invent common memories, values, myths and symbols whose aim would be to generate, where it is absent, or increase, where it already exists, the individual's degree of national consciousness. Turning a small elite into a mass movement including people from different backgrounds is the major challenge faced by nations without states and an indispensable condition if their nationalist movements are to succeed.

In my view, the future significance of nations without states and their chances of becoming new global political actors depend upon two main factors: their economic viability and their capacity to provide individuals with a strong sense of identity. Economic viability is indispensable since it is very hard for nations without states to demand further autonomy or even independence when they are economically dependent on the states which include them. The threat of substantial cuts in state subsidies may act as a deterrent to those who otherwise would be happy for its nation to enjoy further autonomy. The passion awakened by nationalism can certainly be cooled by a state of affairs in which people feel deprived. Without doubt the imminent reduction of British subsidies to Scotland once the Scottish Parliament is up and running will play a major part in determining the success of Scottish devolution. The economic prosperity of Catalonia and its condition as a major contributor to the Spanish coffers from which it receives significantly less than it contributes, is one of the major arguments employed by Catalan nationalists calling for greater autonomy. In a highly competitive world, nations without states need to specialize and offer high-quality products or services based upon high standards.

There are other cases in which nationalist movements have emerged in deprived areas. Corsican nationalism is a case in point. In these circumstances nationalists tend to provide an explanation for the nation's backwardness by blaming the state. The argument for further autonomy or independence rests on the need to break free from a state which is portrayed as a source of constraint for the nation's development. In such areas, state subsidies are poor, non-existent, or considered as insufficient. Secession is often presented as the only feasible alternative for the nation's survival.

So far I have stressed the nation's capacity to equip individuals with a sense of identity and the need to demonstrate its economic viability as two major conditions for nations without states to sustain and enhance their status as international political actors. In my view, nations without states are faced with three main dilemmas, these are:

1 How to deal with internal diversity;
2 How to avoid violence as a strategy to achieve further autonomy and recognition and;
3 How to avoid the creation of an expensive bureaucratic machine adding a further layer of government to an already saturated political structure.

(1) First, one of the major causes of intra-state conflict stems from the nation-state's tendency to neglect its internal diversity and impose a set of homogenizing policies aimed at favouring the emergence of a single united nation under the auspices of a centralized political institution, the state. Most nation-states have failed to acknowledge the resilience of national and ethnic identities co-existing within its boundaries other than the one they were aiming to impose. This line of action has prompted innumerable conflicts creating resentment and dissatisfaction among national and ethnic minorities elsewhere.

Nation-states enjoy varying degrees of power and act according to different structural principles. Yet while some of them have opted for the forced assimilation or even the annihilation of their national minorities, others have chosen to confer on them diverse degrees of recognition. At the same time, while some nations without states have remained silent, buried under the pressure exerted by the state, others have more or less disappeared, their languages and cultures being reduced to a minority status which seriously threatens their survival and a few have generated potent nationalist movements defending their right to participate in the governance of their own communities.

At present we observe the flourishing of nationalism in nations without states. However, due to the transnational circulation of people, culture and financial resources, these nations are confronted with a major challenge, their increasing internal diversity. At the dawn of a new millennium, nations without states should seek imaginative and democratically based alternatives to permit cultural coexistence and at the same time encourage a sufficient degree of civic coherence. In my view, they should aim to promote their own culture and language in the public domain while favouring diversity in the private sphere. This is an extremely delicate matter since most nations without states feel the legitimate need to engage in the active 'nation-alization' of the nation. Often, they have to reverse years of forced assimilation, resist the powerful influences of the state's media, and the unstoppable advancement of a global culture which speaks with an American accent. Yet there is only one way out if further conflict and resentment are to be averted. Ethnic differences in nations without states have to be respected and this has to be the product of a mutual compromise, that is, in practical terms, those who respect others should be respected.

Ethnically distinct people living within a nation other than their own should be welcomed into the host society and allowed to maintain their own cultures and languages, but they should also be expected to engage in a collective project able to unite all the members of the nation. The political engagement of diverse people living within the same nation should be based not upon a shared origin, but on shared values and principles involving the construction of an open society, endowed with democratic, efficient and accountable institutions. The commitment to civic values should operate as a source of cohesion and solidarity among otherwise diverse and free individuals who, as members of the nation, should be recognized as bearers of individual as well as collective rights.

To reach a state of affairs in which individuals share democratic principles and values concerning the type of society they want to live in and regard the institutions governing them as legitimate is not an easy task. Yet it seems to me the only alternative to the challenges posed by a world characterized by an increasing socio-political fragmentation stemming from cultural misunderstandings and confrontation between cultures struggling not to be swept away by the tide of globalization. These are some of the most difficult questions to be answered: How can we preserve and promote a decaying culture and language which has been neglected by lack of resources? How can we preserve a culture and enhance the use of a language wherever a particular nation has received a large number of migrants who, because of the marginalization to which the national culture was condemned at the time of their arrival, did not feel either the need or the wish to appropriate it and make it part of their own identity? How can we harmonize the nationalist claims of a nation without state such as Quebec with similar claims on behalf of the Native nations inhabiting its territory?

Much has been written recently about the concept of multicultural-- ism as some kind of panacea in sorting out cultural differences between groups coexisting within the same state. Rex's concept of multiculturalism is primarily designed to deal with ethnic communities of migrant origin within already established nation-states. Although, in my view, a more comprehensive definition of multiculturalism should account for national as well as ethnic intra-state differences, it is worth considering Rex's argument. In his opinion, 'multiculturalism in the modern world involves on the one hand the acceptance of a single culture and a single set of individual rights governing the public domain and a variety of folk cultures in the private domestic and communal domains'.[1] He points out that, the public domain should be based upon the notion of equality between individuals, while the private domain permits diversity between groups. Law, politics, economics and education, insofar as this is concerned with selection, the transmission of skills and the perpetuation of civic culture are included in the public domain. In contrast, moral education, primary socialization and the inculcation of religious belief belong to the private domain. Rex also stresses the significance of kinship ties that extend back into a homeland, a network of associations and a system of religious organizations and beliefs, stressing once more the use of multiculturalism in dealing with migrant communities within settler societies.

A further interpretation of multiculturalism refers, for example, to its controversial use, from a Quebec perspective, in defining Canada as a multicultural and bilingual society. This assertion, as I have already discussed, was perceived by Quebec nationalists as a strategy to water down the idea of Canada as a state based upon two founding peoples and cultures – the French and the English – thus conferring the same status on all cultures living and developing within Canada. It should also be noted that declarations of multiculturalism almost inevitably spring from members of a particular culture which decide how and when multiculturalism should be applied.

(2) A second dilemma faced by nations without states concerns the strategies chosen by their nationalist movements in order to advance their goals. Such strategies are closely related to the political ideologies held by such movements. Hence, the acceptance of democracy as a guiding principle should discourage the use of violence and favour the emergence of social movements determined to advance their goals through dialogue and participation in democratic channels.

As I have shown, specific socio-political and historical circumstances influence the decision of some groups to turn to violence as a means to attract international attention and hopefully promote their goals. It should be stressed that political terrorism has more often than not proved to be an unsuccessful device in the struggle for self-determination. Whenever identity is constructed upon the portrayal of the other as a potential enemy, violence against ethnic minorities living within the nation's territory is likely to emerge. Building up an identity upon the belief of one's group superiority above others is bound to generate feelings of hatred which can easily turn into xenophobia and racism. At present, there are many circumstances in which nationalist arguments are mixed with racist and xenophobic elements.

In the recent past, non-democratic forms of nationalism have brought destruction and suffering to Bosnia, Croatia, Serbia, Chechnya, East Timor and Rwanda, among many other countries. At the time of writing, it is provoking a massive exodus of ethnic Albanians from Kosovo into Albania. In all these situations, nationalist arguments have been employed as detonators of civil and international wars, ethnic cleansing, oppression and the annihilation of peoples.

Nations without states, to flourish and prosper, need to build up their nationalist discourses upon solid democratic principles stressing the richness and value of diversity and encouraging respect for the different. Only then can nations without states overcome what I consider one of the nation-state's main flaws, this is the failure to accommodate national and ethnic differences within its borders. The constitution of the EU as a pioneering political institution contains a great opportunity for nations without states to be recognized as political actors, but there is also a great danger of reproducing past mistakes which have led to bloodshed and suffering in Europe and in many other parts of the world. The construction of civic forms of nationalism should take precedence and override social exclusion based upon ethnic or national grounds.

(3) A third dilemma faced by emerging nations without states refers to the need to avoid the genesis of a heavy and expensive bureaucratic machine which would seriously undermine their efficiency and pose a burden to their economic viability. In the near future nations without states are bound to exist along with changing classical nation-state structures and newly created supranational organizations. There is a risk of unnecessary duplication of bureaucracy which can only be averted if subsidiarity is taken seriously and a serious restructuring of the distinct functions for which each political institution is made responsible takes place.

Subsidiarity refers to the political principle which establishes that decisions should be taken as close to the citizens as possible. Subsidiarity is based upon the decentralization of power and it primarily refers to the process by means of which the state devolves power to the regions and local governments. But it also applies to regional governments being able to put into practice their own decentralization.

Subsidiarity is favoured by a communication technology which permits an almost immediate flow of information between traditional centres of power and regional decision-making institutions. It could be argued that subsidiarity is encouraged because, although decisions might be taken miles away from traditional centres of power, these can still exert a tight control upon them due to the highly sophisticated technology which permits the storage, selective use, and immediate access to information being generated in distant localities.

Centres of political power continue to exist but they are shifting away from the nation-state to supranational organizations. They are stronger than they ever had been and they determine the rules of government. Subsidiarity consists of applying, interpreting and developing these particular rules to specific scenarios. One of the main advantages of opting for a system based upon subsidiarity resides in the fact that the individuals who are going to take the decisions have a much closer experience of the problems to solve, know better the people's needs, aspirations and limitations, and almost invariably they belong to the communities within which they are operating. Yet, they are not regarded as alien by community members.

A further advantage of subsidiarity is its proven capacity to enable people to take a more active part in the life of their community. Subsidiarity empowers individuals and stimulates their creative capacity, they feel they are actors with specific tasks to accomplish and are endowed with the power to decide upon a limited number of issues.

In my view, to work, subsidiarity requires three main conditions: efficiency, trust and legitimacy.

Decentralization to be efficient has to avoid the duplication of bureaucracy which is often frequent whenever there is an attempt to apply the subsidiarity principle. People will feel that subsidiarity is positive if the institutions generated by it are efficient, that is, they identify the problems, seek and work to eradicate their causes, and promptly respond to the citizens' needs. Matters devolved should be dealt with by a single layer of officials and civil servants, otherwise subsidiarity is nothing more than a very expensive fiction.

Trust is essential for subsidiarity to work. Trust operates in two ways. Downwards from the institutions which opt for decentralization to regional and local institutions; and upwards, from the newly created or empowered institutions to state or supranational institutions which decide which functions are to be devolved. The agents involved in a subsidiarity structure need to trust each other about the common principles and values which inform their actions. Central institutions should regard subsidiarity as a furthering of democracy. Devolved institutions should employ their newly acquired power and resources to the advancement of their communities within the framework set up by decentralization, being aware that the strongest arguments for subsidiarity stem from its efficiency, cost-effectiveness and identification of the people with their regional institutions and rulers.

In the context of the European Union, for instance, subsidiarity is primarily understood as giving power to the regions which are expected to further their own development while contributing to the strengthening of the Union. In contrast with this, there are others who invoke subsidiarity to defend the inalienable power and sovereignty of nation-states within the EU. There is a thin line between those who espouse this position while being truly committed Europeans, and those who adopt it at the expense of weakening the European Union. Trust is a basic requirement for a mode of government which aims to replace a centralized power by devolution and dialogue. Subsidiarity is impossible wherever political actors do not trust each other and do not share a core of principles, values and objectives which guarantee their cohesion. If this is the case, then subsidiarity leads to nothing but fragmentation and hostility.

Once subsidiarity is adopted as a principle for political organization, it is crucial that the people regard the institutions and individuals who work in them as legitimate. The key condition of legitimacy is that people feel represented by the democratically elected rulers of the devolved government and institutions. Identification with and trust in devolved institutions are closely dependent upon the perception of them as genuinely legitimate, that is, considered by the people as their own, and not as something imposed upon them. Legitimacy has to prove effective and this brings us back to the requirement for efficiency mentioned above. Transparency and accountability in decision-making processes and its subsequent implementation are vital to guarantee an efficient and cost effective application of the subsidiarity principle. The future of nations without states to a great extent, depends upon the acceptance and successful implementation of subsidiarity. The fulfilment of the three main conditions I have just outlined, points to some of the major challenges to be faced by nations without states in their quest for recognition as political actors.

Notes

Introduction

1 Smith, A. D. *National Identity*, p. 21.
2 Smith, A. D. *The Ethnic Origins of Nations*, pp. 13–14.
3 Keating, M. *Nations against the State*, p. 217.
4 Ibid., p. 221.
5 Among other works of a similar character it is worth mentioning: on Catalonia, Casassas, X. and Termes, J. *El futur del catalanisme* (Proa-CETC: Barcelona, 1997); on Galicia, Maiz, R. *A idea de nación*; on Scotland, Kemp, A. *The Hollow Drum* (Mainstream Publishing: Edinburgh, 1993) and Brown, A., McCrone, D. and Paterson, L. *Politics and Society in Scotland* (Edinburgh University Press: Edinburgh 1998).
6 Le Galès, P. and Lequesne, C. *Regions in Europe*, p. 263.
7 Ibid., p. 267.
8 See Rokkan, S. and Urwin, D. *Economy, Territory, Identity*.
9 See Held, D. *Democracy and The Global Order* and 'Democracy and Globalization' in Archibugi, D., Held, D. and Köhler, M. *Re-imagining political community* (Polity Press: Cambridge, 1998) pp. 11–27.
10 Held, D. *Democracy and the Global Order*, p. 136.
11 Held, D. Ibid., p. 137.
12 Horsman, M. and Marshall, A. *After the Nation-State*, p. 172.
13 Ibid., p. 185.
14 Hobsbawm, E. *Nations and Nationalism since 1780*; Maffessoli, M. *The time of the tribes* (Sage: London, 1995).
15 See Guibernau, M. *Nationalisms*, ch. 1.
16 See Kant, E. 'Toward perpetual peace' (1795) in *Practical Philosophy* (Cambridge University Press: Cambridge, 1996) pp. 311–52.

Chapter 1   State and Nation

1 Weber, M. *From Max Weber*, p. 78 (my italics).
2 Guibernau, M. *Nationalisms*, pp. 47–8.
3 Ibid., ch. 5.
4 Giddens, A. *The Consequences of Modernity* (Polity Press: Cambridge, 1990) pp. 63–64.
5 Ibid., p. 64.
6 Ibid., p. 64.
7 Albrow, M. *The Global Age* (Polity Press: Cambridge, 1996).
8 Ibid., p. 168.
9 Ibid., p. 170.
10 Ibid., p. 178.
11 Hutton, W. *The State to come* (Vintage: London, 1997), ch. 2.
12 Hirst, P. and Thompson, G. *Globalization in Question* (Polity Press: Cambridge, 1996) pp. 170–1.
13 Albrow, M. *The Global Age*, p. 171.
14 Hobsbawm, E. *Nations and nationalism since 1780*, p. 32.
15 See Van Dyke, V. 'The individual, the state, and ethnic communities in political theory', pp. 31–56.
16 See Guibernau, M. *Nationalisms*, pp. 16–19.
17 Hobsbawm, E. *Nations and nationalism since 1780*, p. 34.
18 Ibid., p. 35.
19 Kedourie, E. *Nationalism*, p. 59.
20 *J. G. Herder on Social and Political Culture*, p. 59.
21 See Nipperdey, T. 'In Search of Identity'.
22 Berlin, I. *The Sense of Reality*, pp. 243–4.
23 Ibid., p. 248.
24 Ibid., p. 252.
25 Ibid., p. 256.
26 Mayall, J. *Nationalism and international society* (Cambridge University Press: Cambridge, 1992 [1990]) p. 50.
27 Ibid., p. 56.
28 Ibid., p. 61.
29 Ibid., p. 63.
30 *La Gazette*, Montreal, 21 August 1998.
31 Durkheim, E. *The Division of Labour in society*, p. liii.
32 Tönnies, F. *Community and Association*, p. 74.
33 Ibid., p. 74–5.
34 Ibid., p. 87.
35 Ibid., p. 88.
36 Ibid., p. 90.
37 Ibid., p. 223.

Chapter 2   Nations without States: different political scenarios

1 See Giner, S. *The Social Structure of Catalonia*, pp. 7–8, and Bisson, T. N. *The Medieval Crown of Aragon*.
2 Elliott, J. H. *The Revolt of the Catalans*, p. 7.
3 Elliott, J. H. *The Revolt of the Catalans*, p. 45. See also, Vilar, P. *Història de Catalunya*, vol. III pp. 217 ff.
4 For an analysis of the process of industrialization of Catalonia, see Vilar, P. *La Catalogne dans l'Espagne moderne*.
5 See Bilbeny, N. *La ideologia nacionalista a Catalunya* and also Colomer, J. M. *Espanyolisme i Catalanisme*.
6 See, Marr, A. *The Battle for Scotland*, pp. 10–11.
7 For an analysis of early Scottish history see, Smyth, A. P. *Warlords and holymen: Scotland AD 80–1000* (Edinburgh University Press: Edinburgh, 1984).
8 Llobera, J. R. *The God of Modernity*, p. 29. For an accurate account of this period see, Barrow, G. W. S. *Kingship and Unity*.
9 See, Grant, A. *Independence and Nationhood*.
10 Quoted in Mackie, J. K. *A History of Scotland*, p. 77.
11 According to Mackie's, *A History of Scotland*, p. 261, the essential points of the Treaty were these: 'The two kingdoms were to be united into one in the name of Great Britain, with a common flag, a common great seal, and a common coinage. The monarchy of Great Britain was to descend to the Hanoverian Princess and her heirs. The two countries were to have one and the same Parliament, styled the Parliament of Great Britain; the Scottish representation in this was reckoned according to a ratio, based both on populations (perhaps five to one), and on taxable capacities (about thirty-six to one), and Scotland was to send only 16 peers to join the 190 English peers and 45 commoners to join the 513 from England and Wales. Scotland was to retain her own law and her own judicature free from any appeal to any court sitting in Westminster Hall; the Privy Council and the existing Court of Exchequer were to remain until the Parliament of Great Britain should think fit to ordain otherwise. The matter of a right of appeal to the House of Lords was left deliberately ambiguous.'
12 Mackie, J. K. *A History of Scotland*, p. 264.
13 Lynch, M. *Scotland: A new history*, p. 324.
14 See Ibid., p. 346ff.
15 McCormick, J. and Alexander, W. 'Firm foundations', pp. 161 62.
16 Smith, G. *Federalism: the multiethnic challenge* (Longman: London, 1995) p. 4.
17 Burgess, M. and Gagnon, A. G. *Comparative Federalism and Federation*, p. 5.
18 Elazar, D. *Exploring Federalism*, p. 12.

19 See Sanguin, A. L. *La Suisse*, and Eschet-Schwarz, A. 'The Role of Semi-Direct Democracy'.
20 'See Gunlicks, A. 'Introduction', Publius, 19.
21 Benz, A. 'German regions in the European Union', p. 113.
22 Ibid., p. 113.
23 King, P. 'Federation and Representation', p. 96.
24 Smith, G. *Federalism*, p. 7.
25 Burgess, M. and Gagnon, A. G. *Comparative Federalism and Federation*, p. 20.
26 Ibid., p. 18.
27 Kriek, D. J. *Federalism: the solution?*, p. 30.
28 Conway, J. F. *Debts to pay*, p. 14.
29 Ibid., p. 42.
30 For a history of Quebec, its politics and policy, see: La Chapelle, G. et al. *The Quebec Democracy*.
31 See Fitzmaurice, J. *Quebec and Canada*, pp. 54–75, and Lévesque, R. *Attendez que je me rappelle*, pp. 201–39.
32 For an historical perspective on the Canadian federation see: Brown-John, Ll. 'The Meech Lake Accord in historical perspective'.
33 Conway, J. F. *Debts to pay*, p. 70.
34 Ibid., p. 73.
35 Tully, J. 'Let's talk', p. 6.
36 Quebec, Chief Electoral Officer, *Rapport préliminaire*.
37 For a thorough analysis of the implications of a new Quebec–Canada partnership beyond Plan B's hard line toward Quebec or on the contingency strategy of a Plan C in the event of Quebec's secession in the near future see Gibbins, R. and Laforest, G. *Beyond the Impasse toward reconciliation*.
38 Gagnon, A. G. 'From Nation-State to Multinational State', p. 16.
39 Klein, R. 'Ethnicity and Citizenship Attitudes'.
40 For an analysis of the possible political scenarios to be faced by Quebec, see Department of Sociology, Quebec's University in Montreal 'Être ou ne pas être Québécois'.
41 See, Guibernau, M. *Nationalism in Stateless Nations*.
42 For an account of the Spanish Civil War and its consequences, see Gallo, M. *Historia de la España Franquista* and Payne, S. G. *The Franco regime 1936–1975*.
43 For an account of Catalan repression and nationalism under Francoism see: Benet, J. *Catalunya sota el règim franquista*; Vilar, P. *Història de Catalunya* vol. II and Termes, J. et al. 'Catalanisme'. For an account of Basque nationalism and repression under the Francoist regime see: Gurrutxaga, A. *El código nacionalista vasco* and Pérez-Agote, A. *El nacionalismo vasco*.
44 Kionka, R. and Vetik, R. 'Estonia and the Estonians', p. 133.
45 Senn, A. E. 'Lithuania and the Lithuanians', p. 172.
46 Smith, G. 'Latvia and the Latvians', p. 153.
47 Citron, S. *L'Histoire de France: Autrement*, p. 142.

48 Ibid., p. 174. Translated by Guibernau, M.
49 Ibid.
50 Ibid.
51 Graff, H. J. *The Legacies of Literacy*, p. 277.
52 See Bowen, J. A. *History of Western Education* vol. III.
53 Sahlins refers to this particular point in exploring the use of the Catalan language north of the Pyrenees. See Sahlins, P. *Boundaries*, p. 289.
54 Ibid., p. 291.
55 Ibid., p. 290.
56 O'Ballance, E. *The Kurdish Struggle 1920–94*, p. xxi.
57 Ignatieff, M. *Blood and Belonging*, p. 136.
58 Zubaida, S. 'Introduction', p. 5.
59 O'Ballance, E. *The Kurdish Struggle 1920–94*, p. xi.
60 Ignatieff, M. *Blood and Belonging*, p. 137.
61 Ibid., p. 138.
62 Human Rights Watch/Middle East, *Iraq's Crime of Genocide*, p. 24.
63 Ibid., p. 4.
64 Ibid., p. xvii.
65 Ibid., p. 8.

Chapter 3   Nations and Nationalism in Native America

1 Wilmer, F. *The Indigenous voice*, p. 97.
2 Quoted in Burger, J. *Report from the frontier*, p. 7.
3 Wilmer, F. The *Indigenous voice*, p. 9.
4 Ibid., p. 168.
5 Ibid., p. 106–7.
6 Spoonley, P. *Racism and Ethnicity*. p. xiii.
7 Burger, J. *Report from the Frontier*, p. 267.
8 Cornell, S. *The Return of the Native*, p. 6–7.
9 Tocqueville, A. de *Democracy in America*, p. 317.
10 Ibid., p. 318.
11 Ibid., p. 328.
12 Ibid., p. 334.
13 Ibid., p. 335.
14 Ibid., p. 336.
15 Ibid., p.324.
16 Berkhofer, R. F., Jr *The White Man's Indian*, p. 158.
17 Ibid., p. 164–5.
18 Ibid., p. 165.
19 Ibid., p. 166.
20 Parman, D. L. *Indians and the American West*, p. 1.
21 Ibid., p. 9.
22 Wilmer, F. *The Indigenous Voice*, p. 84.

23 Cornell, S. *The Return of the Native*, p. 92.
24 Deloria, V. Jr *Behind the Trail of Broken Treaties*, p. 196–7.
25 Wilmer, F. *The Indigenous Voice*, p. 85.
26 Quoted in Berkhofer, R. F. Jr *The White Man's Indian*, p. 144.
27 Quoted in Tocqueville, A. de *Democracy in America*, p. 338.
28 Quoted in Berkhofer, R. F. Jr *The White Man's Indian*, p. 164.
29 Quoted in Deloria, V. Jr *Behind the Trail*, p. viii.
30 Ibid., pp. 23–4.
31 American Indian Capital Conference on Poverty: A Statement made for the Young People by Melvin Thom, May 1964. Quoted in Josephy, A. Jr *Red Power*, p. 67.
32 Josephy, A. Jr *Red Power*, p. 226.
33 Nixon said: 'This resolution would explicitly affirm the integrity and right to continued existence of all Indian tribes and Alaska native governments, recognizing that cultural pluralism is a source of national strength. It would assure these groups that the United States Government would continue to carry out its treaty and trusteeship obligations to them as long as the groups themselves believe that such a policy was necessary or desirable ... For years we have talked about encouraging Indians to exercise greater self-determination, but our progress has never been commensurate with our promises. Part of the reason for this situation has been the threat of termination. But another reason is the fact that when a decision is made as to whether a Federal program will be turned over to Indian administration, it is the Federal authorities and not the Indian people who finally make that decision.' Quoted in Josephy, A. Jr *Red Power*, pp. 228–9.
34 Deloria, V. Jr *Behind the Trail*, p. 252.
35 Alfred, G. R. *Heeding the voices*, p. 7.
36 Robbins, R. L. 'Self-determination and subordination', p. 110.
37 Ibid., p. 111.
38 Parman, D. L. *Indians and the American West*, p. 168.
39 Deloria, V. Jr *Behind the Trail*, p. 250.
40 Alfred, G. R. *Heeding the voices*, p. 13.
41 Ibid., p. 86.
42 Ibid., p. 188.
43 Ibid., pp. 2–3.
44 Ibid., p. 179.
45 Ibid., pp. 180–1.
46 Ibid., p. 182.
47 See Guibernau, M. *Nationalisms*, ch. 5.
48 Alfred, G. R. *Heeding the voices*, p. 102.
49 Ibid., p. 99.
50 See Chapter Two for an account of the legal ruling in Canada.
51 *Royal Commission Report on Aboriginal Peoples*, vol. 5.

Chapter 4   Nationalism as a Social Movement

1 Smith, A. D. *National Identity*, p. 93.
2 Hutchinson, J. *Modern Nationalism*, p. 45.
3 Smith, A. D. *National Identity*, p. 64.
4 See Balcells, A. *El nacionalismo Catalan*.
5 Perin, R. 'Answering the Quebec Question', p. 36.
6 Juteau, D. 'Theorizing ethnicity', p. 47.
7 Conway, J. F. *Debts to Pay*, p. 74.
8 Hroch, M. *Social Preconditions*, p. 23.
9 Ibid., p. 183.
10 Ibid., p. 23.
11 Ibid., p. 179.
12 Ibid., p. 161.
13 Ibid., pp. 162–79.
14 Ibid., p. 180.
15 Ibid., p. 183.
16 Ibid., p. 186.
17 Ibid., p. 186.
18 Martin, W.C. 'The Role of the Intellectual', p. 62.
19 Ibid., p. 73.
20 Smith, A. D. *National Identity*, p. 95.
21 Gellner, E. *Nations and Nationalism*, p. 117.
22 Ibid., p. 143.
23 Ibid., p. 37.
24 Ibid., p. 143.
25 Ibid., p. 38.
26 Kymlicka, W. *Multicultural Citizenship*, p. 50.
27 *Parti Québécois, Programme*, Preface by Jacques Parizeau.
28 IPSO, *Quebec Sovereignty*, pp. 6–7.
29 Ibid., p. 7.
30 Seymour, M. *A letter to Canadians*, p. 12.
31 Scottish National Party, *Programme for Government* 1996, Pamphlet 2, p. 3.
32 Scottish National Party, *Programme for Government* 1996, Pamphlet 3, p. 4.
33 Plaid Cymru. *A Democratic Wales in a United Europe*, Introduction by Dafydd Wigley, president of PC (Playd Cymru: Caernarfon, 1995).
34 Ibid.
35 *CDC X Congrés*, p. 38.
36 Parti Québécois, *Programme*, p. 14.
37 Scottish National Party, *Programme for Government 1996*, Foreword by Alex Salmond.
38 Scottish National Party, *Programme for Government 1996*, Pamphlet 2, p. 3.
39 Guibernau, M. 'Images of Catalonia', p. 103.
40 Pujol, J. Address: 'CDC: Què ha estat', p. 19. See also, Esteve, P. Address:

'Una Política, un Horitzó', Cercle Financer de 'La Caixa', 26 June 1997 (CDC: Barcelona, 1997).
41 Parti Québécois, *Programme 1991*, p. 15.
42 Scottish National Party, *Programme for Government 1996*, Pamphlet 'A Voice for Scotland in the World', p. 47.
43 Plaid Cymru. *A Democratic Wales in a United Europe*, Introduction by Dafydd Wigley.
44 Diamanti, I.. *Il male del Nord*, p. 62.
45 Pujol, J. *Quatre conferències*, p. 80.
46 Thompson, J. B. *Ideology and modern culture*, p. 247.
47 Ibid. p. 319.
48 Ibid., p. 48.

Chapter 5   Cultural Resistance and Political Violence

1 See Fabré, J., Huertas, J. M. and Ribas, A. *Vint anys de resistència catalana.*
2 For a detailed account, see Crexell, J. *Els fets del Palau*; see also Muñoz, X. *De dreta a esquerra*, pp. 135–144.
3 Vilar, P. *Història de Catalunya*, vol. III p. 358.
4 Giner, S. *The Social Structure of Catalonia*, p. 59.
5 For an overall view of Welsh history see Davies, J. *A history of Wales.* For an account of Wales's early history see, Roderick, A. J. (ed) *Wales through the Ages*, vol. I.
6 See Walker, D. *Medieval Wales*, pp. 8–15.
7 See Davies, R. R. *The Age of Conquest*, pp. 272 ff.
8 Ibid., pp. 355–88.
9 Ibid., p. 166 ff.
10 See Rawkins, P. 'Living in the House of Power', pp. 294–314.
11 Jenkins, R. *Rethinking Ethnicity*, p. 129.
12 Ibid., p. 132.
13 Bennett, C. *Yugoslavia's bloody collapse*, p. 242.
14 Ibid., p. 248.
15 Shultz, R. 'Conceptualizing political terrorism', p. 45.
16 See Laqueur, W. *The age of terrorism*, p. 72.
17 Crenshaw, M. 'The causes of terrorism', p. 117.
18 Quoted in Schlesinger, P. *Media, state and nation*, p. 18.
19 Guelke, A. *The age of terrorism and the international political system*, p. 31.
20 Gurr, T. R. 'The political origins of state violence and terror', p. 59.
21 Quoted in Guelke, A. *The age of terrorism*, p. 36.
22 Crenshaw, M. 'The causes of terrorism', p. 119.
23 Ibid., p. 119.
24 Ibid., p. 125. Jáuregui, for instance, acknowledges the need to combine political theory with other disciplines such as social psychology and anthropology to find an answer to the continuing of ETA's armed struggle

more than twenty years after Franco's death. Jáuregui, G. *Entre la tragedia y la esperanza*, p. 72.

25 Gilbert, P. *Terrorism, security and nationality*, p. 99.
26 Leach, E. *Custom, law and terrorist violence*, p. 21.
27 Ibid., p. 36.
28 Ibid.
29 Schlesinger, P. *Media, state and nation*, p. 19.
30 See Guelke, A. *The age of terrorism*, p. 23.
31 Ibid., p. 25.
32 Laqueur, W. 'The futility of terrorism', p. 70.
33 Weber, M. 'Politics as a vocation' in *From Max Weber*, p. 78.
34 Guelke, A. *The age of terrorism*, p. 29.
35 See Ibid., pp. 45–6.
36 According to Conversi, 'although the *Fueros* were slowly eroded, before their abolition the *señorío* ("seigniory") of Bizkaia was working as a state within the Spanish state, and was even expanding its powers (Agirreazkuenaga, 1987)'. Conversi, D. *The Basques, the Catalans and Spain*, p. 45. See also Caro Baroja, J. *Los Vascos*.
37 Ibid., p. 145.
38 See Landa Montenegro, C. *Jesús María de Leizaola*.
39 See Arana, S. *El pensamiento de Sabino de Arana y Goiri*.
40 See Tejerina, B. *Nacionalismo y lengua*. For an in-depth analysis of the Basque Country during the Francoist regime see, Gurrutxaga, A. *El código nacionalista vasco* and Pérez-Agote, A. *El nacionalismo vasco*.
41 Jáuregui, G. *Entre la tragedia y la esperanza*, p. 65.
42 ETA's immediate goal was to force the Francoist state to increase its repressive measures thus prompting a reaction from the Basque people, who had so far adopted a more or less passive attitude. ETA's objective was to achieve a mass following, or at least considerable support for their 'revolutionary war'. See ETA's pamphlet *La insurrección en Euskadi*, quoted in Garmendia, J. M. *Historia de ETA*, p. 110. See also, Letamendía, F. *Juego de espejos; Historia de Euskadi, el nacionalismo vasco y ETA* and Ibarra, P. *La evolución estratégica de ETA (1963–1987)*.
43 The 1998 Basque Country regional election results were: Basque Nationalist Party (PNV) 21 seats, 27.9 per cent of the vote; Popular Party (PP) 16 seats, 20.1 per cent of the vote; Euskal Herritarrok (EH) 14 seats, 17.9 per cent of the vote; Spanish Socialist Workers Party (PSOE-PSE) 14 seats, 17.5 per cent of the vote; Euskal Alkartasuna Party (EA) 6 seats, 8.7 per cent of the vote; Izquierda Unida (IU-EB) 2 seats, 5.6 per cent of the vote; and Unión Alavesa Party (UA) 2 seats, 1.2 per cent of the vote. (*El Pais*, 25 October, 1998).
44 For a good analysis of the different social movements in the Basque Country see Tejerina, B. , Fernández Sobrado, J. M. and Aierdi, X. *Sociedad civil*.
45 Conway, J. F. *Debts to pay*, p. 89.

46 Lévesque, R. *Attendez que je me rappelle*, pp. 323–34.
47 See, Foster, R. F. *The Oxford History of Ireland*, Buckland, P. A. *A short history of Northern Ireland*, Bardon, J. *A history of Ulster*, Falls, C. *The birth of Ulster*, Foster, R. F. *Modern Ireland 1600–1972* and Hennessey, T. *A History of Northern Ireland 1920–1996*. The best-known Republican book is Farrell, M. *The Orange State*. For a Unionist approach, see Wilson, T. *Ulster: Conflict and Consent*.
48 For an account of early Irish history see, Richter, M. *Ireland: The enduring tradition*.
49 See Dáibhí ó Cróinín, *Early Medieval Ireland 400–1200*, pp. 45–49.
50 Richter, M. *Ireland: The enduring tradition*, p. 129.
51 Jenkins, R. *Rethinking Ethnicity*, p. 93.
52 See Hayden, T. (ed.) *Irish Hunger*.
53 See Akenson, D. H. *The Irish Diaspora*.
54 For an account of contemporary Northern Irish politics see: O'Leary, B. and McGarry, J. *The Politics of Antagonism* and, also by the same authors, *The future of Northern Ireland* and *Explaining Northern Ireland*.
55 Jenkins, R. *Rethinking Ethnicity*, p. 127.
56 Bowyer Bell, J. *IRA, tactics and targets*, p. 9.
57 Jenkins, R. *Rethinking Ethnicity*, p. 128.
58 Horowitz, D. L. *Ethnic groups in conflict*, p. 230.
59 Guelke, A. *The age of terrorism*, p. 106.
60 *The Belfast Agreement* (The Stationery Office: London, April, 1998) p. 1.
61 Ibid., p. 2.
62 Ibid., p. 20.
63 Ibid., p. 21.
64 Hayden, T. Pamphlet: *No Border, no cry?*, p. 2.
65 *The Belfast Agreement*, p. 19.
66 Gurr, T. R. 'The political origins of state violence', p. 57. See also Gurr, T. R. 'Ethnopolitical rebellion', pp. 1082–3.
67 Giddens, A. *The nation-state and violence*, p. 295.
68 See Mitchell, C. et al. 'State terrorism', p. 13.
69 Gurr, R 'The political origins of state violence', p. 51.
70 McCamant, J. F. 'Domination, state power, and political repression', p. 42.
71 Schmid, A. P. 'Repression, state terrorism and genocide', p. 25.

Chapter 6 Nations without States as New Global Political Actors

1 Axford, B. *The Global System*, p. 15.
2 Ohmae, K. *The end of the nation-state*, p. 11.
3 See, Ruggie, J. G., 'International regimes, transactions and change' and Krasner, S. 'Sovereignty'.
4 Giddens, A. *The nation-state and violence*, p. 121.

5 Ibid., p. 281.
6 Ibid., p. 282.
7 Giner, S. 'The rise of a European Society', p. 151.
8 Ohmae, K. *The end of the nation-state*, p. 118.
9 See Llobera, J. R. *The God of Modernity.*
10 Ohmae, K. *The end of the nation-state*, p. 42.
11 Ibid., p. 142.
12 Weber, M. *From Max Weber*, p. 78.
13 Albrow, M. *The Global Age*, p. 167.
14 Ohmae, K. *The end of the nation-state*, pp. 11–12.
15 See Urwin, D. *Politics in Western Europe*, p. 236.
16 Ibid., p. 80.
17 Miller, *On Nationality*, p. 101.
18 *The Guardian*, 7 January 1998, p. 13.
19 Anderson, M. *Frontiers*, p. 186.
20 *Treaty of European Union* C 191, 29.7.92, Article J.4. Quoted in Gummett, P. 'Foreign Defence and Security Policy', p. 220.
21 Ibid.
22 See Bennett, C. *Yugoslavia's bloody collapse.*
23 See Kymlicka, W. *Multicultural Citizenship.*
24 *Scotland's Parliament White Paper*, article 3.1.
25 Extracts from *The Guardian*, 1 October, 1997.
26 Durkheim, E. 'Pacifisme et Patriotisme'.
27 See Ohmae, K. *The end of the nation-state*, pp. 89 ff.
28 Ibid., p. 93.
29 Ibid.
30 See *The Guardian*, 11 April 1998, p. 16, and 7 January 1998, p. 1.
31 Ohmae, K. *The end of the nation-state*, p. 136.
32 Ibid., p. 138.
33 See Baubock, R. *Transnational Citizenship* and Roche, M. and Van Berkel, R. *European Citizenship and Social Exclusion.*
34 See Cooke, P. Christiansen, T. and Schienstock, G. 'Regional Economic Policy', pp. 197 ff. For an analysis of different European nationalist movements see, Beramendi, J. G., Máiz, and Núñez, X. M. *Nationalism in Europe.*
35 Cooke, Christiansen and Schienstock, 'Regional Economic Policy', p. 201.
36 See Engel, C. 'Committee of the Regions', pp. 38–40.

Conclusion

1 Rex, J. 'The concept of a multicultural society', p. 210.

Bibliography

AKENSON, D. H., *The Irish Diaspora*, P. D. Meany Company, Inc., Publishers and The Institute of Irish Studies, The Queen's University of Belfast, Belfast, 1996.

ALBROW, M., *The Global Age*, Polity Press, Cambridge, 1996.

ALFRED, G. R., *Heeding the Voices of our Ancestors: Kahnawake Mohawk politics and the rise of Native nationalism*, Oxford University Press, Toronto, 1995.

ANDERSON, M., *Frontiers: territory and state formation in the modern world*, Polity Press, Cambridge, 1996.

ARANA Y GOIRI, S., *El pensamiento de Sabino de Arana y Goiri a través de sus escritos. Antología de textos 1893–1903*, Partido Nacionalista Vasco, 1995.

A Voice for Wales: The Government's proposals for a Welsh Assembly, The Stationery Office, London, July 1997.

AXFORD, B., *The Global System: Economics, politics and Culture*, Polity Press, Cambridge, 1995.

BALCELLS, A., *El nacionalismo catalán*, Historia 16, Madrid, 1991.

BARDON, J. A., *A History of Ulster*, Blackstaff Press, Belfast, 1992.

BARROW, G. W., *Kingship and Unity: Scotland 1000–1306*, Edinburgh University Press, Edinburgh, 1981.

BAUBOCK, R., *Transnational Citizenship: Membership and rights in International Migration*, Edward Elgar, Aldershot, 1994.

BENET, J., *Catalunya sota el règim franquista*, Edicions Catalanes de París, París, 1973.

BENNETT, C., *Yugoslavia's Bloody Collapse: causes, course and consequences*, Hurst & Company, London, 1995.

BENZ, A., 'German regions in the European Union', in Le Galès and Lequesne, *Regions in Europe*, Routledge, London, 1998, pp. 111–29 & 113.

BERAMENDI, J. G., MÁIZ, R., & NÚÑEZ, X. M., (ed.), *Nationalism in Europe: Past and Present*, Universidad de Santiago de Compostela, 1994, 2 vol.

BERKHOFER, R. F., JR, *The White Man's Indian: Images of the American Indian from Columbus to the present*, Alfred Knopf, New York, 1978.

BERLIN, I., *The Sense of Reality: Studies in ideas and their history*, Pimlico, London, 1996.

BILBENY, N., *La ideologia nacionalista a Catalunya*, Laia/L'entrellat, Barcelona, 1988.

BISSON, T. N., *The Medieval Crown of Aragon*, Clarendon Press, Oxford, 1986.

BOWEN, J. A., *History of Western Education*, Methuen, London, 1981, vol. III.

BOWYER BELL, J., *IRA, Tactics and Targets*, Poolbeg Press Ltd., Dublin, 1997 (1990).

BROWN-JOHN, Ll., 'The Meech Lake Accord in historical perspective', in Burgess, M. (ed.), *Canadian Federalism: Past, Present and Future*, Leicester University Press, Leicester, 1990.

BUCKLAND, P. A., *A Short History of Northern Ireland*, Holmes and Meier, New York, 1982

BURGER, J., *Report from the Frontier: the state of the world's indigenous peoples*, Zed Books Ltd., London, 1987.

BURGESS, M., & GAGNON, A. G., *Comparative Federalism and Federation*, Harvester Wheatsheaf, London, 1993.

CARO BAROJA, J., *Los Vascos*, Istmo, Madrid, 1971.

CDC, *CDC X Congrès: La força decisiva per a Catalunya*, l'Hospitalet, 8, 9 and 10 November 1996, CDC, Barcelona, 1997.

CITRON, S., *L'Histoire de France: Autrement*, Les Éditions Ouvrières, París, 1992.

COLOMER, J. M., 'Espanyolisme i Catalanisme', in *L'Avenç*, Barcelona, 1984, 4.

CONVERSI, D., *The Basques, the Catalans and Spain: alternative routes to nationalist mobilization*, Hurst & Company, London, 1997.

CONWAY, J. F., *Debts to Pay: English Canada and Quebec from the Conquest to the Referendum*, James Lorimer & Company Publishers, Toronto, 1992.

COOKE, P., CHRISTIANSEN, T. and SCHIENSTOCK, G., 'Regional Economic Policy and a Europe of the Regions', in Rhodes, M., Heywood, P., & Wright, V., (eds), *Developments in West European Politics*, Macmillan, London, 1997, p. 190–206.

CORCUERA, J., *Orígenes, ideología y organización del nacionalismo vasco (1876–1904)*, Siglo XXI, Madrid, 1979.

CORNELL, S., *The Return of the Native: American Indian political resurgence*, Oxford University Press, Oxford-New York, 1988.

COUTURE, J., NIELSEN, K. and SEYMOUR, M. *Rethinking Nationalism*, University of Calgary Press, Calgary, Alberta, Canada, 1998.

CRENSHAW, M., 'The causes of terrorism', in Kegley, C. W., Kegley, Jr, *International Terrorism: characteristics, causes, controls*, St Martin's Press Inc, New York, 1990, p. 113–26.

CREXELL, J., *Els fet del Palau i el consell de guerra de Jordi Pujol*, La Magrana, Barcelona, 1982.

DÁIBHÍ Ó CRÓINÍN, *Early Medieval Ireland 400–1200*, Longman, London, 1995.

DANDEKER, C. (ed) *Nationalism and Violence*, Transaction, New Brunswick and London, 1998.

DAVIES, J. A., *A History of Wales*, Penguin Books, London, 1993 (1990).

DAVIES, R. R., *The Age of Conquest, Wales 1063–1415*, Oxford University Press, Oxford, 1991 (1987).

DELORIA, V., Jr, *Behind the Trail of Broken Treaties*, University of Texas Press, Austin, 1985.

DE PABLO, S., DE LA GRANJA, J. L., and MEES, L., (eds), *Documentos para la historia del nacionalismo vasco*, Ariel, Barcelona, 1998.

Department of Sociology, Quebec's University in Montreal, 'Être ou ne pas être Québécois', in *Cahiers de Recherche sociologique*, UQAM, 1995, no. 25.

DIAMANTI, I., *Il male del Nord*, Donzelli Editore, Rome, 1996.

DURKHEIM, E., *The Division of Labour in society*, Macmillan, London, 1984.

——, 'Pacifisme et Patriotisme', translated by N. Layne in *Sociological Inquiry*, 1973, 43, 2, pp. 99–103.

ELAZAR, D., *Exploring Federalism*, University of Alabama Press, Tuscaloosa, AL, 1987.

ELLIOT, J. H., *The Revolt of the Catalans: a study in the decline of Spain (1598–1640)*, Cambridge University Press, Cambridge, 1963.

ELORZA, A., *Ideologías del nacionalismo vasco, 1876–1937*, Haranburu Editor, San Sebastián, 1978.

ENGEL, C., 'Committee of the Regions', in Weidenfeld, W., and Wessels, *Europe from A to Z: Guide to European integration*, Office for Official Publications of the European Communities, Luxemburg, 1997, pp. 38–40.

ESCHET-SCHWARZ, A., 'The Role of Semi-Direct Democracy in Shaping Swiss Federalism: The Behaviour of Cantons Regarding Revision of the Constitution, 1866–1981', in *Publius: The Journal of Federalism*, 1989, no. 19, pp. 19–105.

FABRÉ J., HUERTAS, J. M., and RIBAS, A., *Vint anys de resistència catalana 1939–1959*, La Magrana, Barcelona, 1978.

FALLS, C., *The birth of Ulster*, Constable, London, 1936.

FARRELL, M., *The Orange State*, Pluto Press, London, 1980.

FITZMAURICE, J., *Quebec and Canada: Past, Present and Future*, C. Hurst & Company, London, 1985.

FOSTER, R. F., *The Oxford History of Ireland*, Oxford University Press, Oxford, 1989.

——, *Modern Ireland 1600–1972*, Penguin, London, 1989.

FUSI, J. P., *El País Vasco: Pluralismo y nacionalidad*, Madrid, Alianza, 1984.

GAGNON, A. G., 'From Nation-State to Multicultural State: Quebec and Canada facing the challenge of modernity', Keynote speech delivered before the British Association of Canadian Studies April 12 1996.

GALLO, M., *Historia de la España Franquista*, Ruedo Ibérico, París, 1969.

GARMENDIA, J. M., *Historia de ETA*, L. Haranburu Editor, San Sebastián, 1979, 2 vols.

GELLNER, E., *Nations and Nationalism*, Basil Blackwell, Oxford, 1983.

GIBBINS, R., and LAFOREST, G., *Beyond the Impasse toward Reconciliation*, Institute for Research in Public Policy, Montreal, 1998.

GIDDENS, A., *The Nation-state and Violence*, Polity Press, Cambridge, 1985.

GILBERT, P., *Terrorism, Security and Nationality*, Routledge, London, 1994.

GINER, S., *La Societat Catalana*, Institut Català d'Estadística, Barcelona, 1998.

——, 'The Rise of a European Society', in *Revue Européenne des sciences sociales*, 1993, vol. XXXI, no. 95, pp. 146–61.

——, *The Social Structure of Catalonia*, The Anglo-Catalan Society, Sheffield, 1980.

GRAFF, H. J., *The Legacies of Literacy*, Indiana University Press, Bloomington, Indiana, 1987.

GRANT, A., *Independence and nationhood: Scotland 1306–1469*, Edward Arnold Ltd., London, 1984.

GUELKE, A., *The Age of Terrorism and the International Political System*, Tauris Academic Studies, London, 1985.

GUIBERNAU, M., *Nationalism: the nation-state and nationalism in the twentieth century*, Polity Press, Cambridge, 1996.

——, *Nationalism in Stateless Nations: the case of Catalonia*, unpublished doctoral thesis, Cambridge University, 1993.

——, 'Images of Catalonia', in *Nations and Nationalism*, March 1997, vol. 3, 1, pp. 90–111.

——, and Rex, J., (eds), *The Ethnicity Reader: nationalism, multiculturalism and migration*, Polity Press, Cambridge, 1997.

GUMMETT, P., 'Foreign Defence and Security Policy', in Rhodes, M., Heywood, P., and Wright, V., (eds), *Developments in West European Politics*, Macmillan, London, 1997, pp. 205–25.

GUNLICKS, A., 'Introduction', Publius, 19, no. 4, edició especial, *Federalism and Intergovernmental Relations in West Germany*, Gunlicks, (ed.), 1989.

GURR, T. R., 'Ethnopolitical rebellion: A cross-sectional analysis of the 1980s with risk assessments for the 1990s', in *American Journal of Political Science*, October 1997, vol. 41, no. 4, pp. 1079–103.

——, 'The political origins of state violence and terror: a theoretical analysis', in Stohl, M., and Lopez, G. A., (eds), *Government Violence and Repression*, Greenwood Press, New York, 1986, pp. 45–72.

GURRUTXAGA, A., *El código nacionalista vasco durante el franquismo*, Anthropos, Barcelona, 1985.

HARVIE, C., *The Rise of Regional Europe*, Routledge, London, 1994.

HAYDEN, T., (ed.), pamphlet, *No Border, No Cry? The Peace Process and the Causes of Conflict in Northern Ireland*, 1 February 1998, Senator Tom Hayden, State Capitol, Sacramento CA.

——, *Irish Hunger: personal reflections on the legacy of the famine*, Wolfhound, Dublin, 1997.

HELD, D., *Democracy and the Global Order*, Polity Press, Cambridge 1995.

——, *Political Theory Today*, Stanford, Stanford University Press, 1991, & Polity Press, Cambridge, 1991.

HENNESSEY, T. A., *History of Northern Ireland 1920–1996*, Macmillan, London, 1997.

HERDER, J. G., *Herder on Social and Political Culture*, trans. and ed. by F. M. Barnard, Cambridge University Press, 1969.

HERNÁNDEZ, F., and MERCADÉ, F., (eds), *Estructuras sociales y cuestión nacional en España*, Ariel, Barcelona, 1986.

HOBSBAWM, E., *Nations and Nationalism since 1780*, Canto, Cambridge University Press, Cambridge, 1992 (1990).

HOROWITZ, D. L., *Ethnic Groups in Conflict*, University of California Press, Berkeley and Los Angeles, 1985.

HORSMAN, M., and MARSHALL, A., *After the Nation-State: citizens, tribalism and the new world disorder*, Harper Collins, London, 1995.

HROCH, M., *Social Preconditions of National Revival in Europe*, Cambridge University Press, Cambridge, 1985.

Human Rights Watch/Middle East, *Iraq's Crime of Genocide: The Anfal Campaign against the Kurds*, Yale University Press, New Haven and London, 1995.

HUTCHINSON, J., *Modern Nationalism*, Fontana Press, London, 1994.

HUTTON, W., *The State We're In*, Vintage, London, 1996.

IBARRA, P., *La evolución estratégica de ETA 1963–1987*, Kriselu: Donostia, 1987.

IGNATIEFF, M., *Blood and Belonging*, BBC Books, London, 1993.

IPSO Intellectuels pour la souveraineté, pamphlet, *Quebec Sovereignty: A legitimate Goal*, Montreal, 1996.

JÁUREGUI, G., *Entre la tragedia y la esperanza: Vasconia ante el nuevo milenio*, Ariel, Barcelona, 1997 (1996).

——, *Ideología y estrategia política de ETA*, Siglo XXI, Madrid, 1981.

JENKINS, R., *Rethinking Ethnicity*, Sage, London, 1997.

JOSEPHY, A., Jr, *Red Power: The American Indians' Fight for Freedom*, American Heritage Press, New York, 1971.

JUTEAU, D., 'theorizing ethnicity and ethnic communalizations at the margins: from Quebec to the world system', in *Nations and Nationalism*, March 1996, 2, 1, pp. 45–66.

KEATING, M., *Nations against the State: the new politics of nationalism in Quebec, Catalonia and Scotland*, Macmillan Press, 1996.

KEDOURIE, E., *Nationalism*, Hutchinson University Library, London, 1985 (1960).

KEGLEY, Jr, C. W., *International Terrorism: characteristics, causes, controls*, St Martin's Press, NY, 1990.

KING, P., 'Federation and Representation', in Burgess, M., and Gagnon, A. G., (eds), *Comparative Federalism and Federation*, Harvester Wheatsheaf, London, 1993.

KIONKA, R., and VETIK, R., 'Estonia and the Estonians', in Smith, G., (ed.), *The Nationalities question in the post-Soviet states*, Longman, London, 1996 (1990).

KLEIN, R., 'Ethnicity and Citizenship Attitudes in Canada: Analyses of a 1991

National survey', in Laponce, J., and Safran, W., (eds), *Ethnicity and Citizenship: The Canadian Case*, Frank Cass, London, 1996.

KRASNER, S., 'Sovereignty: an institutional perspective', in *Comparative Political Studies*, 1988, 21, 1.

KRIEK, D. J., *Federalism: the solution?*, HSRC Publishers, Pretoria, 1992.

KYMLICKA, W., *Multicultural Citizenship*, Oxford University Press, Oxford, 1995.

LA CHAPELLE, G., et al, (eds), *The Quebec Democracy: structures, processes and policies*, McGraw-Hill Ryerson Limited, Montreal, 1993.

LANDA MONTENEGRO, C., *Jesús María de Leizaola: vida, obra y acción política de un nacionalista vasco 1896–1937*, Fundación Sabino de Arana, Artea, 1995.

LAQUEUR, W., *The Age of Terrorism*, Weidenfeld and Nicolson, London, 1987.

——, 'The futility of terrorism', in Kegley C. W., Jr., (ed.), *International Terrorism: characteristics, causes, controls*, St Martin's Press Inc, New York, 1990, pp. 69–73.

LEACH, E., *Custom, Law and Terrorist Violence*, Edinburgh University Press, Edinburgh, 1977.

LETAMENDIA, F., *Juego de espejos: conflictos nacionales centro-periferia*, Editorial Trotta, Madrid, 1997.

——, *Historia de Euskadi, el nacionalismo vasco y ETA*, 1975.

LÉVESQUE, R., *Attendez que je me rapelle ...*, Québec/Amérique, Montreal, 1986.

LLOBERA, J. R., *The God of Modernity: the development of nationalism in Western Europe*, Berg, Oxford, 1994.

LYNCH, M., *Scotland: A new history*, Pimlico, London, 1998 (1991).

MACKIE, J. K., *A History of Scotland*, Penguin, London, 1991.

MAIZ, R., *A idea de nación*, Xerais, Vigo, 1997.

MARR, A., *The Battle for Scotland*, Penguin, London, 1992.

MARTIN, W. C., 'The Role of the Intellectual in Revolutionary Institutions', in Mohan, Raj P., (ed.), *The Mythmakers: Intellectuals and the Intelligentsia in Perspective*, Greenwood Press, Westport, Connecticut, 1987, pp. 61–77.

MAYALL, J. *Nationalism and international society*, Cambridge University Press, Cambridge, 1992 [1990].

McCAMANT, J. F., 'Domination, state power, and political repression', in Bushell, P. T., et al., (eds), *State Organized Terror*, Westview Press, Boulder, Co., 1991, pp. 41–58.

McCORMICK, J., and ALEXANDER, W., 'Firm foundations: securing the Scottish Parliament, in Tindale, Stephen, (ed.), *The State and the Nations: the politics of devolution*, IPPR, London, 1996.

McCRONE, D., *Understanding Scotland: the Sociology of a Stateless Nation*, Routledge, London, 1992.

MILLER, D., *On Nationality*, Oxford University Press, 1997 (1995).

MITCHELL, C., STOHL, M., CARLETON, D., and LOPEZ, G. A., 'State terrorism: issues of concept and measurement', in Stohl, M., and Lopez, G., (eds),

Government violence and repression, Greenwood Press, New York, 1986 pp. 1–26.

MORENO, L., *Escocia, razón y pasión*, CSIC, Madrid, 1995.

MUÑOZ, X., *De dreta a esquerra: Memòries polítiques*, Edicions 62, Barcelona, 1990.

NIPPERDEY, T., 'In Search of Identity', in Eade, J. C., (ed.), *Romantic Nationalism in Europe*, Humanities Research Centre, Australian National University, 1983.

NÚÑEZ SEIXAS, X. M., 'Radicais e pragmàticos: do nacionalismo galego a finais do século XX', in *Grial*, 1998, núm. XXXVI, pp. 313–348.

O'BALLANCE, E., *The Kurdish Struggle 1920–94*, Macmillan, London, 1996.

OHMAE, K., *The End of the Nation-state: the Rise of Regional Economies*, Harper Collins Publishers, London, 1996 (1995).

O'LEARY, B., MCGARRY, J., (eds), *Explaining Northern Ireland*, Blackwell, Oxford, 1998.

——, *The Politics of Antagonism: Understanding Northern Ireland*, Athlone, London and Atlantic Heights NY, 1993.

——, *The future of Northern Ireland*, Clarendon Press, Oxford, 1990.

PARMAN, D. L., *Indians and the American West in the twentieth century*, Indiana University Press, Bloomington Indianapolis, 1994.

Parti Québécois, *Programme du Parti Québécois*, Montreal, 1991.

PAYNE. S. G., *The Franco regime 1936–1975*, University of Wisconsin Press, Wisconsin, 1987.

PÉREZ-AGOTE, A., *El nacionalismo vasco a la salida del franquismo*, C.I.S. Ediciones Siglo XXI, Madrid, 1987.

PERIN, R., 'Answering the Quebec Question: two Centuries of Equivocation', in Drache, D., & Perin, R., (eds), *Negotiating with a Sovereign Quebec*, James Lorimer & Company, Publishers, Toronto, 1992.

Plaid Cymru, *A Democratic Wales in a United Europe*, introduction by Dafydd Wigley, president of PC, Plaid Cymru, Caernarfon, 1995.

PUJOL, J., *Quatre conferències: analitzar el passat per renovar el projecte*, Edicions 62, Barcelona, 1990.

——, 'CDC: Què ha estat, què és, què volem que sigui', address at Teatre Tívoli, 17 June 1996, CDC, Barcelona, 1996.

Quebec Chief Electoral Officer, *Rapport préliminaire des résultats du dépouillement des votes le soir du scrutin: Rèfèrendum du 30 octobre 1995*, Quebec, Bibliothèque nationale du Québec, 1995.

RAWKINS, P., 'Living in the House of Power: Welsh nationalism and the dilemma of Antisystem Politics', in Tiryakian, E., and Rogowski, R., (eds), *New Nationalisms of the Developed West*, Allen & Unwin, Boston, 1985, pp. 294–314.

REQUEJO, F., *Zoom polític: Democràcia, federalisme i nacionalisme des d'una Catalunya europea*, Proa, La mirada, Barcelona, 1998.

REX, J., 'The concept of a multicultural society', in Guibernau, M., and Rex, J.

(eds), *The Ethnicity Reader: nationalism, multiculturalism and migration*, Polity Press, Cambridge, 1997.

——, *Ethnic Minorities in the Modern Nation-State*, Macmillan in association with CRER, University of Warwick, London, 1996.

RICHTER, M., *Ireland: The enduring tradition*, Macmillan education, London, 1983.

ROBBINS, R. L., 'Self-determination and subordination', in Jaimes, A., (ed.), *The State of Native America: Genocide, Colonization, and Resistance*, South End Press, Boston, 1992.

ROCHE, M., and VAN BERKEL, R., *European Citizenship and Social Exclusion*, Ashgate, Aldershot, 1997.

RODERICK, A. J., (ed.), *Wales Through the Ages*, Christopher Davies Ltd., Llandybie, Camarthenshire, 1971 (1959), vol. I.

ROKKAN, S., and URWIN, D., *Economy, Territory, Identity: Politics of West European Regionalism*, Sage, London, 1983.

Royal Commission Report on Aboriginal Peoples, Ottawa, 1996, vol. 5.

RUGGIE, J. G., 'International regimes, transactions and change: embedded liberalism in the post war economic order', *International Organization*, 1982, 36.

SAHLINS, P., *Boundaries: The Making of France and Spain in the Pyrenees*, The University of California Press, Berkeley and Los Angeles, 1989.

SANGUIN, A. L., *La Suisse, Essai de Géographie Politique*, Éditions Ophrys, Gap, 1983.

SCHLESINGER, P., *Media, State and Nation: political violence and collective identities*, Sage, London, 1991.

SCHMID, A. P., 'Repression, state terrorism and genocide: conceptual clarifications', in Bushell, P. T., et al. (eds), *State Organized Terror*, pp. 23–37.

Scotland's Parliament White Paper, The Stationery Office, London, 1997.

Scottish National Party, *Programme for Government 1996*.

——, *Programme for Government 1996*, pamphlet, 'A Voice for Scotland in the World', September 1996.

——, *Programme for Government*, pamphlet 2, 'Independence in Europe – Best for Scotland', September 1996.

——, *Programme for Government 1996*, pamphlet 3, 'The Constitution and Governance of an Independent Scotland', September 1996.

SENN, A. E., 'Lithuania and the Lithuanians', in Smith, G., (ed.), *The Nationalities Question in the Post-Soviet States*, Longman, London, 1996 (1990).

SEYMOUR, M. A., *A Letter to Canadians*, IPSO, 20 May 1998.

SHULTZ, R., 'Conceptualizing political terrorism', in Kegley C. W., Jr, (ed.), *International Terrorism: characteristics, causes, controls*, St Martin's Press Inc., New York, 1990, pp. 45–50.

SMITH, A. D., *National Identity*, Penguin, London, 1991.

——, *Federalism: the multiethnic challenge*, Longman, London, 1995.

SMITH, A. P., *Warlords and Holymen: Scotland AD 80–1000*, Edinburgh University Press, Edinburgh, 1984.

SMITH, G., 'Latvia and the Latvians', in *The Nationalities Question in the Post-Soviet States*, Longman, London, 1996 (1990).

——, *Federalism: the multiethnic challenge*, Longman, London, 1995.

SPOONLEY, P., *Racism and Ethnicity*, Oxford University Press, Auckland, 1993 (1988).

TEJERINA, B., *Nacionalismo y lengua*, Centro de Investigaciones Sociológicas, Madrid, 1992.

——, FERNÁNDEZ SOBRADO, J. M., and AIERDI, X., *Sociedad civil, protesta y movimientos sociales en el País Vasco*, Servicio Central de Publicaciones del Gobierno Vasco, Vitoria-Gasteiz, 1995.

TERMES., J., et al., 'Catalanisme: història, política i cultura', in *L'Avenç*, Barcelona, 1986.

THOMPSON, J. B., *Ideology and Modern Culture*, Polity Press, Cambridge, 1990.

TONNIES, F., *Community and Association (Gemeinschaft und Gesellschaft)*, Routledge & Kegan Paul, London, 1955.

TOCQUEVILLE DE, A., *Democracy in America*, Fontana Press, London, 1994.

TULLY, J., 'Let's talk: the Quebec referendum and the future of Canada', The Austin-Hempel lecture, Dalhouise University, 23–24 March 1995.

URWIN, D., *Politics in Western Europe today: perspectives, policies and problems since 1980*, Longman, London, 1990.

VAN DYKE, V., 'The individual, the state and ethnic communities in political theory', in Kymlicka, W., (ed.), *The Rights of Minority Cultures*, Oxford University Press, Oxford, 1995.

VILAR, P., (ed.), *Història de Catalunya*, by Borja de Riquer and Joan Culla, Edicions 62, Barcelona, 1989, vol. II.

——, *Història de Catalunya*, by Batlle, C., Edicions 62, Barcelona, 1987, vol. III.

——, *La Catalogne dans l'Espagne moderne*, Flammarion, París, 1977.

WALKER, D., *Medieval Wales*, Cambridge University Press, Cambridge, 1990.

WEBER, M., *From Max Weber: Essays in Sociology*, Gerth, H. H., and Wright Mills (eds), Routledge, London, 1991 (1948).

WILMER, F., *The Indigenous Voice in World Politics: since time immemorial*, Sage, Newbury Park, California, 1993.

WILSON, T., *Ulster: Conflict and Consent*, Basil Blackwell, Oxford, 1989.

ZUBAIDA, S., 'Introduction', in Kreyenbroek, P., and Sperl, S., (eds), *The Kurds: A Contemporary Overview*, Routledge, London, 1992.

Index

Vindication of Scottish Rights 47;
decentralization of Britain 47–50;
Declaration of Arbroath 45;
education 46, 47; emigration 138;
Enlightenment 46; European Union
165; history 44–7, 187n5, 189n7, n11;
identity 44–5, 98; industrialization
46–7; judicial system 46, 47; Kirk 44,
46, 47; labour movement 47; political
autonomy in 44–9; re-emergence 33;
Referendum (1979) 47; Romans 44;
separateness 35–6; subsidies 180;
Union of Crowns 45; Union of
Parliament 46; at war with England
45–6
Scotland's Parliament White Paper 48–9,
165, 166–8
Scottish Assembly 47
Scottish Constitutional Convention 47
Scottish Nationalist Party 47, 105, 107,
165
Scottish Parliament 35, 47–8
secession 27–8, 180
second homes 36–7
Secretary for Scotland 35–6, 47
Secretary of State for Scotland 35, 47
sectarianism 139, 140
security, multi-nation-state 161, 162
self-determination: democracy 37–8;
indigenous peoples 68–9; nation 13;
nation-state 8; nationalism 103–4;
nations without states 25–6, 27,
49–50, 107–8, 178; Native Americans
77; Native nations 86; and political
autonomy 16, 102; violence 136
self-interest 91–2
Serbia 125–6
Seven Years War 54–5
Sèvres, Treaty of 65
Seymour, Michael 105
Shultz, R. 126
Sinn Fein 141, 165
16 October War Measures Act, Canada
136
Slovenia 123, 162
Smith, Anthony D. 2, 90, 94, 100
Smith, Graham 50, 53
Social Democratic and Labour Party
141

social mobility 97–8
social movements 25, 29, 71–2, 78, 178
socialism 178
Socialist Unified Party of Catalonia 95
society 19, 29–32
solidarity 4, 94, 114, 117–18, 171
'solidarity actions' 116, 117, 118
Sons of Glyndwr 122
sovereignty: and centralization 18;
citizenship 151; European Union
153; federation 51, 52; Mohawk
84–5; nation-state 6, 20, 176–7;
popular 8, 24, 27; Quebec 59;
regions 6, 38
Soviet Union 61
Spain 117, 124, 133: *see also* Basque
Country; Catalonia
Spanish Autonomous Communities
System 42–4, 92, 111
Spanish Popular Party 135
Spanish Socialist Workers Party 44, 111
Spanish Succession, War of 40
Spoonley, P. 71
Stalin, Joseph 146
state: changes 16; community 114; and
culture 35, 101–2; internal conflict
30–1; language 35, 101–2; legitimacy
22, 142; multinational 14–15; and
nation 2–3, 13, 17; nationalism 90,
177; regions 171; repression 147–8;
Weber 13
state-building 17, 28
state nationalism 177
state terrorism 145–8
Suárez, Adolfo 118
sub-state nationalist movements 16, 19
sub-state units 3, 5, 9, 16, 19
subsidiarity 111, 124, 172, 184–6
Sunni Muslims 65
Switzerland 51
'symbolic actions' 116

Táin Bó Cuailnge 137
Talon, Jean 54
Tarradellas, Josep 41
technology in media 158–9
television, Welsh language 122
termination policy 78–9
Terra Lliure 136